Baseball/Literature/Culture

ALSO EDITED BY PETER CARINO

Baseball/Literature/Culture
Essays 1995–2001 (2003)

Baseball/Literature/Culture

Essays, 2002–2003

Edited by PETER CARINO

McFarland & Company, Inc., Publishers
Jefferson, North Carolina, and London

LIBRARY OF CONGRESS CATALOGUING-IN-PUBLICATION DATA

Baseball/literature/culture : essays, 2002–2003 / edited by
Peter Carino.
    p.   cm.
Includes bibliographical references and index.

ISBN 0-7864-1851-6 (softcover : 50# alkaline paper)

1. American literature—History and criticism. 2. Baseball in
literature. 3. Baseball stories, American—History and criticism.
4. Baseball—United States. I. Carino, Peter.
PS169.B36B38   2004
810.9'357—dc22   2004003163

British Library cataloguing data are available

©2004 Peter Carino. All rights reserved

*No part of this book may be reproduced or transmitted in any form
or by any means, electronic or mechanical, including photocopying
or recording, or by any information storage and retrieval system,
without permission in writing from the publisher.*

Manufactured in the United States of America

Cover photograph by Mark Durr

McFarland & Company, Inc., Publishers
  Box 611, Jefferson, North Carolina 28640
    www.mcfarlandpub.com

Table of Contents

Introduction   PETER CARINO   1

Part I: Baseball in Literature and Film

1. A Field of Questions: W.P. Kinsella Comes to Ithaca
   ANDREW ANDERSON   9

2. Jon Billman's "Indians" and American Indian
   Exhibition Baseball Teams
   JEFFREY POWERS-BECK   19

3. "Dad—Can We Have a Catch?" Images of Fatherhood
   and Redemption in Three Baseball Films
   SCOTT JENSEN AND JOSEPH SCHUSTER   28

4. Mick Cochrane's *Sport* and the Mythic Symbol of
   Fathers Playing Catch with Sons
   MATTHEW C. BRENNAN   39

5. Nelson Algren's Chicago: The Black Sox Scandal,
   McCarthyism, and the Truth about Cubs Fans
   ANDY HAZUCHA   49

6. "You don't play the angles, you're a sap": John Sayles,
   Eliot Asinof, Baseball, Labor, and Chicago in 1919
   WARREN TORMEY   60

7. "The proper distance for worship": Art Worlds and
   Assimilation Narratives in *The Celebrant*
      RONALD KATES ... 76

8. Nine Assists and No Errors: Rediscovering
   the Baseball Fiction of Charles Van Loan
      TREY STRECKER ... 83

Part II: Baseball in American Culture

9. Baseball, Scholarship, and the "Duty to Justice"
      FRANK D. RASHID ... 93

10. Is Baseball an American Religion?
    A Sociological Analysis
      TOBY ZIGLAR ... 106

11. Home Run Derby Versus the Pitchers' Duel:
    Could the Need for Instant Gratification Ruin Baseball?
      JOAN M. THOMAS ... 116

12. (Caray)^3: Baseball as Narrated on Television
      GERALD C. WOOD ... 124

13. Baseball Immortals: Character and Performance
    On and Off the Field
      RON REMBERT ... 136

14. Forces of Darkness and Light: The Cultural
    Significance of Transitions in Baseball History
      DAVID SHINER ... 146

15. Lessons to Be Learned from *Only the Ball Was White*:
    Similarities Between the Negro Leagues and
    African-Americans in Baseball Today
      DAVID C. OGDEN ... 157

16. From "Game Winning Home Run" to "Walk-Off":
    Baseball Jargon and the Discourse of
    Modern American Life
      WILLIAM A. LEHN ... 166

17. Nineteenth-Century and Black Baseball
   in Indianapolis
      W.C. MADDEN   177

18. Interviewing a Local Legend: Preacher Roe
   and Ozark Culture
      DAVE MALONE   186

19. Which Ball Is in Play? Lasting Images of
   Stan Musial at Wrigley Field
      ROBERT E. MEYER   193

Contributors   201
Index   205

Introduction

Peter Carino

This collection offers a representative sampling of the essays presented at the annual Indiana State University Conference on Baseball in Literature and American Culture for 2002 and 2003. Since 1995, the conference has provided a venue in the Midwest where scholars of the game can gather to share their work on baseball both as literary subject matter and cultural institution. The essays here demonstrate that baseball continues to engage scholars like no other sport, despite the game's supposed loss of stature as the national game. The connection between the game and scholarly thought was again underscored at these two conferences. In 2001, former American League umpire Larry Barnett brought a unique perspective to the conference as the luncheon speaker. In 2002, Milt Pappas, whose statistics compare well with those of Hall of Famer Don Drysdale's, spoke of his career and his candid autobiography *Out at Home*. Like past special guests such as Carl Erskine, Al Hrabosky, Dock Ellis, and Al Oliver, Barnett and Pappas presented firsthand views of Major League Baseball not available to scholars. At the same time, however, the essays in this collection provide ways of looking at baseball not usually considered by players, umpires, or the average fan.

Undoubtedly, given its long history as game and institution, baseball is complex. Despite complaints that it is too slow, too traditional, too much of a business, it continues to persist, more strongly than its detractors would admit, as a companion to multitudes each summer, as a way of marking the movement of time from spring to fall, and as a world unto itself despite its institutional entanglements in culture, economics, and media. The essays here attempt to unknot many of those entanglements, commenting on the way the game has been appropriated in literary texts and film, as well as on its place in various aspects of cultural experience from the politics and economics of stadium building to the effect of the game's language on the national vernacular. Sponsored by the Indiana State University English Department, the primary emphasis of the conference has been baseball in literature, but increasingly scholars from several disciplines have presented essays on numerous aspects of baseball and culture. This shift is reflected slightly in this volume with eight essays primarily on baseball literature and eleven on broader cultural topics.

BASEBALL IN LITERATURE AND FILM

The first section of this collection presents essays on baseball in literature and film. At the top of the lineup is Andrew Anderson's "A Field of Questions: W. P. Kinsella Comes to Ithaca." Anderson sat down for a lengthy interview in the local diner with perhaps the most prolific and well-known writer of baseball fiction when Kinsella was serving as writer in residence at Ithaca College. Moving beyond the obvious attention given to *Shoeless Joe* and its film counterpart, *Field of Dreams*, Anderson reveals Kinsella as fan as well as Kinsella as writer. While offering insights into his views on both writing and the game, Anderson explicates some of Kinsella's lesser known but finely crafted short fiction. Short fiction is also the topic of Jeffrey Powers-Beck's analysis of John Billman's "Indians," the lead story in Billman's well-received collection *When We Were Wolves*. Powers-Beck's project is to place the story against historical accounts of Native-American barnstorming teams of the late nineteenth and early twentieth century. In addition to an insightful reading of Billman's short story, Powers-Beck provides historical commentary on an area of baseball history that has not received much attention.

A more widely explored topic—fathers playing catch with sons—receives new examination in one essay by Scott Jensen and Joseph Schuster, and another by Matthew Brennan. Jensen and Schuster trace the role of this image in two baseball films based on literary texts, *The Natural* and *Field of Dreams*, and one popular film based loosely on true events, *The Rookie*. In all three they find the metaphor a bracing "context in which one can seek and find redemption." Matthew Brennan complicates this metaphor, conceding its potential to be fulfilling but also exploring the tensions in father-son relations in the maturation process of the son. His analysis treats both the text and film versions of *Fear Strikes Out*, as well as a sampling of baseball poems, but his primary example of a new take on fathers playing catch with sons is *Sport*, a contemporary first novel by Mick Cochrane.

An equally fascinating subject on baseball has been the Black Sox scandal, and both Andrew Hazucha and Warren Tormey take up the scandal once more but from fresh angles, demonstrating the continuing fascination it holds for artists and scholars alike. Hazucha finds substantial interest in it in Nelson Algren's *Chicago: City on the Make*. Algren, as Chicagoan and political radical, saw in attitudes about the fall of the beloved Sox of his boyhood connections to McCarthy era persecution of those who choose to think differently. Hazucha uncovers how Algren's account of being a Sox fan in a Cub neighborhood, written during the time of McCarthy's ascension to power, draws several parallels between 1919 and the early 1950s. At the same time, Hazucha raises some pointed questions about Sox and Cub fans as representatives of social relations in Chicago today. It is a commonplace in commentary, in whatever media, on the Black Sox to view the actions of the banned eight as a type of labor action. Warren Tormey takes this commonplace far beyond the obvious in his examination of John Sayles's *Eight Men Out* in the context of both Eliot Asinof's historical account of the fix and Sayles's earlier and openly labor oriented film *Matewan*. The essay also points out several means Sayles employed to compress Asinof's detailed history into the more dramatic medium of film.

Ronald Kates's contribution continues discussion of literary works set in the early part of the twentieth century, with a reading of Eric Rolfe Greenberg's fine novel, *The Celebrant*. Well known as a literary portrayal of Christy Mathewson and an analysis of the role of baseball for immigrants, the novel, Kates shows, also concerns itself with the tension between art and commerce, a theme that entwines with that of the American assimilation of the Kapinski brothers, Jews who find themselves attracted, in different ways, to America's game and its larger than life heroes. Closing the section on baseball in literature in film, Trey Strecker calls for a revival of interest in Charles Van Loan, a writer Grantland Rice dubbed "baseball's comic genius." A prolific writer of sports fiction in general, Van Loan penned four baseball novels and nine collections of short stories on the game. Though Van Loan wrote with an eye for the mass audience, Strecker makes a case for him as a writer worthy of scholarly attention and a precursor to Ring Lardner, whose work Van Loan first recommended to the *Saturday Evening Post*.

Together these essays attest to the intelligent use of baseball as metaphor by both talented writers and filmmakers. In addition, in their careful and complex analyses, they confirm that artistic treatments of the game are as worthy of scholarly discussion as the literature of more mainstream subject matter.

BASEBALL IN CULTURE

Baseball has been a powerful cultural institution for a long time—and continues to be. The game is a profession, a leisure activity, a source of television programming, a business, and a metaphor of cultural relations in America and, to varying degrees, in several foreign countries. The essays collected in this section reveal many of the ways in which the game is more than just a game. In fact, they illustrate how this "game" has insinuated itself into various cultural domains and dynamics, sometimes happily, sometimes ominously, but always in ways relevant to the daily activities and relations of the social structure.

Leading off this section, Frank Rashid gives a first-hand account of the difficulties of preserving an old ballpark and opposing the construction of a new one at taxpayers' expense. Taking a cue from Elaine Scarry's work on the scholar's civic responsibility to defend beauty and justice, Rashid recounts his long experience as a member of the Tiger Stadium Fan Club and his role in its embattled political efforts against the powerful in Detroit. Though his and his colleagues' efforts ultimately failed, the story of their work and the opposition to it is a sobering reminder of the power of money and special interests on civic decisions in a supposedly democratic society.

Moving from the political to the spiritual, Toby Ziglar unpacks the often repeated commonplace that baseball can be a religion. Ziglar rigorously subjects this claim to three codified, sociological definitions of religion. While thinking of baseball as religion is relatively innocent, Ziglar demonstrates that to claim so requires more than just a strong attraction to the game. Joan Thomas's paper also considers aspects of the game in terms of societal habits, desires, and perceptions, tracing the penchant for home runs of the last few years to the fast pace of American culture. Arguing that most Americans suffer from a vast case of attention deficit disorder, she laments the passing of many fans' appreciation for good pitching. However, she finds some hope for a more leisure game in young men's participation in the budding phenomenon of vintage league baseball.

Gerald Wood returns the discussion to the contemporary with a focus on broadcast media, particularly the three generations of Careys: Harry, Skip, and Chip. In analyzing each announcer and his relation both to the game and the television audience, Wood poses some intriguing questions about how broadcasts reimagine and reshape the viewer's experience of the game. While Wood is interested in the character of the announcers, Ron Rembert engages himself with the character of the players, analyzing how character and performance interact in both fan and media perceptions as well as in terms of a player's candidacy for the Hall of Fame.

David Shiner concerns himself with the ways in which cultural metaphor—in this case blackness and whiteness, dirtiness and cleanliness—have shaped both racial attitudes and styles of play in Major League Baseball throughout the twentieth-century. His expansive treatment of this subject includes discussion of the effect of the Black Sox scandal and Jackie Robinson's breaking the color line in terms of how each helped transform the game and the culture. David Ogden, who has done much work on African-American youth in baseball, is also concerned with race. His essay traces significant parallels between the problems faced by Negro League teams and players and the absence of African-American players in youth select baseball. Drawing on history of the Negro Leagues and extensive field work with select team coaches, Ogden delineates the difficulties baseball faces in reviving interest in the game among African-American fans and potential players.

William A. Lehn addresses a subject known to all—the entrance of baseball terms into public discourse—but goes beyond obvious terms such as "getting to first base" or "ballpark figure." Rather he traces how the terms "walk-off home run" and "Tommy John surgery" have come to pervade baseball discourse and have begun to enter public discourse. In addition, he discusses terms as they cross cultures, and he speculates on how football terms compete with those of baseball in a post 9/11 society.

Both W.C. Madden and Dave Malone write of baseball in terms of place. Madden recounts the history of early teams and Negro squads in Indianapolis, compiling a register of the many nineteenth-century white teams in the city and the city's ups and downs in maintaining a presence in leagues then considered major. His treatment of Negro teams, of course, touches on famous nines such as the ABCs and the Clowns. Malone analyzes the reciprocal relationship of giving and receiving between Preacher Roe and the area of the Ozarks from which he hails. Combining an interview with the former Brooklyn Dodger pitcher with textual sources, Malone shows how the generosity of Roe's family, friends, and neighbors helped nurture his talents and how his generosity contributed much to the Ozark community in return.

In the closer's role, Robert E. Meyer delivers a lyrical memoir on his boyhood experience of seeing Stan Musial at Wrigley Field, with his dying father, a closet Cardinal fan living in Chicago. In addition to offering a portrait of the dignity of one of baseball's greats, Meyer tenders a loving tribute to the dignity of his father, but all this is lightened by of his account of Stan the Man's involvement in one of the most humorous and unusual plays in baseball history.

As editor of this collection and coordinator of the Indiana State University Conference on Baseball in American Literature and Culture, I am happy to compile these essays for those who have not been able to attend the conference and those who have. I would be remiss if I did not thank those who have helped make it a success over the years: English Department Chair and indefatigable Red Sox fan Ronald Baker; my good friend, sometimes co-coordinator, and fellow devotee of good baseball Matthew Brennan; Gary Mitchem and the rest of the editorial staff at McFarland; but most of all, the many fine scholars whose work here and at past conferences confirms once again that baseball is "the thinking man's (and woman's) game."

Part I
Baseball in Literature and Film

1

A Field of Questions: W. P. Kinsella Comes to Ithaca

Andrew Anderson

> Baseball is very conducive to supernatural kinds of things because on a true baseball field there is no limit to how far a batter could hit a ball or how far a fielder could run to retrieve it and it makes for myth and larger than life characters.
>
> —W.P. Kinsella

In his fiction, W.P. Kinsella has made baseball a powerful, imaginative, yet gentle metaphor that transcends the barriers of time. In *Shoeless Joe* and *Field of Dreams*, Ray Kinsella's troubled soul is redeemed by a simple game of catch between a son and the soul of his father, suddenly, magically alive again. In so many of his other stories, too, Kinsella weaves real and fictional characters in ways that defy the mundane and day-to-day. In "Eggs," we see an aging pitcher haunted by retirement in nightmares about the Ukrainian Easter eggs his wife makes. In "Searching for January," Roberto Clemente is alive again—still in his prime—rowing a raft around the Caribbean, trying to catch-on with another ball club, since he's been gone from the Pirates too long. And in "K Mart" (Kinsella's personal favorite), old friends, like sandlot children, recapture the wonder of the game inside the mega-store that has replaced their old baseball field (home plate's in lingerie, second in house wares, the outfield in furniture). All of these are baseball stories of haunting, super-natural power and the softest metaphors of inner peace.

In April 2002, W.P. Kinsella taught a week of master classes in fiction writing as part of the Ithaca College Distinguished Writers series.

During that time, he also met with Writing Department Faculty, offered a public lecture on his life and work, and presented a reading from his own work. I interviewed him on March 12, 2002, and had breakfast with him (he loved the potato pancakes with sour cream at Hal's Diner in downtown Ithaca). These were memorable times of great baseball talk.

We began the interview with discussion of Kinsella's take on the craft of writing baseball fiction. His first response was surprising: "My characters are always much more intense [about baseball] than I am personally. In 1980, I wrote *Shoeless Joe* and discovered on publication that there was a market for baseball fiction. I said 'all right; if there are readers out there I can certainly fulfill their needs.' So, I wrote another eight or ten baseball books."

His typical workday, Kinsella says, is a very business-like, "buns on the chair" enterprise based on a "set quota of four new pages or fifty pages of editing per day. If I made that quota in half an hour, I was able to take the rest of the day to do whatever I wanted. If I didn't get it and had to write the last ten lines after the 11 o'clock news, then that's what I did." When blocked, he said he never changes the routine. "Some days, I could write four pages in forty minutes, and on other days every word was like pulling a tooth, and I would work on ten different projects, writing a couple of sentences on each, just to advance things." What advice does Kinsella offer to other writers?

> What I tell would-be writers you have to keep your buns on the chair and work whether you feel like it or not. Flannery O'Connor used to say 'I sit at my typewriter from ten to twelve every day, so just in case something comes I'll be there to receive it.' That's the key to writing. I've seen more good writers go by the boards because they don't have the stamina to finish their work. If you have a job, you don't just work when you feel like it, and it's exactly the same when you're self-employed.

For Kinsella, getting a story going often seems a matter of luck—and all its perversions. "Eggs" is his story of Webb Waterman, an aging pitcher facing the specter of retirement, its imminence as cold and desolate as the Alberta winter outside his massive Vegreville estate. He tells his agent "I'll work all winter developing a knuckleball, maybe try a split-finger fastball, perfect the screwball. Get me a contract, with anybody" (*Dixon* 71). His Ukrainian wife, Maika, is no help—she thinks it's time to move-on: "don't be a Steve Carlton, begging to try out in Japan, a pathetic shadow of yourself. We have no financial worries. You'll be elected to the Hall of Fame the first year you're eligible" (74). Webb begins having colorful, full-dimensional nightmares of being chased into retirement by hundreds of the Ukrainian Easter eggs Maika and Halya, his mother-in-law, make.

The seed for this story, Kinsella remembered, came on an ill-advised trip to a small town in Canada to present a reading of his work:

> The "Eggs" story is ... loosely based on Steve Carlton, who married a Ukrainian girl who was an airline stewardess, and they actually lived in a little town in northern Ontario, sort of the asshole of the earth where her family came from. I once mistakenly—I didn't know where this was—agreed to do a reading there. They held the reading at noon on a Saturday for about twenty people who had never been to a reading before and didn't know how to act, and they sat there while I did all my best material and didn't make a sound while I died.

After the ill-fated lecture, as he was on "the drive back to the nearest civilization," the woman driver said, "I bet you would've liked to have met Olga. Olga is Steve Carlton's mother-in-law, and her house is just like a shrine to Steve Carlton." Kinsella never met her but "wrote a little blurb for *USA Today* called 'How I Almost Met Steve Carlton's Mother In Law.' The story 'Eggs' came from that."

When I asked him what story he would most like to see in an anthology of the greatest baseball writing, Kinsella said that after "Shoeless Joe Jackson Comes to Iowa," "K Mart" is his favorite short story. His theme is once again the spiritual redemption of three middle-aged old friends from the many losses of growing up and now growing old. Meeting at the funeral of Cory Mazeppa, a beautiful, supposedly "easy" girl who used to watch their sandlot games and who is now dead to suicide after a failed marriage, the friends grow suddenly in need of a baseball game. The kind of game that began "when it was April, and the snow was barely gone ... the fine green tendrils emerging from the brown fuzz of winterkilled grass" (*Distance* 80) and ran all day, every day, all summer, "long, sunny afternoons on the field where our endless game went on from the time the dew left the grass until it was too dark to see the ball" (85).

After Cory's funeral, Kaz, Eddie, and Jamie, the narrator, yearn for those days, so they visit the K Mart that has been built over their old ball field. As they layout a field amid the clothes racks and shelves of the discount store, Kaz grooves Jamie a fastball, and the ghosts of the past all appear.

> All the players were in place now, my team along the sidelines, Kaz's team in the field. All the baseball boys. All the accoun-

tants, thugs and TV producers and packing-plant workers and railroad section men. And Cory was sitting on the grass a few yards behind the bench, alone as always, her black hair snarled about her face [102].

As he hits a long drive to Eddie in the furniture department, Jamie thinks about after the game when he will "walk Cory to the end of the sidewalk" and "kiss her so gently in the lilac shadows" (103). Baseball has brought them back together. They all know Cory never "did it" with any of them, and Jamie, at least in his reverie, can finally tell her how much he loves her.

Kinsella says that *Shoeless Joe* was actually suggested by a young man at Houghton-Mifflin "right out of editor's school and didn't know any better than to contact authors ... hadn't learned yet that more material than he could read in seven lifetimes comes over the transom." Having read "Shoeless Joe Comes to Iowa," he suggested Kinsella turn it into a novel. "How can I make a novel out of this damn thing?" Kinsella told me he asked himself. Again, luck and "buns on the chair" hard work came next. It took "nine months, just like a baby" to complete the novel, and it is still, Kinsella says, the "only book I've ever written straight through."

> I knew I had notes and wanted to write about J.D. Salinger because he makes himself conspicuous by hiding. I said, "all right, I'll have my guy go off to New Hampshire and visit Salinger." I knew I wanted to write something about Moonlight Graham because I discovered his entry in *The Baseball Encyclopedia* and here was a guy who for one instant in 1905 played major league baseball and never came to bat. I wondered how that affected his life—if he was an American Legion drunk who sat around boozing and bragging about playing major league baseball. We actually went up to Chisholm, Minnesota and discovered Doc Graham was more wonderful in real life than anything I could have invented.

Eddie Scissons, the major league liar who never played a day in the Majors, was another character born of dumb luck. "I met an old guy on the streets of Iowa City one day," Kinsella says, who told him he was "87 years old and used to play for the Chicago Cubs." Kinsella remembers having "all sorts of wonderful ideas that Ernie Banks, then a PR man for the Cubs, would want this old dude to throw out the first pitch, and I'd get a free trip to Chicago and an article in *Sports Illustrated* and something for *The Chicago Tribune*." So, he "got the guy's name and arranged to go interview him, and of course, when I went to the library to check him out he was just a storyteller like I am; he's never been near the Major Leagues, and that was where Eddie Scissons came from. I just kept saying 'what if, what if, what if?'"

The "what if" about Eddie Scissons comes out harshly in Kinsella's story "The Eddie Scissons Syndrome." The story is in part an allegory for his own dislike of "university people who make their living writing ludicrous papers about ludicrous interpretations of [my] work. I think that's scary ... so I always try to put a couple of intentional mistakes in my books because there are people who live for finding factual errors. It's very weird." Professor Willis of "Syndrome" is one of these weird, ultimately cruel, academics. His research (based on his admiration for *Shoeless Joe* by an "author at some university town out in Iowa") is to find "how many old men, all across America, were lying through their teeth every time they talked of their careers in the big leagues" (*Distance* 141–42).

The search leads him to a VA hospital in South Carolina, to interview Kiley, a light-skinned old black man who swears he passed for white and filled-in as catcher for Ray Schalk on the 1917 Chicago White Sox. There's no record, he says, because "'it was Charles Comiskey [who always knew Kiley was black] tore up my records so nobody'd ever know I played in the Bigs'" (150). Since for Willis baseball is no more than the countless record books and newspaper archives he can use to catch liars, he attacks the helpless old man in the most vile way—the destruction of his sweet, imaginary baseball dream:

> "I wrote to *The Chicago Tribune* and I got the box scores of White Sox games for the two months you claim to have played. Charles Comiskey couldn't destroy the back issues of the *Chicago Tribune*. You never played a day of major-league baseball in your life!"
>
> Professor Willis moved closer to the old man, his mouth snapping out words, his fleshy lips like red meat in the old man's face.
>
> "I wanted to see what a stone-cold liar looked like, I wanted to get down your lies on tape for everyone to hear."
>
> The old man shrunk into his pillows; he covered one ear with a hand, but seemed to lack the strength to cover the other [150–51].

All Kinsella remembers about the legal hassles with J.D. Salinger while writing *Shoeless Joe* were lots of attorneys exchanging threatening letters: "The lawyers at Houghton-Mifflin went over the book several times and made me make a few changes." They were convinced that Salinger's only legal accusation would be "false light—the sixth definition of libel." To contest the novel's publication, he would have had to go to court himself and say:

> "Look, in this novel I am being portrayed as a kindly, loving, humorous individual. In reality, I am a surly son of a bitch who sits in a bunker on the side of a hill and shoots at tourists when they drive by my house and am therefore being portrayed in a false light." Houghton-Mifflin's lawyers got a grumbling letter from Salinger's lawyers saying he would be "outraged and offended to be portrayed in the novel and would be very unhappy if it were transferred to other media."

The change from Salinger to Terrence Mann in the screenplay for the film, Kinsella says, was

> cowardice on the part of Hollywood. They were afraid he [Salinger] would take some legal action to delay the release of the movie. They probably could have gotten away with it. Essentially there was nothing they could do. But Hollywood, being the cowards they are, decided not to take any chances and created Terrence Mann instead.

The phenomenal and continuing impacts of *Shoeless Joe* and *Field of Dreams* still surprise—and delight—Kinsella. He still appreciates Philip Alden Robinson's work as the screenwriter and director of the film that "captured the essence of what I was trying to do." Kinsella remembers his reaction to the first draft of the screenplay: "he [Robinson] sent me the screenplay, and I had tears in my eyes when I read it, and I said my gosh, if this is my own work, and this can do this to me, if they can only translate this to the screen." The "genius" of the project was leaving it in Robinson's hands—only the young director's second feature film—and Kinsella believes he got it right.

> They let Phil direct the movie. They could have brought in Altman or Coppola or some big name director who would have said, "well, yes, this is pretty good, but it's not the way I see it. We need a car chase here and a fistfight here and some hot sex here," and it would have been just another movie. But Phil was able to keep what he had written and it worked out beautifully.

We talked about his favorite scene (when the young Moonlight Graham crosses the foul line and becomes the old Doc) and mine (the game of catch at the end of the story). He still feels "disappointed that Burt Lancaster didn't get an Academy Award nomination" for the role and wonders why, when the actor died, the "people who did his obit didn't have the common sense to use the scene when he disappears into the cornfield. It would've been so wonderful."

Kinsella has received "thousands of letters from people who said how much that [game of catch] affected them. How some guy drove from Connecticut to New Mexico ... to make up with his father who hadn't been seen for fifteen years and take him to a baseball game." This is the "universal thing," he says, about the chance to "redo the past," to take things back even when in real time you can't. He is pleased that the farm in Dyersville, Iowa, has remained sort of a shrine to the love of baseball we see in the novel and film. "My fans!" Kinsella nearly shouted, "My fans are really kind and gentle people. They are really, really nice people who come to the field there. They like to run around the bases and bat, and everyone shares and takes pictures with each other, and it's just really a nice experience."

Next we talked about some of Kinsella's favorite baseball stories. His meeting with Major League Baseball Commissioner Bud Selig is at the top of his list:

> Selig is a bean counter. I was sitting in the box with him at the Toronto World Series with Morley Safer and the owner of the Seattle Mariners. I was telling a story that I had applied to be a pitching coach for the Mariners and how I was going to see that by April they would be writing complete sentences and by August they would be writing complete paragraphs and essays. We wouldn't worry about their pitching because Seattle's pitchers weren't much good anyway, so we'd just see that they became competent essayists by the end of the season. Selig just looked at me. He didn't have a clue what I was talking about.

Kinsella has always claimed, he says, that he "should have been the next baseball commissioner. I know a fair amount about baseball. I'm Canadian. We haven't had a Canadian commissioner. I'd immediately move the office from New York to Palm Springs. I mean, why do they want to have something like that in a cold place?"

His first act as Commissioner, Kinsella says, would be to reinstate Pete Rose and Shoeless Joe Jackson. They have both been victims, he believes, of the changes in sports journalism from player-protective to tabloid exploitation:

> That came around in the 70's when they stopped protecting sports people. You know Babe Ruth could get drunk and have seven women every evening and they kept it all out of the papers— the same with all of the evil things Ty Cobb did. Ty Cobb and Tris Speaker both had their hands in the till, and all they did was become sick for the rest of the season. But then somehow the tabloid journalism somehow became regular journalism, and now

players can't fart without making the newspapers, and I find that abominable. I mean. It doesn't really matter what kind of person you were when you weren't on the field. Your reputation as an athlete is made between the foul lines. Pete Rose was a jerk personally, but he should be in the Hall of Fame because he is one of the greatest players who ever lived. I just don't know why they don't leave guys like DiMaggio alone. Leave the guys alone. Let their reputations as ballplayers be what counts.

We next talked about Kinsella's favorite "good days at a ballpark stories." One was when he "heard the one about the Japanese rookie pitcher on the San Francisco Giants." It goes like this. "I like the story about the first Japanese pitcher [Masonuri Murakami], whose name I can't say, who pitched for the Giants. Herman Franks was the manager, and the kid spoke virtually no English. Willie Mays and Willie McCovey gave him a line to say when the manager came out to visit him. The kid bowed and said, 'get lost, fatso!'"

One of his best days, he told me, was when he saw Bob Forsch pitch a no-hitter in St. Louis. "That was when, '82? Willie McGee was just becoming a star. Forsch missed the perfect game because the last time they had played the Expos Gary Carter had done something they didn't like. So the first time he came up, Forsch plunked him. It turned out that cost him a perfect game. So I think that was my perfect baseball day." Another great yet sad day was when he paid for tickets in the rightfield bleachers at Yankee Stadium but somehow got tickets eight rows back, just behind home plate. "Thurman Munson came right face-to-face with me to catch a foul, and this was like a month before he died. I mean I hated the Yankees. I was there to cheer for whomever they were playing against, but you admire a great ballplayer and it was sad to see him cut down in the prime of life." This incident found its way into *Shoeless Joe* when Ray stops at Yankee Stadium on his way to New England to find Salinger.

We finished our discussion with some quick "love-hate" questions. Kinsella's favorite baseball novel is Eric Rolfe Greenberg's *The Celebrant*, the story of a family of Jewish jewelry makers whose son is fascinated by Christy Matthewson and "makes a piece of jewelry every time [the pitcher] does something spectacular." For non-fiction, his choice is Tom Boswell's *How Life Imitates the World Series*. He thinks Roger Angell's work is "too slow" for him. After *Field of Dreams* (which he *really* thinks *is* the best baseball film ever), he likes *Rhubarb*, a film he saw when he was twelve about a cat that inherits a major league baseball team. He also likes *Bull Durham*, although the "last forty minutes are probably unnecessary. Once

Nuke Laloosh gets called-up to the big leagues, the story was over." He found Ken Burns's *Baseball* an "unwatchable documentary. I found it really boring. The Civil War piece was held together by the letters which made it so authentic."

Kinsella's selections for the title of "world's greatest living ballplayer right now is Ichiro. He is dynamite! It depends if he can hold on or not. I mean, if he can have a six- or seven-year career he'll be Hall of Fame material!" For veterans, it's between Ted Williams, who "was pretty good," and Sandy Koufax, "if he had just pitched a couple more years." His best player ever is still Shoeless Joe Jackson.

His favorite ballpark is Dodger Stadium, and he really hates "those cookie-cutter stadiums [formerly] in Cincinnati and Philadelphia and Pittsburgh." He never saw "the Houston concrete dome, but it was probably pretty bad, too." He thinks the absolutely worst stadium was in Seattle: "I saw more games at the Kingdome, so I would probably give it the edge. It was kind of like playing baseball in your basement. It was very bad."

I asked him how he felt about Barry Bonds versus Mark McGwire as the new home run king. "They are at opposite ends of the world. I mean, McGwire, he's a nice guy. He's good for baseball. He goes out of his way to be nice to people. Bonds is a surly SOB. Even his own teammates didn't care if he made the record or not. It was very bad for baseball when he broke the record. I was sorry to see it happen." Kinsella holds-out hope that Sammy Sosa still has a chance at the record.

> I would hope that maybe Sammy Sosa would break the record. It has nothing to do with [Bonds] being black, it's just he's a surly SOB. They [the fans] would have been thrilled if he [Sosa] had won the duel with McGwire, because he is, you know, the kind of guy you'd like to go to lunch with. He just comes off as so happy and friendly, and he plays hard and he's just an all-round good guy.

W.P. Kinsella seems like an all-round good guy too. Later, over our eggs and potato pancakes at Hal's Diner, Kinsella (by now "Bill" to everyone in the place) paused, and took time to remember another great baseball day. "Another no-hitter I saw when I was 17," he remembered. "in a Class-C league in Alberta and a kid named Kirby Paine pitched a no-hitter." Maybe some day this unknown pitcher will make the Major Leagues, or play catch with Clemente, or relieve Fidel Castro when the Senators are against it. In W. P. Kinsella's baseball league anything's possible—even in the depths of the Canadian minors.

WORKS CITED

Field of Dreams. Dir. Philip Alden Robinson. Screenplay by Philip Alden Robinson. Perf. Kevin Costner, James Earl Jones, Burt Lancaster. Universal, 1989.
Kinsella, W.P. *The Dixon Cornbelt League and Other Baseball Stories.* New York: Harper-Collins, 1993.
_____. *Go the Distance.* Dallas: Southern Methodist UP, 1995.
_____. Personal interview. 12 March, 2002.
_____. *Shoeless Joe.* New York: Houghton-Mifflin, 1982.

2

Jon Billman's "Indians" and American Indian Exhibition Baseball Teams

JEFFREY POWERS-BECK

Jon Billman's "Indians" is the first story in his favorably reviewed debut collection, *When We Were Wolves*. Set in Dust-Bowl South Dakota, the story is part legend, part allegory, of a barnstorming Indian team led by a one-armed pitcher named Job Looks Twice. In the climactic scene, the Indians play the renowned House of David team in the drought-stricken town of Faith. In the summer of 2000, as I was researching the history of the Nebraska Indians exhibition baseball team, I corresponded with Jon Billman. So little historical research had been published about the Indian barnstorming teams, I was curious about the sources that he had used in writing his story. He replied that he had based his story on histories of the black barnstorming teams and on South Dakota legends of Indian teams and the Dust Bowl. Or as he put it:

> I'm from South Dakota, and there are apocryphal stories of touring Indian ball teams. I started with this seed and put it with my grandfather's stories of the Dust Bowl, and researched the hell out of the barnstorming negro teams. But as far as actual print on the Indian clubs, I never did find a lot. But since baseball was more ingrained in the culture then, nearly anything was possible [Billman, "Re: Native American Baseball"].

It is hardly surprising that Billman did not find print sources concerning the Indian barnstorming teams, since only two such pieces have been published over the past two decades: one chapter in Harold Seymour's *Baseball: The People's Game* and an article by Barbara Gregorich on John Olson's Cherokee Indian Baseball team in *Michigan History Magazine* in 1995. How accurately, then, does Billman's story represent the lives of players on Indian exhibition baseball teams in this period?

To answer this question, I will briefly recall the plot and major characters of "Indians" and then identify how Billman's Indian team differed considerably from the most successful touring pan–Indian teams of the early twentieth century, Guy Wilder Green's Nebraska Indians (1897–1917) and John Olson's Cherokee Indians or Cherokee All-Stars (1903–1914). Although "The Mud Butte Indians" of Billman's tale are perpetual winners, they are beset by financial crisis, and indeed seem to live on crisis alone. While the account of the team's rugged existence seems exaggerated for the sake of allegory, Billman's account of the players' treatment by white opponents and fans holds true to the experiences of many American Indian ballplayers in this period. In both Billman's story and in Guy Green's accounts of his Indian team, the players suffered segregated accommodations, racial harassment, threats of violence, and badly biased umpiring. This essay will argue that "Indians," though not a strictly accurate historical account of the Indian barnstorming teams, is a triumph of the imagination that captures the social and spiritual isolation of the Indian ball players.

In Billman's "Indians," a team of nine players, eight members of the Lakota Nation of the Pine Ridge Reservation, and the white team manager and narrator of the story, travel the dirt and gravel roads of South Dakota in a single, broken-down model T. The author imagines the narrator, the son of a Presbyterian missionary, growing up in Porcupine, South Dakota, and adopting baseball as his new religion and his boyhood Oglala friends as his teammates. When the Depression comes, and there is no work to be found, they receive a donation of used flannel uniforms from a women's aid society in Mud Butte and so become the "Mud Butte Indians," setting out across the state to play other reservation teams, semipros, barnstorming Blacks, town all-stars, prisoners, and Rotarians "for whatever beans, chickens, Grain Belt beer, and gasoline we could get" (4). Barred by prejudice from most hotels, the Indians sleep under the stars and wander from desperate town to desperate town, looking for games. The team is led by its white manager and catcher, who grows a pony tail and pretends to be an Indian when on the baseball field, and its one-armed, left-handed pitcher, Job Looks Twice, a man of deep convictions and paradoxes. Though Job is a solemnly religious man, his best pitches are the illegal spitball and the mysterious needleball. The Mud Butte team is so successful that local teams increasingly fear to play them, and so the manager coaxes opposing teams to play by allowing winning teams to take all gate receipts, and by convincing them that defeating the Indians would bring an end to drought. Job Looks Twice disapproves of the rainmaking ruse, but he does begin to feel the coming of rain in the aching stump of his right arm as they prepare to play in Faith, South Dakota.

In the climactic scene, the Indians face the House of David team, who are depicted as all devout members of a Michigan religious settlement, dressed in blue and gray flannel: "They let their hair and beards grow long and God-like and kept Bibles with them in the dugout.... Their fervor for God turned into a fervor for baseball and winning.... The games were as intense as firefights. It was like facing Jesus at every position" (12). The usually unbeatable Indians are finally meeting a worthy opponent, and the game is made even tougher for them by the Faith town umpire, who refuses to call Job's pitches as strikes, and Job himself, who, hoping to end the drought, offers easy fastballs to the "Whiskers." With the Indians ahead 13–12 in the bottom of the ninth, two out, and runners on first and second, Job lobs an easy one to cleanup hitter Joe Garner, who hits a "rainmaker" into the deep outfield in the midst of thunderclouds and lightning. However, to the surprise of Garner and the entire town of Faith, a sudden blast of wind pulls the ball back toward centerfielder Otis Downwind, who makes the catch and rushes away to the Model T, for fear of the angry crowd. As the Indian team escapes in its chugging jalopy, the town of Faith is then pelted "with hailstones the size of baseballs" (16).

Billman's treatment of the House of David team is very much like his treatment of the Indian barnstorming teams—true in some historical respects but also exaggerated for the purposes of mythmaking and allegory. The team did hail from the religious settlement of Benjamin Purnell in Benton Harbor, Michigan, and was famed for its apocalyptic beliefs, its abstinence from sex and alcohol, and the players' wearing of long hair and beards (Hawkins and Bertolino 7). One of the first great players for the team, Paul Mooney, was a pitcher who allegedly received a $20,000 offer from the Chicago Cubs, but he refused to cut his hair in order to join a major league team (57). By the 1930's, however, the House of David and City of David teams, which wore light-colored and pinstriped uniforms, were national barnstorming attractions. The House of David management, understanding the team's ability to draw large crowds and publicize the colony, hired outstanding athletes to join the team, including former big leaguers such as Grover Cleveland Alexander and Cy Perkins, and Negro League star Satchel Paige, as well as drawing cards like Babe Didrikson (7). Traveling in its team bus and using portable electric lighting units for night games, House of David teams packed the bleachers in cities such Denver, Chicago, Gary, Akron, and Santa Cruz, California. Seldom did they stop in towns as small as Faith, South Dakota, with populations under a thousand. Nor did anyone named Benson or Garner play on the 1930s House of David teams. Here, as elsewhere in "Indians," Billman is less concerned with precise historical details than with his spiritual allegory of Dust-Bowl South Dakota. And his rootless Lakota ballplayers are at the center of this allegory. The allegorical elements of "Indians," which make Billman's Indian team an alienated and spiritually exhausted group of baseball drifters, belie some of the economic facts of Indian baseball teams, such as Guy Green's Nebraska Indians and John Olson's Cherokee All-Stars. Touring exhibition teams required considerable budgets and planning, involving everything from game scheduling and contracting and ticket sales promotions to team travel and lodging and souvenir sales. As such, Billman's story does not attempt to recreate the financial and management conditions of the successful Indian exhibition baseball teams.

A new graduate of the University of Nebraska law school, Guy Green founded his Nebraska Indians touring team in 1897 after noticing the large crowds that assembled for Genoa Indian and Agricultural School games in Genoa, Nebraska. As he put it, "I observed that even in Nebraska, where an Indian is not all a novelty, a base ball organization composed of red men drew everyone who was alive" (5). An effective recruiter, Green hired talented Indian ballplayers from Genoa, Flandreau, Haskell, and Carlisle Indian schools, as well as players from reservations throughout the Midwest. Also an eager promoter, Green created posters, handbills, and newspaper notices to advertise his teams and occasionally staged team processions in buckskin and headdresses to drum up large crowds for his games. Always, Green took a large percentage of the 25-cent admission charged for Nebraska Indian games. The Nebraska Indians averaged over 150 games per season from 1897 to 1917, in towns and cities of all sizes, sometimes drawing crowds in the thousands. They toured throughout the Midwest and East Coast, although they almost never ventured into South Dakota, the home of Billman's fictional nine (Powers-Beck).

As Billman's "Indians" were perpetual winners, so were Green's "Indians," winning more than 70% of their games in seasons for which records are available, and gaining a reputation as one of the top barnstorming teams in the Midwest (Powers-Beck). As a canny scout of baseball talent, Green signed a series of tremendous Indian athletes. These players included George Howard Johnson (the burly Winnebago pitcher who anchored the Cincinnati Reds' staff in 1913), John Bull Williams (an Oneida outfielder with a long minor-league career), and Jacob Burkhardt (a big Shawnee from Oklahoma, who caught for Carlisle Indian School and played minor league ball before joining the Nebraska Indians in 1898) (Powers-Beck). Green occasionally added to his profits by taking wagers on Indian games against town teams and local all-stars, and enhanced his odds by hiring talented white players to join his team for a series (he hired future Hall of Famer Wahoo Sam Crawford to play against the University of Nebraska in 1898) (Powers-Beck).

The Nebraska Indians' owner also wrote two dime pamphlets about the team, *The Nebraska Indians: A Complete History* and *Fun and Frolic with an Indian Ball Team*. These small books were filled with seasonal narratives, records, anecdotes, illustrations, and advertisements, and Green sold them at games by the thousands, along with picture postcards of the team and of individual players. The Nebraska Indians generally toured with a squad of twelve to fourteen players, a player manager (Dan Tobey), a baggage handler (Sandy Leach), an umpire (Olson), and a business manager (usually Green himself). The large staff was needed to schedule and promote games, purchase train fares, cook meals, and set up the team camp, as the team slept in tents on town fairgrounds or ball fields in order to economize and avoid conflicts with hotel owners who routinely refused to lodge Indians. Players were paid weekly from gate receipts but at lower salaries than minor league teams offered, so Green was zealous in keeping his players away from minor league scouts and managers. While Green continued to work as a lawyer in the off-season from 1897–1911, his success with the Nebraska Indians enabled him to buy the Lincoln Western League franchise in late 1907. For two years, from late 1907 to mid–1909, when he sold his Western League team, Guy Green considered himself primarily a baseball magnate.

Following a similar formula, John Olson of Waterliviet, Michigan, toured with a bloomer girls baseball team in 1901, and finding success, added an Indian team, apparently in 1903. Though known as the "Cherokee Indians" or "Cherokee All-Stars," the team had few if any Cherokee players, as Olson recruited most of his players from the Menominee and Stockbridge reservations in Michigan and from Indian boarding schools. According to Barbara Gregorich's account, Olson's 1905 Indian team traveled with eleven players and four canvas-men in a Pullman car, named the Clementine, purchased by Olson and his partner L.C. Figg of Chicago (39). The specially-equipped coach held an undercarriage with "a 1,200-foot-long, 12-foot-high canvas fence; a portable grandstand that would seat 1,000; and a complete light plant for night games" (39). The canvas fence was designed to prevent spectators from watching games without paying for attendance, and the portable lights enabled the team to play night games and day-night double headers. Like Green, Olson also sold postcards of his team, and apparently profited, touring annually with the team through 1914.

In telling his story of the "Mud Butte Indians," Billman styles them, like Green's and Olson's teams, as a group of fleet-footed, talented players, capable of competing with the best exhibition teams in the country. The management of the "Indians" team by the white catcher is a realistic detail, as game scheduling depended on working with small town officials, who were often reluctant to make financial agreements with Indian players. However, the financial and living conditions that Billman describes are very unlike those of Green's and Olson's teams. Receiving payment only for wins, accepting payment in chickens and gasoline, playing without substitutes in case of injury or illness, wandering from town to town in search of games, catching dinner from nearby streams, and carrying all nine players in a single Model T—these are hardly the ingredients for a winning exhibition team, even during the Depression. Green himself found during his first season that when he required his players to do all the work of driving, carrying equipment, and setting up the team camp, they soon grew exhausted and their play faltered. Billman's team, miraculously, appears to thrive on crisis, living on nothing, playing for nothing, but still winning and sputtering off to play another day. Although this element of the narrative is not realistic, it does help recreate the atmosphere of spiritual and social alienation that Indian ballplayers faced early in the twentieth century.

In "Indians," as in the other stories in *When We Were Wolves*, Billman is often at his best in describing the hardscrabble lives of people in the West. In "Sugar City," a story later in the collection, the narrator, a drifter, seeks "true happiness in living like coyotes," but finds himself having "to face all Idaho with nothing but a windbreaker and a pocket comb" (137, 147). These are lives made harder by prejudice and personal misunderstanding as well as by the characters' hopeless but unquenchable desires for transcendence. Although the allegory in "Indians" of Job's joyless victory over the House of David in the God-cursed town of Faith borders on parody, Billman's account of the Indian players' struggles rings true. The narrator comments: "Job never argued with umpires, because he knew it was fruitless. The umps had the support of the fans, who sometimes resembled angry mobs" (8). Just as the Mud Butte Indians suffer from unfair umpiring and a hostile crowd in the town of Faith, so Guy

Green complained of town umpires: "Sometimes they were ignorant; sometimes willfully unfair" (69). For this reason, the Nebraska Indians furnished their own umpire for games (a man named Olson), who at times traded bum calls with town umpires. Likewise, the crowds that the Nebraska Indians faced were occasionally hostile like the local umpires. For one game in Hopkinsville, Kentucky, Green recalled that his team captain Roberts argued a call by a local umpire: "The umpired produced a knife about a foot long and threatened to cut somebody's 'innards' out while the crowd yelled, 'Stick 'im. Stick 'im. We'll stand by you'" (69). So the Mud Butte Indians' fleeing in their Model T from games for fear of the crowd fits Green's account of his team.

Although the Mud Butte Indians play baseball with real passion, they drift from game to game like exiles. Their rootless existence is directly attributed to the prejudices and economic circumstances they face. Like Green's teams, Billman's fictional players sleep outside, shut out of hotels and motor lodges by anti–Indian biases. Publicity of the Mud Butte Indians' games is largely handled by the local communities themselves and indulges in anti–Indian stereotypes, as the narrator notes:

> We'd ... speak with the mayor, the sheriff, barkeeps, the undertaker, the men who planned the games. They ran ads in the local newspapers, cartoons of feathered savages with big teeth and tomahawks running bases. Word of our winning preceded us, and opposing teams shot beanballs at our heads in the early innings [9].

This fictional account squares with the factual, day-to-day racism that Indian exhibition teams faced in contemporary media and in game situations. When the Nebraska Indians played the University of Nebraska team in late June of 1897, Lincoln's *Evening News* indulged in the following lurid anti–Indian stereotypes:

> With wild yells and flourishing tomahawk, with unsheathed knives and poisoned arrows, with plenty of war paint but no fire water, a band of Indians from western Nebraska and Kansas swooped down upon a small encampment of Lincoln baseball players yesterday afternoon, and in less time than it takes to enunciate John Robinson's cognomen, nine bloody scalps were dangling from the belts of the savages ["In a Bloodless Battle" 1].

Unfortunately, the anti–Indian prejudice was not limited to newspaper stories but erupted frequently in the derisive chanting and jeers of crowds. Billman comments about the hostility of baseball crowds toward Indian players, as in Custer, South Dakota, where the "Mud Butte Indians," are "downright thankful to make it out of town with our hides" (10). Green also describes the occasional hostile crowd, but by his account, the Nebraska Indians constantly faced derisive laughter. In an interview with the *Sioux City Journal* in 1909, Green reflected upon George Johnson's experience as an Indian pitcher with the Nebraska Indians and the Lincoln Western League franchise:

> Johnson, my Indian twirler ... pitched for my Nebraska Indian team three seasons. During that time we played an average of 150 towns annually in the United States and Canada. That makes 450 towns. Johnson is now pitching his second season in this league. He has never yet stepped to the mound to pitch a game anywhere on earth that three things have not happened. Numerous local humorists have started what they imagine to be Indian war cries; others have yelled "Back to the reservation," and the third variety of town pump jester has shrieked "Dog soup! Dog soup!" If you were at the game Tuesday you heard this. If you see him pitch in Pueblo or Sitka or Kamchatka you will hear the same thing. You would think people would get all that kind of patent inside stuff out of their systems after awhile, wouldn't you? But they never do ["Raps Bleacher" 9].

While Billman does not depict this kind of crowd derision, he does hint at the attitude as his narrator schedules "rainmaking" games with local officials: "Hell, their faces would say, if we can't beat a one-armed Indian baseball team, we don't deserve rain" (9). That kind of mocking prejudice, disguised as jocularity, frequently confronted American Indian athletes early in the twentieth century.

Jon Billman's "Indians" is not a strictly realistic historical account of Indian exhibition baseball teams of the early twentieth century, but it is an imaginative triumph. While the story does not convey the financial and management conditions of teams like the Nebraska Indians and Cherokee All-Stars, it does portray the spiritual and social alienation of American Indian players. In the story, as on the diamonds of federal Indian boarding schools during this time, baseball provided an athletic compensation for peoples whose languages, religions, and cultures were being pervasively assaulted. "Indians" does not dwell on this assault itself but on the Job-like conditions suffered by the players, who having lost so much and been given so little, cling tightly to the seams of a baseball. Billman's one-armed Job, devoutly Christian but still more deeply Lakota, imagines that the "stitched horsehide" of the baseball possesses "the spirit of the horse" (15), a powerful recuperation from a deep loss. Baseball does not lift these proud people from poverty or social alienation, but it does provide a temporary, nine-inning "miracle." The crowd at "Faith" yells, "The miracle! Do you smell the rain!" (15). The crowd at Faith is mistaken about the rain, but they do intuit the imaginative compensations of baseball for the people of the Depression, even for the most economically and socially disadvantaged of those people.

WORKS CITED:

Billman, Jon. *When We Were Wolves*. New York: Random House, 1999.
_____. "Re: Native American Baseball." E-mail to Jeffrey Powers-Beck. 3 Aug. 2000.
Green, Guy. *The Nebraska Indians: A Complete History of the Nebraska Indian Base Ball Team*. Lincoln, NE: Woodruff-Collins, 1903.
Gregorich, Barbara. "John Olson and His Barnstorming Baseball Teams." *Michigan History Magazine* 79.3 (May/June): 38–44.
Hawkins, Joel, and Terry Bertolino. *The House of David Baseball Team*. Chicago: Arcadia Publishing, 2000.
"In a Bloodless Battle," *Lincoln Evening News*, 28 June 1897: 1.
Powers-Beck, Jeffrey. "'A Role New to the Race': A New History of the Nebraska Indians," *Nebraska History* 84.2 (Summer 2003): 30 pages ms. forthcoming.
"Raps Bleacher Jokesters," *Sioux City Journal*, 3 June 1909: 9.
Seymour, Harold. *Baseball: The People's Game*. Oxford: Oxford University Press, 1990.

3

"Dad—Can We Have a Catch?" Images of Fatherhood and Redemption in Three Baseball Films

SCOTT JENSEN AND JOSEPH SCHUSTER

An inexorable relationship binds baseball and fatherhood. Jack Petrash, in his *Covering Home,* writes that "there is a place in us where our passionate commitments converge, and it is there that fathering and baseball intertwine" (x). For myriad and often unexplainable reasons, fatherhood shares a relationship with baseball that differentiates the game from other sports. Perhaps the relationship is fashioned because baseball is played as school ends, summer ensues, and school begins again. Then again, baseball's poignant and lengthy history, or its rich characterizations of heroes may offer the best explanation. Whatever the reason, the significance of fatherhood and baseball in our national culture is undeniable. In their critique of baseball films, Marty Most and Robert Rudd write that these stories demonstrate "the power of baseball to fuse a heterogeneous assembly into a unified community—a family—pursuing a common goal" (245).

Baseball films that depict images of fatherhood to tell stories of redemption often follow the structure of a heroic journey. Most and Rudd write that in contemporary baseball films, we often see "individuals who, having first made the commitment to the good of the community as a whole, are in turn able to realize their individual dreams" (250). Baseball films provide insights into problems facing fathers, and the game itself the means through which these issues are resolved. In addition, as Most and Rudd contend, "the fact that the fulfillment they [the fathers] achieve is loftier than mere materialistic success completes a picture congruous with baseball's ideological vision" (250). This paper analyzes three prominent baseball films that depict images of fatherhood and baseball—*The Natural*, *The Rookie*, and *Field of Dreams*—arguing that baseball is uniquely suited as a context in which one can seek and find redemption

THE NATURAL

Few baseball films celebrate the journey toward fatherhood and the connection the game allows between fathers and sons more than Barry Levinson's 1984 paean to the sport, *The Natural*. The film's principle narrative is even framed with a paradigmatic image: a father and son playing catch. At the beginning, after a brief prologue, in which we see a weathered Roy Hobbs waiting for the train that will take him, an aged rookie, to the New York Knights, the film flashes back to the pastoral scene of a young, golden-haired Roy Hobbs playing catch with his father in a wheat field. It's an idyllic scene, and the film punctuates the moment by a distinct contrast in light. While the prologue is dominated by muted tones—in a station of browns and rusts, Roy Hobbs sits alone and cast in shadow—the scene in which the young Hobbs plays a game of catch with his father is cast in the brilliant yellows of the wheat and the sun, creating a halo effect around young Hobbs. The scene seems a juxtaposition of earth and light, immanent and transcendent. In a way, it lays the foundation for the journey Hobbs will take through the film, as he moves from callow, self-centered young man to the altruistic mature father-hero he becomes by the end of the film—a journey made clear by the film's final image, which echoes that earlier one: a father playing catch with a son in a wheat field on a brilliant day. Only this time, Hobbs is the father.

In many ways, the journey Hobbs takes from son to father mirrors the hero's journey that Joseph Campbell describes in *The Hero with a Thousand Faces* and that Christopher Vogler applies to the film's story in his book, *The Writer's Journey*. Without straying too far onto this path, it is useful to consider Campbell's work, and Vogler's translation of it, as a framework to discuss the film. Briefly, the hero's journey centers on the following structure: A hero abides in an ordinary world and is forced to separate from it; often the separation comes as a result of some trauma: the death of a parent, for example, or some sort of familial estrangement.

Think of all of the fairy tales in which an orphan sets off to make his fortune in the world, or of jealous stepmothers who reject the child of their spouses and send them off on a dangerous errand.

As Vogler says, "The journey of many heroes is the story of separation from the family or tribe.... The Hero archetype represents the ego's search for identity and wholeness." (Vogler 35) It is only by leaving the familiar world of childhood behind that the hero can achieve wholeness; in *The Natural*, and other baseball films, that wholeness manifests itself in a transformation from son to father. The separation from the familiar is accompanied by a call to adventure, which the prospective hero refuses, but then later accepts. Eventually, the hero undergoes a supreme trial, perhaps facing some sort of death or ultimate failure, but then, if successful, he returns to the familiar world with an elixir that somehow makes for a better world.

Roy Hobbs' story in *The Natural* unfolds within the structure of the heroic journey. Initially, we see him with his father: playing catch, being tutored in the game. "You've got a gift, Roy," his father says. "But it's not enough. Rely too much on your own gift and you'll fail." Shortly, as happens often in these kinds of stories, his father dies suddenly, while Roy watches, helpless from a distance as his father collapses at the base of a tree. Later, the sky echoes his grief, as it explodes into the first of several violent thunderstorms that will punctuate many of the key moments in his journey. Abruptly, through the black sky, a flash of lightning strikes the very tree that marked the place where his father fell. From the smoldering remnant of the trunk, Roy makes himself the bat he will take with him into the game, a bat he names (fittingly for this stage of his journey) Wonder Boy.

Not long after, he leaves home for a tryout with the Chicago Cubs—but not before he has a tryst with Iris, a girl with whom he grew up. On his trip to Chicago, he encounters a mysterious woman in black who asks him what he wants out of the game. He replies that, when he walks down the street, he wants people to say, "There goes Roy Hobbs, the best that ever was." She asks him, "Is that all?" He replies, "What else is there?" His answer is not a good one; he fails the test, gets shot and disappears.

When he reemerges from his exile sixteen years later and joins the Knights, he is older but not yet much wiser. He still desires to be the best that ever was—and soon appears to be on track to do just that—but although his outstanding play helps to elevate what had previously been an inept team, he has his self interest at heart. The film even signals that Hobbs still has not matured fully when his immaturity and pursuit of self-interest soon brings about a fall, as it did on his interrupted trip to Chicago

3. "Dad—Can We Have a Catch?" (Jensen & Schuster)

earlier. Again, a woman to whom he is attracted leads to his fall. The seductive Memo, in league with gamblers, distracts him from the game and he slips into a slump, pulling his team with him.

His salvation comes partly through the agency of Iris, his childhood sweetheart whom he has unknowingly impregnated before he left home many years before. He encounters her on the Knights' first trip to Chicago—interestingly the city that in the beginning of the film was the location of his initial failure. She attends a game and, after seeing Hobbs strike out early on, stands as he bats in the ninth inning, a woman in white, bathed in sunlight—the light of this moment again echoing the earlier scene in the film when Hobbs and his father played catch. Hobbs hits a majestic home run that destroys the scoreboard clock in centerfield, and afterwards, she and Hobbs are reunited, although she does not disclose that he is the father of their son. "He [the father] lives in New York," Iris tells him, but goes on to say that she has been thinking that the boy had reached the age where he needs contact with his father. Ironically, Hobbs assents.

From here on, Hobbs finds himself in a clear conflict on a number of levels—but the central conflict is between selfishness and altruism, and the tension manifests itself partly through his relationship with the two women in his life, Memo and Iris, whore and mother. Eventually, he makes his choice clear: he comes down on the side of altruism and honor—rejecting the Judge's bribe that he throw the championship game—and Memo poisons him. Fittingly, he ends up recovering in a maternity hospital—the film explains that it was the nearest hospital—where the doctor informs him that, because of his earlier gunshot wound, if he continues to play ball, it likely would kill him. In the hospital, both Memo and Iris visit him. Memo selfishly begs him to take the bribe: "Think what we can do with the money, Roy," she pleads. When Iris visits, Roy confesses that he fears he has been a failure. She tells him, "Think of all the young boys you have influenced—so many of them," and also tells him that his life is not over: "I believe we have two lives. The life we learn with and the life we live with after that." These lines constitute her invitation for him to accept his rebirth—in Campbell's and Vogler's models, the hero's death is often followed by a rebirth—this time into a life of mature responsibility and eventually fatherhood, a perfection of the mature male.

Despite the risk to himself, Hobbs goes to the ballpark and plays in the game—which Iris and their son have chosen to attend. At first, things go badly as Hobbs plays poorly and the Knights trail until Iris sends him a note during the game revealing his fatherhood and the presence of his son at the ballpark Almost immediately after, Hobbs comes to the plate in the bottom of the ninth inning. As he cracks a long foul down the rightfield line, his bat—Wonder Boy—splits. He tells the team's batboy, Bobby Savoy, to pick out another one for him, and Savoy brings Hobbs a bat that the boy, himself, had made under the guidance of Hobbs. The choice is appropriate—Hobbs is putting aside his own boyhood, as he is no longer that same person. Additionally, the bat he now uses was produced by a protégé, a sort of surrogate son who foreshadows the appearance of his natural son.

When Hobbs hits the home run to win the game, breaking a stadium light and setting off a chain reaction that showers the field with light, the final shot from the game tracks the ball as it continues its flight into space, and the film dissolves into a ball coming down from a blue sky to settle into the glove of Hobbs' son, who is transplanted along with Hobbs and Iris into the golden wheat field of the film's opening—the journey and family now complete.

THE ROOKIE

The Rookie offers a different sort of fatherhood narrative than does *The Natural*. Although in the latter film, the hero's salvation is connected with his recognition of his role as father, he achieves his greatest heroic moment immediately after learning he is a father. In *The Rookie*, the fact of the hero's fatherhood provides the agency for the realization of his dreams of playing in the Major Leagues, and leads, indirectly at least, to his embracing of his role as son.

Unlike Roy Hobbs, Jim Morris has a father who fails to support his dreams as a ballplayer. The tension between father and son surfaces several times in the film's first act, which centers on Morris' boyhood, during which his father is an obstacle to his achieving his ambition in the game. His father's job in the military, for example, forces Morris to move often. At one point, he goes to see his father after pitching a winning Little League game, but his father is too busy to talk about it; as Morris describes his success on the mound, his father continues to go about his work, and then informs the boy that the family will be moving in a few weeks' time. When Morris tells him that it would mean his missing the last half of the season, and suggests that he live with friends until it is over, his father refuses: "We move as a family."

When they arrive at their next destination, a small Texas town that worships football to the near exclusion of baseball, Morris discovers that they have left his glove behind them in Florida. His father regards him for a moment and then snaps, "Oh quit moping. There are more important things in life than baseball. The sooner you figure that out, the better."

The grown-up Morris is a doting father, especially to his older son, Hunter, who appears in nearly every moment of the film that marks a significant step on Morris' road to the Major Leagues. For example, Hunter draws from Morris the information that, although his earlier professional career ended because of a shoulder injury, he no longer suffers pain in his arm. Later, when Morris is at practice with the high school team he coaches, and the team's catcher invites him to try out his pitching arm, Hunter is there again and, after a few easy tosses, when the catcher cajoles him to throw as hard as he can, Morris is reluctant until his young son exhorts from the bleachers, "Yeah, dad, bring the heat." Still later, when Morris attends the tryout with the Tampa Bay Devil Rays, and loses heart before he has the chance to actually try out, Hunter protests that he ought to stay until he has a chance to pitch.

Later, when the Devil Rays offer him a minor league contract, and Morris' wife tells him that it would be a mistake for him to play minor league ball for $600 a month when he has a family to support and a good job offer from a better school, Hunter, again, saves Morris' dream. Immediately after offering her opinion that Morris give up his dream, his wife goes into Hunter's room to tuck him in for the night. He's asleep already, and as she smoothes the blanket over him, she takes in the decorations on his walls: posters of Major League players and a large photo of his father as a pitcher. When she returns to Morris and tells him that she was wrong to discourage him, she says, "We've got an eight-year-old boy inside this house who waited all day in the sun and the rain to see his daddy try to do something that nobody believed he could do. What are we telling him if you don't try now?"

Interestingly, Hunter also provides the bridge that allows Morris to reconcile with his own father. After a long estrangement, Morris takes Hunter to his father's to receive the gift that he's bought for his grandson. Fittingly, it is a baseball glove—but, also fittingly (given Morris' father's failure to support his own son's baseball ambitions), it is an inappropriate one, a first baseman's mitt, something that disappoints Hunter. While there, however, Morris discovers that his father has a number of pictures of him on his walls—all snapshots of him as a ballplayer when he was a boy. "Your mother gave them to me," Morris' father says. Morris nods. "She'd be the one to have them." This response is a slap at his father's lack of interest when Morris was a boy.

The two eventually reconcile—in one of the film's most sentimental and perhaps most false moments. After Morris has pitched his first game in the Major Leagues, he comes out of the clubhouse where he finds a swarm of reporters. As he responds to a question, he sees his father in the background and excuses himself from the cameras and microphones. Though Morris is surprised to see his father, his father responds that he wouldn't have missed the game and adds, "Watching you tonight—not many fathers get a chance to do that. I guess I let too many of those get away." "So did I," Morris responds and then gives him the ball. His father walks off, tossing it into the air and catching it, the first time we have seen him happy in the film. Though the two men separate, baseball has been the vehicle for the reconciliation that the film suggests redeems the past and will continue into the future.

FIELD OF DREAMS

The relationship between father and son is at the heart of the 1989 Phil Alden Robinson film, *Field of Dreams*. While the primary backdrop of the film appears to be a cornfield in rural Iowa, the essential background is Ray Kinsella's memories of his father and the way those memories both consciously and subconsciously shape Ray's life as an adult. The film depicts two fathers—one as a memory who unknowingly guides the son, and the other the son who is "scared to death I am turning into my father" as he tells his wife at one point in the film.

The film opens with photographs and Ray's narration of his childhood. He recounts hearing bedtime stories of the White Sox and Shoeless Joe that helped to define his childhood with his father who raised him after his mother died. Shoeless Joe plays a central role in Ray's journey to redemption. Interestingly, Ray passes on his father's stories of Shoeless Joe to his daughter, evoking the outfielder's greatness and the injustice dealt to him when he was banned from baseball after the infamous Black Sox scandal of 1919. This glorification of Shoeless Joe is compensatory because, as Ray admits later, his last memories of his father were when he left home after pronouncing that he "could never respect a man whose hero was a criminal." Ray's regret about the comment marks his journey to redemption—his desire to take it back by glorifying both his father and his father's hero by building a baseball field.

When the movie begins with Ray hearing the disembodied voice tell him, "If you build it, he will come," though first puzzled, he eventually sees an image of Shoeless Joe and realizes that the voice is telling him that if he builds this field, he can resurrect the banned outfielder to play baseball again. For obvious reasons, his wife, Annie, resists taking away a portion of the family's only source of income to build a field because a mysterious voice is instructing Ray to do so. In his defense, Ray tells Annie that the field will "let him play ... right an old wrong." This desire to "right an old wrong" foreshadows the relationship between Ray's father and his dreams and Ray's wish to mend their relationship. As Ray persuades Annie to let him build the field, the impetus for his journey to redemption gradually emerges. In his effort to win over Annie, Ray tells her, "He [Ray's father] never did one spontaneous thing in the years that I knew him. Annie, I'm afraid of that happening to me. And something tells me this may be my last chance to do something about it."

Once Ray convinces Annie to allow him to build the field, it becomes clear that he shares his father's admiration of Shoeless Joe, who becomes the vehicle for the reconciliation of the two. With great enthusiasm, Ray tells his daughter, "My pop called him the greatest left fielder of all time ... he said his glove was the place where triples go to die." After building the field Ray reflects on his motivation for building it when he tells Annie, "Dad used to say no one could hit like Shoeless Joe." Annie's response frames the dissonance Ray feels: "I think that's the first time I've ever seen you smile when you mentioned your father." While Ray smiles at her, he also changes the subject by observing that he has "just created something totally illogical." Ray's failure to continue the conversation about his father leaves the audience with some question as to the nature of the relationship they had.

The financial difficulties Ray and Annie face as a result of the portion of crop lost to the field provide the challenges for Ray when he hears the voice again, this time telling him "Ease his pain." Predictably, Ray determines that the pain to be eased must be that of the great writer Terrance Mann when Mann appears in a dream Ray and Annie share that features the two men together in Fenway Park. Though facing financial ruin, she endorses Ray's plan to trek to Boston to find Mann and carry out the task given by the mysterious voice.

At this point, the narrative of the film adopts the structure of the journey and return. Mann's pain, like Ray's, is grounded in dreams not pursued and regrets he wishes could be reversed, specifically a dream of playing for the New York Giants. As Mann and Ray sit in Fenway Park, they see a message about an unknown Giant of the past, Moonlight Graham, and hear the voice tell them to "Go the distance." The journey now moves to Chisolm, Minnesota, and again, the regrets of a former baseball player serve as the crux of the message. Now known as Doc, not Moonlight, Graham provides the poignant observation that validates Ray's illogical adherence to the voice: "You know, we just don't recognize the most significant moments of our life when they're happening." Reflecting on his leaving baseball after an inning of playing defense in the outfield, Doc crystallizes his own regrets when he says, "I thought, well, they'll be other days. I didn't realize that was the only day."

At this point in Ray's journey Terrance Mann has decided to continue on with him to Iowa, while Doc Graham, now dead for several years, has told Ray that he actually felt no regrets in his decision to leave baseball and become a doctor in the small Minnesota town. Ray and Terrance, on their return to Iowa, pick up a hitchhiker looking for a place where he can play baseball. The young man's introduces himself as Archie Graham—the same Moonlight who, in a backdrop of 1972, told Ray that he was satisfied with his life as he had lived it—without continuing his pursuit of his baseball dreams.

On this same return, the central motivation behind Ray's journey to redemption is revealed. A dialogue between Mann and Ray reveals a difficult relationship that resulted in the voice, the field, and the pursuit of redemption.

Mann: "What happened to your father?"

Ray: "He never made it as a ball player so he tried to get his son to make it for him. By the time I was ten playing baseball was like eating vegetables or taking out the garbage. So when I was fourteen I started to refuse. Do you believe that? American boy refusing to have a catch with his father?"

Mann: "Why fourteen?"

Ray: "That's when I read *The Boat Rocker* by Terrance Mann."

Mann: "Oh God—"

Ray: "Never played catch with him again."

Mann: "That's the kind of crap people always lay on me. It's not my fault you wouldn't play catch with your father."

Mann's chastising of Ray further highlights Ray's need to reconcile with his father. Rejecting the role of surrogate father, in which his book supplants Rays's father's narrative of baseball, Mann goes on to crystallize Ray's motivation, telling him that the field and his journey are his "penance," an attempt to bring back his father's hero because he can't bring back his father.

As the three men arrive at Ray's farm, they are greeted by Annie, Karen, and a field full of baseball players who shared a generation with Shoeless Joe. Shoeless Joe, who has been expecting Graham, tells him to suit up to play. The significance of the players throughout the film is that only those who share faith in the voice and Ray's journey can see or hear them. Terrance Mann immediately sees the players, while Annie's family interpret the references to the players as some cruel joke or ruse that not only mocks them but also will condemn her to poverty. However, when Graham leaves the field, transforms back into the figure of Doc Graham, and saves Karen from choking on a bite of hot dog lodged in her throat, he not only validates his decision years earlier but enables Annie's mother and brother to see the players and believe in the magic of the field. Their inclusion further validates the notion of familial reconciliation central to Ray's plot.

But Ray faces one more test before the vision of the film is complete. As the day ends, Shoeless Joe invites Mann to come with him and the players. Ray mistakes the invitation as being directed to him. When he learns that Mann, not he himself, is being given the opportunity, he asks, for the first time, "What's in it for me?" Shoeless Joe tells Ray he had better stay and states, "If you build it, he will come," prompting Ray to turn and see his father taking off his catcher's gear at home plate. When Ray asks Annie what he should say to him, she responds in a way that links Ray's father's stories to him with those he has told his daughter, "Why don't you introduce him to his granddaughter?"

As Annie and Karen return to the house, Ray visits with his father, John Kinsella. Ray tells his father that he "catches a good game," and his father responds, "It's so beautiful here. For me, well, for me it's like a dream come true." The father then asks Ray if they are in heaven. Ray tells him that it is Iowa, but then asks his father if there is a heaven, who answers, "Oh yeah. It's the place dreams come true." Upon that response, Ray looks to the field, his wife and daughter on the porch of his farmhouse, and then suggests, "Maybe this is heaven." The reuniting of a mature son and a wronged father is complete as the before unknown motive for building the field becomes clear to Ray. The line of cars seen parading toward the field validates Ray's dream beyond his personal circumstances before his journey to redemption culminates when he calls to John, "Hey Dad, you wanna have a catch?" and the father says "I'd like that." Ray reaches home both literally and metaphorically.

Conclusions

While Roy Hobbs, Jim Morris, and Ray Kinsella represent the literal role of fatherhood, they also portray the metaphor of fatherhood as an altruistic role present in mature males who have the potential to nurture a child. In each case, baseball helps these men to appreciate their roles as fathers; baseball connects them with dreams and realities, each central to defining their responsibilities to their children and families. While redemption is not at all a conscious goal of any of these characters, these fathers, it becomes clear to each once it is achieved. In each film, the main characters transcend their dissonance between immaturity and dreams unfulfilled and accept realities seemingly incompatible with their baseball-connected dreams. Ironically, in each case, the acceptance of responsibility and maturity makes their baseball dreams an enduring element in the relationships between the fathers and their families.

These films provide the lessons that are offered by Petrash in his book that presents baseball as a text for effective fathering. While "good" fathers must live in the present and the reality, their nurturing ways can (and, perhaps, should) celebrate dreams that unfold on a baseball diamond. In the end, baseball provides fathers with lessons that can shape approaches to fatherhood, helping dads to overcome exigencies and achieve their own redemption. Baseball films continue to tell these stories, as we have seen in *The Natural, The Rookie,* and *Field of Dreams.*

WORKS CITED

Field of Dreams. Dir. Phil Alden Robinson. Perf. Kevin Costner, Amy Madigan, James Earl Jones, Ray Liotta, and Burt Lancaster. DVD Video. Universal, 1989.

Most, Marty and Rudd, Robert. "The America That Was Meant to Be: Images of Community in Baseball Films." *Take Me Out to the Ballgame: Communicating Baseball.* Ed. Gary Gumpert and Susan J. Drucker. Cresskill, NJ: Hampton, 2002. 241–271.

The Natural. Dir. Barry Levinson. Perf. Robert Redford, Robert Duvall, Glenn Close, Kim Basinger, Wilford Brimley. DVD Video. Tri-Star Pictures, Inc., 1984.

Petrash, Jack. *Covering Home: Lessons on the Art of Fathering from the Game of Baseball.* Beltsville, MD: Robins Lane Press, 2000.

The Rookie. Dir. John Lee Hancock. Perf. Dennis Quaid, Rachel Griffiths, Jay Hernandez, and Brian Cox. DVD Video. Disney, 2002.

Vogler, Christopher. *The Writer's Journey: Mythic Structures for Writers.* Studio City, CA: Michael Wiese Productions, 1998.

4

Mick Cochrane's *Sport* and the Mythic Symbol of Fathers Playing Catch with Sons

MATTHEW C. BRENNAN

In a classic essay poet Donald Hall defines baseball as "fathers and sons playing catch" (30). This image typically evokes deep sentiment in fans, if not a fit of sentimentality. For example, in Edwin Romond's fine poem "Something I Could Tell You about Love," the speaker captures the bond between him and his dad by describing them playing catch over the hood of a truck whose freight his father must yet deliver. Despite this responsibility, when the son asks his father for five minutes more, the man who never liked baseball simply "nods," thus wordlessly conveying a depth of emotion (20). This warm-hearted portrayal of fathers, sons, and baseball is a staple of Hollywood directors, who often are less restrained than Romond in controlling sentimentality. Simply recall the endings to the films *Field of Dreams* (1989) and *The Natural* (1984), both of which present nostalgic images of fathers and sons playing catch that are absent from the less sanguine resolutions of the novels on which they are based.

Even Hall's essay, though emphasizing associations of sentiment, actually describes the game of catch with his father as both "tender and tense" (28). In the same vein, Mick Cochrane's *Sport* (2001) gestures toward the tense and tender symbols of fathers playing catch with sons. Ultimately, though, the novel is revisionary: Cochrane supplants the romanticized image through Harlan "Sport" Hawkins' rejections of both his father, a violent alcoholic and liar who abandons the family, and his well-meaning neighbor, coach, and quasi-surrogate father, George Walker, who once pitched in the high minors. In place of this mythic symbol of father and son playing catch, Cochrane instead underscores the gritty image of Harlan's disabled but resilient if wacky mother, who caught his pitches before MS ravaged her lobster-like hands. Thereby, Cochrane represents the adolescent boy's maturation and acceptance of reality, as he has learned to love his broken home.

THE LIVING SYMBOL

Russell Hollander maintains that "Fathers playing catch with sons" is "a living symbol" linked "to the mythic dimension of baseball" (311). To explain the resonance of this symbol, Hollander imports the story of Iron John in which a boy loses his golden ball and enacts the hero's journey to retrieve it. By way of Robert Bly, Hollander claims that this journey symbolizes the quest to recover a lost unity of personality (312). So in our culture, according to Hollander, what "a father and son throw back and forth" is "the golden baseball ... the child's first heroic dream of himself" and "vision of male completeness" (313). Like a realistic novel, Bernard Malamud's baseball classic, *The Natural*, resists the sentimental in its dénouement, but the work in many ways also insists on being read in the tradition of the romance. Its mythic dimension appears in the second paragraph, where Malamud twice invokes the symbol of the golden ball: first, a boy whipping "a glowing ball to someone hidden under a dark oak," perhaps his father (3); and then, Roy's dreamlike vision of himself "standing at night in a strange field with a golden baseball in his palm" (4). Playing catch for Donald Hall also evokes the mythic, for he connects fathers and sons playing catch not only to "the generations looping backward forever" but also to "the profound archaic song of birth, growth, age, and death" (30).

This tender symbol is most memorably depicted in the Hollywood productions of Malamud's *The Natural* (1952), W.P. Kinsella's *Shoeless Joe* (1982), and Jimmy Piersall's memoir *Fear Strikes Out* (1955). The film *Field of Dreams*—unlike its source, the novel *Shoeless Joe*—concludes with Ray Kinsella resolving his ambivalence about his father, the phantom catcher who plays with Shoeless Joe on the field Ray has carved from his farm in obedience to his vision, "If you build it, he will come" (6). Significantly, before his dad disappears into the afterlife of a cornfield, Ray asks him to play catch. To illustrate the powerful piety of this ending, Hollander quotes Robert Mayer's account in *Baseball and Men's Lives* of weeping while watching this scene (306–7). Mayer remarks that during his first viewing of the film's end his "throat was choked" and he "found" himself "fighting back tears" and that when he rewatched it in private two years later "huge sobs burst forth" from him "without warning" (270–71). The film's reference to playing catch with the long-lost father mythically amounts to Ray's finding the golden ball and thus a sense of elusive completeness. In Kinsella's novel, of course, he speaks to his dad but cannot hear his dad's reply. He is left thinking of all he'd like to converse with him about (254–55). But this dialogue never happens and when the father retreats into the corn one last time, Salinger, not Ray, is by his side (264).

The cinematic adaptations of Malamud's novel and Piersall's memoir provide similarly warmhearted connections of fathers and sons through the image of playing catch. *The Natural* as cinema ends with a trumped-up, wordless tableau of Roy Hobbs in a wheatfield playing catch with the son he first meets during his final game. The director Barry Levinson implies that despite the heroics of a season-ending walk-off homer, Roy has subordinated glory on the diamond to a future of fatherhood. In the novel, however, Malamud provides no redemption. Roy's career ends bitterly with a strikeout and subsequent loneliness, not a long ball and family reunion. After striking out on a bad pitch, Roy returns the bribe to the Judge and hits the streets alone, where "nobody recognized him" and he thinks "now I have to suffer again" (205–6). Even the movie version of Jimmy Piersall's *Fear Strikes Out* (1956) appropriates the family romance of baseball myth. For though the director Robert Mulligan explicitly blames the father (played by Karl Malden) for Piersall's breakdown, he also uses the father to signal the son's recovery. When Tony Perkins in the role of Piersall finally lets his father visit him at the hospital, the two repair to the grounds and rebuild their bond by playing catch, barehanded, with a rubber ball, a scene the director invents to dramatize the major leaguer's return to psychic health. In Hollywood's myth, then, Piersall, like Hobbs in Levinson's film, achieves unity of personality by finding again the golden ball.

The "Tender" and the "Tense"

While literature is not immune to romanticizing the portrayal of fathers and sons playing catch, many belletristic depictions balance this image with realities more tense than tender. Hall, for instance, admits that his father *demanded* that he "be good" but in truth the young Hall "was wild" (28). Similarly, Robert Collins's "Catch," dedicated to the poet's father, presents images of both the tender and the tense, of both anger and unacknowledged love. The poem narrates the speaker's yearly homecoming, which includes a game of catch between the two adults that ends when the son throws "the curve you wouldn't teach me" into "the dirt, / bouncing past" his father into shadows behind him (96–97). And whereas Edwin Romond's "Something I Could Tell You about Love" provides a moment of father and son bonding like Roy and his boy in the fields of gold, David C. Ward's "Isn't it pretty to think so?" deliberately undercuts the tender with the tense. First, he delineates the mythic symbol of fathers and their sons playing catch "as American as wheatfields mown / into ball fields," but next Ward juxtaposes this image from *Field of Dreams* to one of a specific Maldenesque dad, of a "beaten" father "beating" his son (95).

Piersall's memoir also balances the tender and the tense. When recurrent psychological problems remove Jimmy's mother to the Norwich State Hospital, Malden's model in the book helps Jimmy weather her long absences by playing catch in the back yard for hours (15). However, this mute expression of paternal concern is subverted by an earlier description that anticipates Ward's "Isn't it pretty to think so?" When the boy tells his father that "Catching a ball is fun," the domineering dad commands, "I don't want you thinking about fun ... I want you to become a slugger like Jimmy Foxx." As a result, Piersall soon reveals that "There were times when I loved my father and times when whatever emotion I felt for him was anything but love" (8–9). Though uncharacteristic of Hollywood, the film faithfully captures this unvarnished image of the tense. In the scene when the young boy plays catch with his dad, the father's fierce throws make the boy wince, his palm hurting so badly that, when out of sight getting the ball behind a shed, he bursts into tears. Like these parts of both the Piersall book and film, and like the examples from poets Hall, Collins, and Ward, Mick Cochrane's *Sport* embraces the ambivalence of the mythic symbol of fathers playing catch with sons—so much so that the novel ultimately rejects the father altogether, replacing him with the mother, a symbol of self-reliance.

Rejecting the Father in Cochrane's *Sport*

Harlan "Sport" Hawkins, the protagonist-narrator of Cochrane's novel, loses his golden ball or unity of personality when his alcoholic father abandons the family, a desertion that leads the 12-year-old Twins fan to reject his father altogether. Harlan recalls little of his dad before his mother contracted multiple sclerosis, but he can't forget the deadbeat's later bouts of drunken violence, which persuade him "Something terrible" is "happening" (6). For instance, one night the boy is wakened by breaking glass. He finds his divorced father, armed with Harlan's Louisville Slugger and framed by the back door's shattered window, screaming he'd kill them. Simultaneously, he was pounding the mother's numbed hand as she covered the lock (35–36). Two other baseball-related moments etch themselves in Harlan's memory of his father. In the first Harlan Hawkins, Sr., purportedly a brilliant lawyer, actually attends his son's ballgame. The father calls his son "Sport" and encourages the boy throughout a quick three-strike at-bat, but once repositioned at first base Harlan looks vainly in the stands for his dad (93–95). In the second memory, Hawk—as the father is affectionately known—pulls the kid out of school one day and drags him to his favorite saloon. Here, where an abusive radio sports personality also wastes his afternoons, Hawk tells bald bragging lies about Harlan's "two no-hitters" (146–47). On the way home Hawk hits something indefinable with the car, which leads Harlan to conclude that his father is a man who runs over things that get in his way, who "destroyed things, and [who] never looked back" (157).

However, the turning point in Harlan's understanding of his dad comes when he must write an essay for his application to a local prep school, which the coach Mr. Walker is trying to get him into so he'll have "role models" (202). The assignment is to portray a memorable character, and surprisingly Harlan chooses his father. But instead of focusing on the alcoholic man his mother says will die in a rented room (189), Harlan invents "the kind of man any boy would be proud to claim as his father" (184). To evoke this kind of father Harlan resorts to some "sentimental crap": "my dad playing catch with me." Like much in the essay, this claim had foundation in truth, but the unembellished facts starkly lay bare why the boy—who so loves baseball he can identify a Milt Pappas card from glimpsing just an ear (16)—ultimately rejects his father. His description, bereft of tenderness, teems with tension. His father did actually play catch with him, "but," Harlan qualifies, "only once, a quick, impatient game years earlier, my mother standing in the doorway supervising, something sort of court-ordered about the whole thing, maybe a half dozen throws in all, that ended—much to the relief of both of us—when a client called" (185). As for Donald Hall and Edwin Romond, for Harlan the image of fathers and sons playing catch symbolizes their bond and its depth of emotion, but for Harlan his dad can express only "what he must" think is "fatherly feeling" (218). Significantly, at one point while shagging flies during practice Harlan considers Hawk's antithesis, Jimmy Piersall's overbearing father in *Fear Strikes Out* (91–92). The comparison to Hawk is telling, for the omnipresent Mr. Piersall drives his son into a psychiatric ward, but he nevertheless makes Jimmy believe, like Romond's speaker but unlike Harlan, that he is genuinely loved, at least sometimes (9).

Rejecting the Surrogate Father

After Hawk deserts his family, the neighbor George Walker acts as Harlan's surrogate father. Walker has no children of his own and is recently widowed, so his adoption of Harlan is not completely selfless; still, he consciously responds to Harlan's broken home by becoming in Harlan's words "Mr. Fixit" (236). He steps into this role when, while Hawk is trying to break in the blood-spattered back door, Harlan runs to get him. By the time Harlan and Walker reach the house, the crisis has past: Hawk is gone and the mother tells the coach, "There's really no trouble" (41). Harlan wants him to stay, but Walker returns only the next morning to replace the glass, clearly a symbol of repairing Harlan's broken home life. And Walker gets the boy to promise to let him know if there's anything else he can do (42, 46). Walker continues to forge a bond with the boy through other fatherly acts as well. He hires Harlan to do chores with him, landscaping the yard, washing the car, and teaches him how to handle tools (63–64); he even lends Harlan tools to refurbish his family's badly overgrown property (105–6). Besides paying Harlan for his work, a kind of allowance given the weekly routine, he also gives him things—a windbreaker, pens, Cokes, even a pair of Adidas sneakers, which his mother makes him give back (70–71). Walker's most important gesture of fatherly influence comes when he recommends Harlan to his own alma mater, a prep school where he still has ties and where he believes Harlan's future prospects can be secured (202–3).

Through these various involvements Walker plays the surrogate father, but the foundation of his role in Harlan's life significantly lies in baseball. As already mentioned, George Walker coaches Harlan's Little League baseball team. Unlike Hawk who can't even watch an entire game his son plays in, Walker gives the boy rides to and from the fields; as an extension of their Saturday yard work, he enlists Harlan in helping him prep the diamond before each game (67) and then throws him batting practice (68). Again, unlike Hawk who lies about his boy's no-hitters and can't endure his strike-outs, Walker accepts that Harlan will "never hit a home run" (12) and rewards him one night with an extra-large cone at Dairy Queen after Harlan wins a game by executing Walker's sign for the suicide squeeze bunt (12). Off the field, their conversations revolve around the Twins, and through them Harlan realizes that his mentor is, like him, a true-believing fan, an optimist; Harlan lacks Walker's athletic talent and his "baseball smarts" (66), but their mutual support of the Twins links them like kin. Eventually Walker takes Harlan to a game at Metropolitan Stadium; the boy has been to just a few games before and never with his father. They watch Dean Chance spin a perfect game, but one shortened by rain to five innings (86–90), which implies both Harlan's idealization of Walker and the truth that their bond, like Chance's mini-masterpiece, is "asterisked."

Accordingly, Harlan acknowledges Walker as his surrogate father, but ultimately he rejects him, just as he has rejected his real father. Harlan indicates that he sees the coach filling a paternal role when he narrates how his teammates taunt him about the obviously close relationship he's formed with Walker in the wake of Hawk's absence. At a practice Eddie Doyle informs Harlan his father saw him with the coach at the Twins game and asks, "Has George *adopted* you?" and "So is he like your father now?" By having Harlan think of "adopted" as "an innocent word" given an ugly spin, Cochrane suggests that Harlan does feel like Walker's unnatural son (92–93). Harlan later makes this fantasy of adoption explicit when he explains, "In the storybook version of my life ... George Walker and my mother would ... get married. It would be perfect," and they would be "united in their affection for me" (136). However, even as Harlan advances this wish, he admits the scenario has problems and opts for the reality principle in finally shunting aside his desire for a substitute dad. After getting accepted to Walker's prestigious alma mater, the boy turns down the academy and in doing so knows he's also rejecting Walker's paternal influence. When he breaks the news to Mr. Walker, he stresses that he still wants to take the coach's classes at the public high school (236), and we know that he expects to follow his mentor into the teaching profession (208). But he no longer wants Walker to fix his broken home, for as Marylaine Block asserts in a review in *Library Journal*, Walker's efforts to help—and I'd add his *fatherly* help—"are oblique criticisms of his mother" (132). Harlan is "a broken window refusing to be fixed," but he loves his "broken home" (236).

MOTHERS PLAYING CATCH WITH SONS

Russell Hollander excludes mothers from his elucidation of the symbol of parents playing catch with sons (307), but Harlan rejects his father and surrogate father in part because his mother shares his love of baseball. Her boyfriend before Hawk had been a pitcher on the St. Paul Saints (84), and as a girl she had played catch with her brother (83–84). Now she watched Twins games with Harlan on a portable black-and-white TV she adjusted with a butter knife and a hairbrush (83). More important, unlike her husband, Mrs. Hawkins has supplied Sport's other childhood memory of playing catch. "When I was nine or ten," he recalls, "and still had aspirations to be a pitcher, she'd spent hours catching while I attempted to perfect my delivery. She used to sit in a lawn chair, a cigarette in her mouth, give me an open palm for a target—she refused a mitt—and would call out balls and strikes against an imaginary batter" (84).

Her refusal to protect her hand with leather is like her refusal to indulge in romantic fantasies that life is anything else than hard. She constantly undermines Harlan's colorings of imagination. For instance, when he gets home from the trip with Walker to see the Twins, he can't wait to tell his mom about Chance's perfect game; however, having listened on the radio, she quickly qualifies the achievement as "semiperfect" and "partially perfect," then adds, "what's so great about perfect?" (90). In fact, she teaches him to face reality and to prize sheer grittiness over glamour through her favorite players. In contrast to Hawk who invented athletic heroics for Harlan, Mrs. Hawkins implicitly accepts his journeyman status. Rather than pull for stars such as Killebrew or Oliva or Kaat, she liked the role players—Sandy Valdespino and Rich Reese—who are scrappy like Harlan (85). Accordingly, when Jose Santiago wins a game for Boston that helps the Red Sox nose out the Twins for the 1967 pennant, Harlan calls him "just the sort of player my mother loved," for Santiago hadn't enjoyed a winning season in seven years, and that came in the minors (100).

Consequently, at the end of the novel, when Harlan explicitly chooses his mother over Mr. Walker, he acknowledges her tenacity in the face of hardship. Just before he receives his letter from the prep school, she asks him if he knows what to do when he feels like giving up. Harlan asks to be told and she quips, "Don't" (210). While Walker's answer is to fix things, Mrs. Hawkins' is to hold on. If Harlan's family is broken, he finally understands that his mother has held them together nonetheless. And she has done it through her humanity. His final image of his mother subsumes his earlier memory of her playing catch with him, and her hands become his living symbol. They were "broken down and broken in like an ancient and beloved baseball mitt. I understood—that's what human means. Those hands had caught my fastballs, repaired household appliances with a hairbrush and a fork ... had grabbed the backdoor lock and in a shower of broken glass and blood and murderous curses, held on, held on and on" (246). From his mother he learns self-reliance and thus finds the golden ball.

Cochrane's *Sport* is a rich and moving novel that convincingly gives new life to the living symbol of fathers playing catch with sons. Through this symbol Cochrane defines the failings of Harlan's father Hawk and the generous efforts of George Walker to compensate for Hawk's neglect. For much of the novel Walker works as a foil to Hawk, especially since Harlan's search for identity depends on the vehicle of baseball. Ultimately, though, as Harlan comes of age, he comes to understand his crippled, eccentric mother's unlikely heroism, which embodies the same scrappiness he already puts to good use on the ball field. The novel *Sport*, then, is revisionary and while it embraces the deep tradition of fathers and sons playing catch—from Donald Hall to Jimmy Piersall, from Roy Hobbs to Ray Kinsella—it animates the tradition by replacing the father with a mom whose very hands resemble mitts with which to catch the son's throws.

WORKS CITED

Block, Marylaine. Rev. of *Sport*, by Mick Cochrane. *Library Journal* 1 Nov. 2000: 132.
Bly Robert. *Iron John: A Book about Men*. Reading, MA: Addison-Wesley, 1990.
Cochrane, Mick. *Sport*. New York: Thomas Dunne-St. Martin's, 2001.
Collins, Robert. "Catch." Horvath and Wiles 96.
Fear Strikes Out. Dir. Robert Mulligan. Perf. Anthony Perkins and Karl Malden. Paramount, 1956.
Field of Dreams. Dir. Phil Alden Robinson. Perf. Kevin Costner, Amy Madigan, Ray Liotta, and Burt Lancaster. Universal, 1989.
Hall, Donald. *Fathers Playing Catch with Sons: Essays on Sport (Mostly Baseball)*. New York: North Point, 1985.
Hollander, Russell. "Fathers Playing Catch with Sons: A Living Symbol." *Nine: A Journal of Baseball History and Social Policy Perspectives* 5.2 (1997): 305-15.
Horvath, Brooke, and Tim Wiles, eds. *Line Drives: 100 Contemporary Baseball Poems*. Carbondale: Southern Illinois UP, 2002.
Kinsella, W. P. *Shoeless Joe*. Boston: Houghton Mifflin, 1982.

Malamud, Bernard. *The Natural.* 1952. New York: Perennial Classics-Harper-Collins, 2000.

Mayer, Robert. *Baseball and Men's Lives: The True Confessions of a Skinny-Marink.* New York: Delta Books, 1994.

The Natural. Dir. Barry Levinson. Perf. Robert Redford, Robert Duvall, Wilford Brimley, Glenn Close, and Kim Basinger. Columbia-Tristar, 1984.

Piersall, Jim, and Al Hirschberg. *Fear Strikes Out: The Jim Piersall Story.* 1955. Lincoln: U of Nebraska P, 1999.

Romond, Edwin. "Something I Could Tell You about Love." Horvath and Wiles 20.

Ward, David C. "Isn't It Pretty to Think So?" Horvath and Wiles 95.

5

Nelson Algren's Chicago: The Black Sox Scandal, McCarthyism, and the Truth about Cubs Fans

ANDREW HAZUCHA

In his long prose poem entitled *Chicago: City on the Make*, Nelson Algren discusses the personal humiliation of growing up as a diehard White Sox fan on the south side of Chicago and then moving to the north side in the summer of 1920, just months before the Black Sox scandal broke in late September of that year and dishonored his boyhood heroes forever. For Algren, however, the scandal achieves greater significance as a symbol for American political culture: not only is it symptomatic of local Chicago political corruption, but on a grander scale it serves as a metaphor for McCarthyism and the Red-baiters' program of denigrating artists nationwide three decades later. Writing in 1951, Algren had already been blacklisted (along with fellow Chicagoan Richard Wright) as a member of the Communist party, and even though he had renounced his affiliation with the party in the late 1930s, he was still regarded as a subversive in literary circles (McCarrell 378).

In *City on the Make*, Algren illustrates how his boyhood association with the Black Sox ruined him in his new neighborhood on Chicago's north side, and how his new group of friends—all of them Cubs fans— played the role of the House Un-American Activities Committee, interrogating him as though he were a dangerous traitor. On one level, then, Algren's work is about what it means to be an artist in an era of such strident political intolerance that the serious writer must publish at his own risk. Like the neighborhood boys who charged the young Algren with disloyalty during the summer of 1920, McCarthyite cold warriors thirty-one summers later have made Algren's Chicago the "most American of cities," a quasi-fascist state that intimidates and maligns its artists (56).

Although the celebrated televised Army-McCarthy hearings that led to Joseph McCarthy's censure by his Senate colleagues in 1954 came three years after Algren wrote *City on the Make*, he was certainly aware of McCarthy's previous and equally notorious anti–Communist stances, since the Wisconsin senator was making news headlines as early as February 1950 by charging the State Department with harboring Communists. In late July of 1951, when Algren was at work composing the early drafts of his book, the *Chicago Tribune* carried an article about McCarthy's intention to publicize the names of twenty-nine individuals who worked for the State Department and whom McCarthy considered grave security risks to the United States. According to a *Tribune* article dated 25 July 1951, Senator McCarthy announced that he had already sent a letter to Secretary of State Dean Acheson in which he named twenty-nine State Department employees who had never been cleared by the Civil Service Commission's loyalty review board, chaired by Hiram Bingham. McCarthy threatened to name these employees as government subversives if Acheson could not assure him that all of them had been either suspended from their jobs or removed from positions where they might have contact with sensitive government documents ("M'Carthy"). Algren, who read the Chicago newspapers assiduously and singled out the *Tribune* for its "mediocrity" and "counterfeit values" in his afterword to *City on the Make*, surely was following this story (88). The FBI had been keeping files on Algren for over a decade by this point, and his own political activity that very year included his being a signatory to a full-page advertisement in the *New York Times* dated 15 January 1951 that urged American citizens to take measures to protect their individual freedoms (Drew 146, Peddie 141n6).

It might be tempting for the popular reader to imagine Algren as shrinking from contemporary political events and sequestering himself at his typewriter in 1951 in order to write a kind of love poem to Chicago, a panegyric that sketches the cultural history of the city from its genesis to its emergence in the mid-twentieth century as the "Second City." If we read *City on the Make* through only this lens, however, Algren's wistful musings on the 1919 White Sox season seem merely nostalgic and almost entirely apolitical. Inasmuch as Algren was ten years old in 1919 and uneducated in the ways of a world that he would later see as irredeemably fallen, he depicts the season quite lyrically as a kind of prelapsarian period in Chicago history, but it is also true that he sees the 1919 season as an analogue to the time when Chicago "used to be a writer's town" (62). By the summer of 1951, of course, the political winds had changed and the climate was anything but encouraging for writers of his persuasion. As a former member of the Chicago chapter of the John Reed Club, a cultural arm of the American Communist Party, Algren had been involved with writers and writings that had expressly subversive political purposes (Drew 50). Given this reality, the modern reader of Algren's book would do well to listen carefully to a narrative voice that necessarily mixes nostalgia with a keen political consciousness honed by the persecutory atmosphere of the McCarthy era.

Chicago, 1919: The Season and Its Aftermath

The centerpiece of *City on the Make* is a chapter entitled "The Silver-Colored Yesterday," a narrative that, among all the chapters in the book, most reads like a short story. The chapter begins with a nostalgic look back at an idyllic moment in Chicago sports history, the glittering summer that preceded the most publicized scandal in all of professional sports. Algren's tone is generally elegiac throughout his narrative, but at this juncture a note of optimism sets the scene: "The year was 1919, Shoeless Joe Jackson was outhitting Ty Cobb, God was in his Heaven, Carl Wanderer was still a war hero, John Dillinger was an Indiana farm boy and the cops were looking cautiously, in all the wrong corners, for Terrible Tommy O'Connor" (30).

Algren's juxtaposition of Shoeless Joe with the homicidal outlaws Carl Wanderer, John Dillinger, and Terrible Tommy O'Connor, all of whom would later become high-profile Chicago public enemies, suggests that from the very beginning he wishes to establish a link between sports, criminality, and Chicago politics. The summer of 1919, however, was still an innocent era when criminals were not yet criminals, a time when the political culture of Chicago had little need to define what was criminal behavior on the public stage. And although even the most naïve defender of the city would never claim that its political machinery was free of corruption, for the young White Sox fan that summer the face of Chicago could not have appeared more pure.

The inescapable merging of the criminal and the political occurs for Algren the following summer when he moves from the far south side neighborhood of 71st Street to North Troy Street. As Algren notes, "North Troy

Street led, like all Northside streets—and alleys too—directly to the alien bleachers of Wrigley Field" (34). It is here, in his newly adopted neighborhood, where the young Algren gets interrogated and ultimately "outed" by a gang of youths playing stickball in the streets. They ask him a series of probing questions before they will allow him to join their game, the central query sounding like a test of National League—that is, *American*—patriotism. "Who's yer fayvrut player?" the leader of the ring asks him, and when he names the current White Sox shortstop, Swede Risberg, the boy brusquely retorts, "It got to be a National Leaguer" (34). Referring to the ringleader of this neighborhood gang as the "chairman" of "the local loyalty board," Algren from the outset politicizes his narrative, consciously drawing upon the language of Cold War anti–Communist witch-hunts to establish the unsavory political machinations that will soon brand him a criminal. As he says of his uneasy assimilation into that north side neighborhood, "The reason I never got to play anything but right field the rest of the summer I attribute to National League Politics pure and simple" (35–36).

Algren's trial and conviction for conspiracy in the neighborhood kangaroo court occurs at the end of that summer, in October 1920, when the National League stickballers find out that Swede Risberg, Algren's alterego during the daily games they play on Troy Street, roomed with Eddie Cicotte during the 1919 World Series the previous fall. The Black Sox scandal had become public a month earlier, when a Cook County grand jury indicted Risberg and seven other White Sox players on September 28, 1920 for conspiring to lose the 1919 World Series (Cottrell 221–222). Only one day after another jury acquitted the indicted ballplayers of all charges, on August 3, 1921, newly elected Baseball Commissioner Kenesaw Mountain Landis banned the eight White Sox players from professional baseball for life for their role in throwing the World Series to the Cincinnati Reds (Nathan 5). Caught at the precise moment between the White Sox players' indictment and banishment, then, Algren himself soon faced his own banishment, since his destiny was irrevocably linked with the Swede's. Algren's identification with his boyhood hero had so compromised his reputation in his north side neighborhood that his playmates now considered him an outright traitor. He describes his ostracism in explicitly political terms:

> It wasn't till a single sunless morning of early Indian summer that all my gods proved me false: Risberg, Cicotte, Jackson, Weaver, Felsch, Gandil, Lefty Williams and a utility infielder whose name escapes me—wasn't it McMillen? The Black Sox were the Reds of that October and mine was the guilt of association.
> And the charge was conspiracy [36].

In this brief passage Algren has linked the Black Sox scandal with the Red Scare of 1919, using the rhetoric of McCarthyism to describe the judicial travesty that has impugned his honor. A few paragraphs later, when one of the stickballers examines Algren's White Sox scorecard, signed by Swede Risberg during a game dated July 1920, the neighborhood gang interprets the card as textual evidence of Algren's treason. Noting that Risberg went 0-for-4 at the plate, was charged with an error for throwing wildly to first, and was "caught sleeping off second" on this particular day, one member of the gang points at the tell-tale card and says, "What kind of American *are* you anyhow...? No wonder you're always in right field where nothin' ever comes—nobody could trust you in center" (37). Algren's public disgrace thus happens when he is exposed as a card-carrying member of an immoral, un–American party, the party of post–1919 true-blue White Sox fans. It is a shameful society that his north side peers believe both knew about and approved of the Black Sox scandal.

THE INQUISITION: SENATOR TOBEY

Algren's depiction of this signal event in his boyhood becomes unequivocally politicized when he describes the young interrogators as "The Committee" (36) and the main inquisitor as "[t]he Tobey" of that committee (37). Senator Charles W. Tobey, Republican Senator from New Hampshire at the time of *City on the Make*'s publication in 1951, served most famously that summer on the Senate Special Committee to Investigate Organized Crime in Interstate Commerce. Algren's pointed reference to Tobey suggests that he was familiar with the public proceedings of this committee; it was the first committee ever to hold televised hearings, and Tobey often cut a spectacular figure as a kind of fist-shaking moral prophet (Coren et al 220, Huitt 352). An outspoken and at times irate member of this committee, which began its public hearings on organized crime in the spring, Senator Tobey made his name as an indefatigable interrogator of mobsters involved in gambling activity. Significantly enough, during one of the televised senate hearings Tobey ordered Morris Kleinman, a leader of the Cleveland crime syndicate, arrested and held on $10,000 bond for refusal to answer his questions (May, pars. 25–26). It is important to note that Algren may very well have been watching Tobey's oracular performances even as he paused at his typewriter while composing *City on the Make*. The hearings began on May 1, 1951 and ended on September 1, 1951, a span of time that would have coincided with Algren's writing of the book, which he first published as a long essay in the fall of that year in a popular magazine. Although *Holiday* may seem like a strange publication for Algren to place his highly poetic piece on his native city, the travel magazine had devoted its entire October 1951 issue to the subject of Chicago, and Algren was ready with a finished draft of his first version just as Tobey's committee was finishing its own highly publicized work (Schmittgens and Savage 130).

Senator Tobey's moralizing outbursts clearly serve as the prototype for the inquisitions of the north side gang that surrounds the young Algren and stares at his scorecard during this crucial episode in his narrative. Algren's assertion that he is now presumed guilty, a hapless victim of the local Tobey's interrogations, is underscored when he laments not having chosen Shoeless Joe Jackson to emulate in the local stickball games. (Jackson, it should be pointed out, hit .375 and played errorless ball during the 1919 World Series.) Algren writes, "I hadn't picked Shoeless Joe. I'd picked the man who, with Eddie Cicotte, bore the heaviest burden of all our dirty Southside guilt" (38–39). Algren's dishonor among his peers is therefore irreversible, not only by his association with Swede Risberg and the Black Sox players' public confessions of wrongdoing but also by a rabid north side political climate that will stop at nothing short of his own public humiliation and forced confession.

At the end of this chapter Algren completes the connection between political corruption and the politicians' false accusations of criminality in those who, like Algren, are presumed guilty by association. Just before the local Tobey administers a beating to him, Algren admits with resignation, "The Black Sox had played scapegoat for Rothstein and I'd played the goat for The Swede" (39). Arnold Rothstein was the New York gambler who was widely believed to have fixed the 1919 World Series, and Algren's recognition that the players paid with their careers for the sins of organized crime sets up an opposition between the powerful moneyed elite and those who do their bidding. The chapter ends with Algren offering a critique of a social and political hierarchy that forever convicts the lowly for the crimes of the affluent. Algren asks, "However do senators get so close to God? How is it that front-office men never conspire?" (39). If, as most historians now agree, White Sox owner Charles Comiskey was aware of the fix as early as game two of the World Series, then he ought to have shared some of the blame and some of the punishment for not heading it off at the pass. That Comiskey was a notoriously stingy owner who grossly underpaid the best players on the most dominant team in baseball—Cicotte, for example, made only $5,000 for the 1919 season, when he won 29 games (Cottrell 199)—only reinforces Algren's perception that Comiskey, who never served a day in jail or paid a cent in fines for the scandal, ought to have stood shoulder to shoulder with the White Sox players during their indictment.

Late in his narrative, in a chapter entitled "Bright Faces of Tomorrow," Algren suggests quite strongly that the Black Sox scandal and such corrupt figures as Charles Comiskey might serve as a useful metaphor for totalitarian politics. Arguing that Chicago in 1951 is "more a soldier's than an artist's town" (55), Algren makes the point that it is difficult for art to flourish in a climate that places under suspicion any artist who dares to speak unassailable truths about those who wield the economic and political power. For Algren, literature is broadly defined as "any occasion that a challenge is put to the legal apparatus by conscience in touch with humanity" (81). By this definition, any coherent resistance against a corrupt political system is an act of literature, and any official attempt to stifle that act is indicative of a society gone awry, a society that cannot tolerate art and will destroy it at all costs.

During the McCarthy era myriad artists were suspected of being Communist sympathizers who sought to undermine the values of the American way of living, and Algren points out that to live in such an era is to live under a regime that devalues art, denigrates artists, and ultimately creates a "cultural Sahara" (54). In one of the most crucial passages in the book Algren makes his case against McCarthyism:

> You can live in a natural home, with pictures on walls, or you can live in a fort; but it's a lead-pipe cinch you can't live in both. You can't make an arsenal of a nation and yet expect its great cities to produce artists. It's in the nature of the overbraided brass to build walls around the minds of men—as it is in the nature of the arts to tear those walls down. Today, under the name of "security," the dark shades are being drawn [55].

Besides the obvious fact that Algren may as well have been describing the rapid erosion of civil liberties under the administration of George W. Bush and the climate of fear enveloping the President's critics, his point is clear: a society that walls in its artists is no longer free. The Black Sox scandal was a scandal only insofar as eight artists of the diamond, walled in by Charles Comiskey's apparent judgment that they were not worthy of a standard wage and Commissioner Landis's apparent judgment that they were un–American for wanting it, dared to get market value for their services. Thus Algren's unfortunate boyhood association with Swede Risberg and the rest of the Black Sox branded him an ingrate, an infidel, a dissident who wished to subvert the American way.

THE TRUTH ABOUT CUBS FANS

If Algren sets up a dichotomy between victimizer and victim, between ruling elite and artist, between the powerful owner of the White Sox and the players who ultimately betrayed him, then what are we to make of the similar dichotomy of Cubs fan and White Sox fan in *City on the Make*? On one level, Algren's characterization of White Sox fans and Cubs fans in the first half of the twentieth century sets up a dialectic between what he terms the "hustlers" and the "squares." As the two great forces that have forever fought for the city's soul, the hustlers and the squares come to represent the two opposing faces of Chicago: the con artists and entrepreneurs and industrialists who built the city with their ingenuity, and the moralizing reformers who continually have tried to amend its evil ways. Algren describes the duality of Chicago in a humorous vein, showing his south side baseball loyalty in the process. He sees Chicago as having "One face for Go-Getters and one for Go-Get-It-Yerselfers. One for poets and one for promoters. One for the good boy and one for the bad.... One for early risers, one for evening hiders. One for the White Sox and none for the Cubs" (24). For Algren, the Cubs fan at mid-century was nothing more than a self-aggrandizing do-gooder who represented Chicago at its moralizing worst, while the White Sox fan represented the genuine article, the working class or even sub-working criminal class which, although dishonored, nevertheless persisted and managed to survive in a world ruled by the wealthy and the powerful—indeed, by such politically powerful people as Charles Comiskey.

It is difficult to determine whether Algren's characterization of the polarizing differences between Cubs fans and White Sox fans is entirely accurate and rooted in clearly observable behavior patterns. What is not debatable, however, is that the recent spate of unruly fan behavior at U.S. Cellular Field—the successor of Comiskey Park and the current home of the White Sox—is not unprecedented in White Sox history. Indeed, during the very summer when Algren was writing *City on the Make* an ugly incident occurred at Comiskey Park that cost an abusive south side fan $200 in fines for disorderly conduct. The episode spanned several days and came to a head on July 3, 1951, when nineteen-year-old Louis Passi and a group of his friends began heckling White Sox pitcher Marvin Rotblatt. According to the courtroom testimony of Rotblatt, Passi had been heckling him with racial and religious epithets for several days during a White Sox home stand. The White Sox management informed Chicago police of the incident, and when they confronted Passi and his friends in the stands at Comiskey Park on July 3, a brawl ensued in which three fans were injured, including a twenty-seven-year-old Jewish man who suffered a dislocated shoulder while scuffling with Passi ("It Costs"). Whether this incident was isolated or represented a pattern of fan misbehavior, it reinforces Algren's contention that to be a White Sox fan is to be a rough-hewn, unrefined, but ultimately more true-to-life Chicagoan than your average north side rooter.

If recent events over the past two seasons at U.S. Cellular Field are any indication, White Sox fan behavior at the turn of the twenty-first century is not much changed from that of the mid-twentieth century fan. One need only recall the night of September 19, 2002, when a father and son duo jumped out of the stands and attacked Kansas City Royals firstbase coach Tom Gamboa, pummeling him with their fists until they were subdued by Royals players and arrested by police (Rogers). Only six months later, on April 15, 2003, a White Sox fan jumped out of the stands during another game with the Royals and attempted to tackle first-base umpire Laz Diaz, grabbing him by the leg (Greenstein). These contemporary examples of White Sox fandom gone awry ought not suggest that today's Cubs fans by contrast are mild-mannered and perfect exemplars of polite behavior. Wrigley Field has seen its fair share of disorderly conduct. A twenty-seven-year-old fan attacked Cubs reliever Randy Meyers on September 28, 1995, after Myers had surrendered a home run. In other incidents, a fan stole a Los Angeles Dodgers player's cap during a May 16, 2000 game and provoked a melee in the stands involving four fans and sixteen Dodgers players, and on April 24, 2003, a Cubs fan threw his cell phone onto the playing field from the upper deck, nearly hitting San Diego Padres third baseman Sean Burroughs on the fly (Hirsley and Bush, Kapos).

Despite these examples of reckless and unruly activity at the "Friendly Confines" on Chicago's north side, however, the common perception among many south siders is that Wrigley Field in the modern era has the feel of a large, innocuous beer garden, and that the average Cubs fan goes there as much to drink as to see Sammy Sosa hit a home run or Kerry Wood strike out the side (Haugh). Legendary Chicago writer Studs Terkel, a long-time White Sox fan and intimate friend of Algren, describes himself as "anti–Cub" on the grounds that the Cubs are "a tourist attraction, like Buckingham Fountain or the [Chicago] air show." According to Terkel, the character of the two ball clubs and their fans contrasts so starkly that it would not be inaccurate to cast them as polar opposites. "The Sox," says Terkel, "are a Carl Sandburg poem. The Cubs are Edgar Guest" (Rapoport). That Terkel would associate the White Sox with Sandburg's gritty working-class poem "Chicago" while the Cubs get linked with the effete, sentimental poetry of British-born Guest suggests that Terkel sees the 2003 White Sox fans-Cubs fans dichotomy in almost exactly the same terms that Algren envisioned it in 1951. In Algren's case, though, the relative propriety of Cubs fans was always duplicitous in that beneath the genteel manner was an imperative to conform or be damned. It was a benign McCarthyism, but McCarthyism nonetheless.

In the end, then, the north side neighborhood boys who ostracize the young Algren from their daily stickball games are representative of the modern Cubs fan circa 1951, the moment at which Algren is writing his narrative. And if, as Algren argues, Chicago at mid-century is "still a Godforsaken spastic, a cerebral-palsy natural among cities, clutching at the unbalanced air" (33), then the working-class White Sox fan is Chicago incarnate. This is not to say that the Chicago Cubs never claimed a working-class fan base but that a qualitative difference has always existed between the two types of fans, who remain a worldview apart half a century after Algren wrote *City on the Make*. For Algren, the inquisitorial, self-serving posture of the average Cubs fan on the street is indicative of a larger failing: an association with the political and corporate elites of the city, a membership with the ruling party—which is now, at the dawn of the 21st century, the party of WGN, the *Chicago Tribune*, and Goose Island beer, a pricey microbrew for the yuppie palate.

The White Sox fan, on the other hand, is still on average a south side working stiff who swills mass-produced, rot-gut beer and works a twelve-hour shift. Such a fan base does not translate easily into Michigan Avenue window shoppers, and indeed Algren inadvertently points to this phenomenon late in his narrative when he celebrates the laborers who built Chicago with their brawn. "And all the stately halls of science," writes Algren, "the newest Broadway hit, the endowed museums, the endowed opera, the endowed art galleries, are not for their cold pavement-colored eyes. For the masses who do the city's labor also keep the city's heart" (68). At the end of the day, in other words, the south sider is much more likely than his north side counterpart to exhibit a coarse but authentic dignity which, as Algren phrases it in his afterword to *City on the Make*, "is not the prerogative of the economically empowered" (106).

WORKS CITED

Algren, Nelson. *Chicago: City on the Make*. Ed. David Schmittgens and Bill Savage. Fiftieth anniversary ed. Chicago: U of Chicago P, 2001.
Coren, Robert W., Mary Rephlo, David Kepley, and Charles South. *Guide to the*

Records of the United States Senate at the National Archives 1789–1989. Bicentennial ed. (S. Doc. No. 100–42). Washington, DC: National Archives and Records Administration, 1989.

Cottrell, Robert C. *Blackball, the Black Sox and the Babe: Baseball's Crucial 1920 Season.* Jefferson, NC: McFarland, 2002.

Drew, Bettina. *Nelson Algren: A Life on the Wild Side.* New York: Putnam's, 1989.

Greenstein, Teddy. "Fan Attacks Ump; Royals GM: We Might Not Play." *Chicago Tribune* 16 April 2003, sec. 4: 1+.

Haugh, David. "For City's Fans, Game's Name Is One-Upmanship." *Chicago Tribune* 23 June 2003, sec. 3: 7.

Hirsley, Michael, and Rudolph Bush. "Man, Son Charged in Comiskey Attack." *Chicago Tribune* 21 Sept. 2002, sec. 1: 1+.

Huitt, Ralph K. "The Congressional Committee: A Case Study." *The American Political Science Review* 48.2 (1954): 340–365.

"It Costs Fan $200 to Jeer Sox Pitcher." *Chicago Daily Tribune* 11 July 1951, final ed., sec. 1: 1.

Kapos, Shia. "Man Dials Up Apology to Cubs." *Chicago Tribune* 26 April 2003, sec. 3: 6.

May, Allen. "Refusing to Refuse the Kleinman/Rothkopf Testimony." 10 Jan. 2000. 37 pars. *American Mafia.com.* 7 July 2003. <http://www.americanmafia.com/Allan_May_1-10-00.html>.

McCarrell, Stuart. "Nelson Algren's Politics." *The Man with the Golden Arm.* Eds. William A. Savage, Jr. and Daniel Simon. Fiftieth anniversary critical ed. New York: Seven Stories Press, 1999. 377–79.

"M'Carthy Plans to Name 29 as Security Risks." *Chicago Daily Tribune* 26 July 1951, final ed., sec. 1: 11.

Nathan, Daniel A. *Saying It's So: A Cultural History of the Black Sox Scandal.* Urbana: U of Illinois P, 2003.

Peddie, Ian. "Poles Apart? Ethnicity, Race, Class, and Nelson Algren." *Modern Fiction Studies* 47.1 (Spring 2001): 118–141.

Rapoport, Ron. "Yard Times: Studs Terkel Weighs in on Cubs-Sox." *Chicago Sun-Times* 23 June 2003, late ed.: 97.

Rogers, Phil. "Comiskey Assault: 2 Spectators Come Out of Stands, Jump Royals Coach Gamboa." *Chicago Tribune* 20 Sept. 2002, sec. 4: 1+.

6

"You don't play the angles, you're a sap": John Sayles, Eliot Asinof, Baseball, Labor, and Chicago in 1919

WARREN TORMEY

Based loosely on Elliot Asinof's 1963 historical narrative of the same name, the 1988 film *Eight Men Out*, directed by John Sayles, explores the circumstances of the banished White Sox players accused of throwing the 1919 World Series. Both book and film depict the exploitation of Charles Comiskey's chronically underpaid team, whose grievances are largely ignored by a public eager to celebrate the national pastime after a period of wartime privations. Sayles' account follows Asinof's lead in exploring the ballplayers' position as wage earners in a series of larger profit-generating networks that continually deny them their fair share. Both Asinof and Sayles show interest in labor economics, and it is easy to note the direct influence of the former's book on the latter's film.

However, while Sayles follows Asinof's historical narrative in important ways, the filmmaker's depiction of the plight of the banished eight can also be understood as an outgrowth of his earlier film *Matewan*, itself based on his novel *Union Dues*. This 1987 film, which displays the struggles of West Virginia coal miners, portrays a world contemporary to the events of 1919 and provides a vivid context to examine the exploitation of the Black Sox. Critics have noted the connection, even if only in the most rudimentary terms. For instance, in her review of the baseball film *Wash-*

ington Post critic Rita Kempley observed that "Sayles gives us *Matewan* at Comiskey Park. It's wage earners vs. employers, his same old pitch. No curveballs, no spitballs, no surprises." When examined as a depiction of contemporary events, however, *Matewan*, a film about exploited miners, enables one to understand *Eight Men Out*, a film about exploited ballplayers in a context that connects the Black Sox scandal to the labor struggles then taking place on a national scale in major industrial and civic sectors.

Asinof, whom Sayles credits with having done most of the research legwork, connects the struggles of the Black Sox to the volatile climate of post World War I labor relations by alluding to other labor conflicts. In describing the eagerness of Americans to celebrate the end of the war, Asinof describes the generational and social conflicts that developed. Young people rebelled against Victorian morality. The cost of living rose. Race riots tore up many major American cities. And the world of the laborer was in turmoil. Close to one million workers were on strike as the Communist threat became a more tangible presence in American factories (Asinof 32–3). Closer to home, the city of Chicago, along with Gary and Hammond, the mill towns to the immediate south, saw a tense steelworkers strike. Southsiders, seeing the turmoil of these events, followed the developing struggles of miners and factory workers in close proximity (31–2).

Asinof's book provides this contextual information in order to frame the initial meeting between the Black Sox ringleader, first baseman Chick Gandil, and the go-betweens Nat Brown and Sport Sullivan, who represent gambler Arnold Rothstein. The meeting comes on the heels of Asinof's comparison of the underpaid Sox' salaries with their less accomplished cohorts' and in their enduring of the petty indignities under the Old Roman's charge—low allowances for daily meals, bogus promises for bonuses, and the like (20–1). With this sequence, Asinof indicates his alignment with the short sighted and fiscally unsophisticated ballplayers. He also clearly demonstrates that their awareness of their exploitation extends only as far as the salaries of their less talented Major League contemporaries. Asinof thus implies that their limited perception precludes the conspirators from recognizing the intangible benefits that come with being the best and the eventually greater rewards—financial and otherwise—that such stature often brings.

If the banished eight themselves could understand their exploitation by their owner only in the most rudimentary terms of salary, Asinof saw it clearly. *Eight Men Out* was published eight years after his first baseball publication, the 1955 novel *Man on Spikes*, a realistic account of the networks of institutional exploitation that victimize ballplayers arbitrarily and prevent their measure by the only standard that would matter in an ideal world: their talent. Asinof's sympathies are clearly with the ballplayer in this work. As in *Eight Men*, he is sensitive to the plight of those who suffer from the game's imbalances. Sayles, whose pro-labor sympathies are retained in his film, supplements the story with the research he has done into the struggles of pre-and post–WWI organized labor. As a result, his characters are more aware of and more connected to the labor tensions of this era in Chicago labor history.

In other words, Sayles portrays the eight conspirators much like he portrays the miners who unite to strike against the Baldwin-Felts agency in *Matewan*. In his version of *Eight Men Out*, Sayles creates a world in which fans see baseball as both an expression of post-war patriotism and as the national institution those who ran the business claimed it to be. However, Sayles invites viewers of the film to see the game also as a place where underpaid wage earners—players and fans alike—are not above supplementing their income with the occasional bet. As the "no betting" signs painted around the cinematic Comiskey Park reveal, the public occasionally sees through the innocence and purity bestowed on the national pastime and the incorruptibility of its heroes. However, this vision continues to obscure the sport's essential identity as an entertainment business, where the related ethics of profit making and income supplementation are preeminent. In speaking of this intersection of the ideals of post-war baseball and its stature as a profit-generating institution, Sayles observes that "the moment it becomes professional, it's already corrupted. The moment you get into something that's a labor situation, it's automatically not just plain fun anymore, and that is just too much to ask of something" (Smith 143).

Significantly, the West Virginia coal miners of *Matewan* know their baseball, hold their Major League heroes in high esteem, and maintain their belief in the incorruptibility the game. This belief in the national institution is established in an exchange between Danny Radnor, the teenager who preaches the Word when he's not working the mines, and Joe Kenehan, the self-educated IWW operative. Both are baseball fans, and this conversation takes place in a camp where striking miners, displaced from company housing, reside in the hills outside of town. Revealing his soon-to-be challenged idealism, Danny alludes to the then-ongoing speculation that would soon result in the banishment of eight members from American League pennant winners. Danny opines that "Some say the Sox just laid down but I don't believe it. You just lookit the Series Joe Jackson had. My favorite on the Reds is Ed Roush and Heinie Groh, even if they is Germans."

While the dialogue serves as a contextual element to place this conversation somewhere in the summer of 1920, it also reveals the disjunction between ballplayers and their fans, a large proportion of whom are workers from the mines, mills, packing houses, police forces, and sweatshops. Workers in these environments were struggling to organize, and sought to bargain for better and safer working conditions, higher pay, and greater degrees of employee representation in company affairs. These were the individuals who turned to baseball for their diversion, and, if aware of its connection to gambling, still held to what Sayles describes as "the idea of True Belief surrounded by gambling and money" (Smith 145). Danny subsequently observes that his favorite pitcher, Hod Eller, is from nearby Logan County. When the mines are open, he doesn't get much chance to indulge his other passion, which is to play ball.

One significant and revealing chance comes in a later scene in *Matewan*, when the striking miners—an uneasy combination of Italian immigrants, displaced African Americans, and West Virginia town folk—enjoy an impromptu ballgame game in a cinematic interlude from the movie's focus on labor tensions. In this scene, the diverse group, united by common experience and hardship, and defined by a common enemy, realize their connectedness. In his series of interviews with Sayles, Gavin Smith alludes to this brief but significant image of the national pastime. Describing the scene as "a brief interlude of utopian community," Smith asks Sayles if he was "in some sense anticipating *Eight Men Out*," and if he "buy[s] the idea as some kind of idealistic expression of coexistence?" In reply, Sayles observes that "in the alleged melting pot of America, music and sports are the first places that people start to melt" (123). He describes an event in 1913 in a Baldwin-Felts-operated mine called the Ludlow Massacre, in which National Guardsmen played ball against striking miners a week before killing them.

Ultimately, *Matewan* represents the link that enables Sayles to connect the Sox to the labor struggles of their era. Of course, in a film focused on the labor struggles of coal miners, baseball and other communal pursuits—in this case, food and music—occupy a secondary position. The narrative's principal concern is in the emergence of Danny into a resonant and defiant voice for the miners. In the face of constant harassment from the Baldwin Felts agency, embodied in the hard-drinking, morally vacuous agents Griggs and Hickey, Danny's growth counterposes the challenge to the pacifist principles of the Wobbly organizer Kenehan, whose aversion to violence results in his Christ-like sacrifice to the miners' struggle. This moment is captured in the film's final few scenes, where Joe's death in the climatic gun battle between miners and agents is followed immediately by a voice over from an aged miner—implied to be an older Danny Radnor. As the film ends, he recalls the organizer's words: "'Hit's just one big Union, the whole world over,'" Joe Kenehan used to say, and from the day of the Matewan Massacre that's what I preached. That was my religion." Danny's declaration captures labor's pro-organization sentiments of the twenties. Organizations like the IWW, the AFL-CIO, the Amalgamated Association of Iron, Steel, and Tin Workers, and other unions were gaining a foothold in the American workplace in the face of often violent opposition. A central feature of the depiction of Danny's fellow miners, this rhetoric has echoes in *Eight Men Out* as well.

The idea that sports supersedes social tensions and provides interludes from them is, of course, challenged in *Eight Men Out*, even as several baseball scenes simultaneously comprise a montage that preserves the harmonious image of the game as used in *Matewan*. Again in *Eight Men*, Sayles uses these scenes, with notable exceptions, mostly as interludes to express the game's essential incorruptibility. Similarly capturing the spirit of this sentiment in his book, Asinof describes how even Gandil, the scandal's ringleader, had his moments as a hero. But both author and director also use the game to show disharmony. Asinof shows how Cicotte discovers early in game one that making a crooked game seem on the level was "a feat as difficult as throwing a no hitter" (105). In the movie version, Sayles expresses the disharmony and even the difficulty of the conspiring Sox' effort to throw the series in a cinematic sequence in which glares, glances, and occasional invectives pass among the players as they ambivalently work to lose the games. A useful contrast is evident in the film's presentation of Series games one and three.

In the Series opener, while Cicotte struggles to make his control problems and fielding miscues look legitimate, he glances uncertainly at teammates—particularly those on the level, such as fiery catcher Ray Schalk (played by Gordon Clapp, who also appeared as *Matewan's* Baldwin agent Griggs). In contrast, in game three, with the Sox down two games to zero, newcomer and conspiracy-outsider Dickie Kerr experiences the bliss of pitching mastery to give the Sox their first win. The temporary (though forced) harmony of the team is depicted in the upbeat ragtime music that captures quick scenes of the Sox clubbing hit after hit as even Kerr's conspiring teammates follow his masterful lead. Generally, Sayles' baseball interludes in *Eight Men Out* capture the same harmonious character as those in *Matewan*, revealing that in their natural environment—on the field of play—professional ballplayers' instincts and competitive drives consistently interfere with any forced efforts to play to lose.

6. *"You don't play the angles, you're a sap"* (Tormey)

In the film's opening frames, however, the connection of the game to money immediately threatens its innocence. Southside street urchins, who later elicit Buck Weaver's pangs of conscience, jubilantly head to their bleacher seats to the sounds of fans betting on the action in the thick of the pennant race: "Two bills says he do!" "Two bills says he don't!" The camera pans around Comiskey Park to reveal the "no betting" signs painted on the grandstand walls. The next scene shows a colleague joining sports writers Ring Lardner (played by Sayles himself) and Hugh Fullerton (Studs Terkel), claiming that the Sox owner is ready to entertain his team's unofficial publicists in the Stadium's posh Bard's Room. Lardner's reply is "Sportswriters of the world unite! You have nothing to lose but your bar privileges!"

The scene shows Comiskey's effort to ingratiate himself with the sportswriters while his truer nature as a penurious penny pincher extends only to his ballplayers. Later, the owner sings the praises of his nine to his assembled retinue of well-fed writers: "I got the horses! " By juxtaposing Comiskey's animal metaphor with Lardner's parody of the IWW slogan, Sayles hints at the pervasiveness of the larger climate of labor tensions and union movements resonating in the steel industry throughout South Chicago, and in nearby Hammond and Gary, Indiana (Taft 348). On September 22, 1919, just as the pennant race was winding down, steelworkers throughout the industrial heartland—in Chicago, Western Pennsylvania, and Ohio—went on strike. Some 279,000 workers left their jobs that day. By October 9, the day after Lefty Williams, preoccupied by threats made by gamblers toward his wife, failed to get out of the first inning against the Reds, the strike "reached its greatest effectiveness with 367,000 workers out" (Taft 357).

Providing a historical perspective on the Sox plight, Asinof recounts the early attempts of ballplayers to organize and lobby for better pay: the Players League of 1890 (50), The Federal League of 1914–5 (224), and the influence of gambling throughout the game's early history (13–14). He even notes the irony of Charles Comiskey's involvement in the labor struggles of players during his playing days, who "were in the vicelike grip of severe, uncompromising businessmen" (49)—the sort that he, himself, would later become. This early attention to the labor economics of the game frames the book's subsequent exploration of the scandal's legal, political, and human dimensions.

Though less frequently than Asinof, Sayles makes overt and powerful allusions to the labor struggles concomitant with the 1919 Series itself. But the film's exploration of labor's plight is located more in the portrayals of individual players, in their discussions of their salaries, and in the vernacular that they use to discuss these circumstances. In this way, Sayles aligns the struggles of disgruntled ballplayers with the striking steelworkers, miners, factory workers, cops, and longshoremen who, like Danny of *Matewan*, ironically see baseball only as a diversion from their troubles. As a sore-armed Cicotte gamely makes his way through the lineup of the second-division Browns to clinch the pennant for the Sox, Comiskey praises his talents to the writers he's hosting. Lardner wryly observes to Fullerton that a pitcher so esteemed by his owner should be paid a living wage.

Lardner's remark is significant, as Cicotte becomes one of the story's central figures. Like *Matewan's* Joe Kenehan, Cicotte's principles are challenged by the circumstances he faces, and along with Weaver's, his inner conflict is the most significant in the film. His stature as a wage-earner is largely subsumed by the game's place in the post-war patriotic climate, a development that has kept his salary down throughout his career, and the film's subsequent scenes are arranged to show the pitcher's difficult position. In the stands, former pitcher turned gambler Bill Burns confides to cohort Billy Maharg that Cicotte's role with the Sox is so significant no conspiracy would float without the knuckleballer's complicity.

At the pennant-winning celebration in a nearby barroom, the wife of Joe Jackson reads him the paper, revealing the mood with which Chicagoans saw their baseball: with the Germans subdued, the nation's attention is once again focused on the comforting diversion of its national pastime. Meanwhile, Gandil holds consecutive conferences with gamblers: first Sport Sullivan, and then Burns and Maharg. He and Risberg agree to do business with both sets of gamblers but keep each set unaware of their arrangements with the other. What results among ballplayers and gamblers alike is a confusing network of agreements, half-truths, and threats that a Chicago grand jury needed months to untangle, and Asinof took several chapters to explain.

However, Sayles, as a filmmaker, is required to condense matters. He does so by repeatedly casting the ballplayers in the vernacular of exploited wage-earners: to the Boston gambler Sullivan, who later becomes the front for gambling kingpin Arnold Rothstein, Gandil implies that he is open to offers to throw the series. Describing his pugilistic past, he reveals that he figured out too late how to make the fight game work for him. At this point, he declares, "you don't play the angles, you're a sap"—a sentiment that reveals his perceptions about the systems of profit making that capitalize on his labor. Having bounced around the American league for almost a decade, the first baseman would have had more than a token familiarity with the wage-supplementing tactics of his contemporary Hal

Chase, who successfully manipulated plays around the first sack for much of his fifteen-year career. When Sullivan seeks to understand his willingness to proceed with the fix, Gandil bitterly remarks on his club's owner's parsimony.

Throughout this smoky barroom scene, the rest of the Sox simultaneously celebrate their pennant and carp about the tight-fisted Comiskey. As Weaver protests Risberg's claim that "Comiskey *owns* you," Gandil plays another "angle." Mum about his recent arrangement with Sullivan, he brings the second pair of schemers, Burns and Maharg, into his plans, promising them that he can bring Cicotte into the conspiracy, all agreeing that the star pitcher's inclusion is most essential to its execution. At this moment Sayles cuts to Cicotte, the sore-armed pitcher at home getting a rubdown from his wife. His arm spent after a long season's labor, he expresses hope that he'll hold up for the three starts he'll see in the nine-game series. By relating their plight in the wage earners' vernacular, Sayles consistently aligns the banished eight with the maligned laborers who constitute much of their fan base. He thus captures the tenor of the times, in which tense labor struggles shaped all interactions between owners and workers. Although well paid in comparison with their wage-earning fans, the ballplayers fully understand their connection to those who watch them, as well as the precariousness of their own good fortune in the hands of the powerful who control their labor.

This condition of their world reverberates when Gandil then goes to work on Cicotte. Even though the pitcher seems grateful for his $6,000-a-year salary while others are unemployed, Gandil stays on him. On his way to meet with Comiskey to ask for his 30-win bonus, Cicotte painfully confronts the meanness of his owner. He has been held out of key starts during the pennant race, supposedly to rest his arm for the Series but really to prohibit his collecting the bonus. As a result, the Old Roman tells the pitcher that his 29 wins are not sufficient to claim it. Despite the pitcher's contributions to the team's pennant run, he'll only get the salary stipulated by his contract.

Cicotte's position as a maligned laborer exploited by a penurious owner becomes apparent to him, as well as to the film's viewers, in this sequence. Rebuffed, he seeks out Gandil, who sits in a hotel lobby reading the newspaper. "Defy Strike; Open Mill" screams the headline, showing the paper's suspicion of unionized labor. Less directly, this brief allusion hints at the connection between the underpaid Sox pitcher, his teammates, and the striking steelworkers. The grievances of both groups contradict the pro-business ethos of this patriotic time, in which labor agitation was treated by the popular press as a mutant strain of European culture and an affront to American values, supposedly best embodied in the national institution of baseball. In this context, Cicotte makes his demands from Gandil, the scandal's ringleader. He is to get ten grand, in cash, before he throws a single series pitch. Out of pressure to supplement his income, and still smarting from his eye-opening encounter with his exploitive boss, the aging knuckleballer realizes the significance of his position as a starter of three games in the extended nine-game Series. In accordance with the grievances of his teammates and against his better judgement, he decides to act.

The challenge to the principles and beliefs of both Joe Kenehan and Eddie Cicotte represents a major narrative thread of their respective stories. Both the pacifist and the pitcher experience a traumatic epiphany when they recognize that the power of their convictions is challenged by the necessity to respond to the actions and beliefs of equally determined but less just men. Christ-like and pleading for peace, Kenehan tries to prevent the movie's climactic gun battle between Baldwin-Felts detectives and striking miners—the so-called Matewan Massacre. Walking into its crossfire, Kenehan is sacrificed to its violent outcome. Angered over the brutal execution of one of their own sons, the striking miners lose their tolerance for his message of non-violence, and his plea for peaceful resolution leads to his demise.

Like Kenehan, Cicotte is at the center of his story's escalating tensions, and his struggles with his principles dictate the course of its progress. Unlike Kenehan, who holds on to his pacifist ethos at the cost of his life, Cicotte chooses to compromise his professional and personal ethos after dramatically confronting the reality of his own exploitation. Yet when Cicotte agrees to the fix, he becomes property of a different kind: in liberating himself from Comiskey's grip, he comes under control of the gamblers.

The idiom of ownership becomes a central feature of the film with the gamblers, like Comiskey, envisioning their power over the players as a means to generate profit. Shortly after Comiskey rejects Cicotte's request for the bonus, the notion of ownership resurfaces in a subsequent dialogue between the New York gambler Arnold Rothstein, and his go-between, Abe Attell. Rothstein expresses his contempt for the athletes in recounting a childhood story in which, as "the fat kid," he was kept out of his cohort's games: "Pretty soon I *owned* the game. And those guys I come up with? They come to *me* now with their hats in their hands." Rothstein then tells Attell, an ex-boxing champion, that, "All together, I musta made ten times more betting on you than you did slugging it out. And I never took a punch." When Attell replies "yeah, but I was *champ*, and can't

6. *"You don't play the angles, you're a sap"* (Tormey)

nothing take that away," Rothstein shows no understanding of the athletic code inherent in the fighter's claim, but his disdain is apparent as he pretends no interest in the fix.

In the awkward silence that follows, Attell realizes that he is dealing with someone who sees through wins and losses to the matter most essential to owners of people and property: profit. As a former athlete turned gambler, Attell retains at least a shred of residual admiration for those who subscribe to an ethic where merit is determined by physical ability and competitive savvy. Rothstein holds no such belief, seeing the Sox as grown up versions of the brutes that kept him out of the game as a child. With Attell's departure, Rothstein calls his cohort Nat Brown and proceeds to set up a meeting with Sport Sullivan, who will serve as his new go-between in the fix.

Meanwhile, Attell meets with Burns and Maharg, who have come to New York themselves to seek Rothstein's backing. Using the gambler's name though lacking his support, Attell goes about raising the funds to buy the players, not knowing that his boss has other plans, which exclude him. Rothstein himself meets with Sullivan and tersely indicates his interest. Waiting for his return trip back to Chicago, Sullivan is visited by the hulking Monk Eastman, who delivers the cash: forty grand up front, forty grand when the deal goes through. Following Gandil's lead and playing an "angle" of his own, Sullivan promptly takes thirty grand of Rothstein's money and places it on bets of his own, demonstrating a mindset characteristic of one accustomed to controlling the wages (and the world) of others. When Sullivan's wide-eyed assistant wonders how the money can be used to buy off the Sox if it's all out on bets, Sullivan explains: "you know what you feed a dray horse in the morning if you want a day's work out of him? Just enough so he knows he's hungry." His remark encapsulates the idea of ownership, recalling Comiskey's earlier claim that he's got the horses and underscoring the connection Sayles wants to make between the gamblers and the Sox's owner. By this time, the Sox are on two payrolls, both of which are controlled by greedy and demanding executors. Whether under the control of a stingy owner or on the gamblers' payrolls, the ballplayers are property. Whether they are laborers earning a wage far below their value, or bought conspirators whose payments are dwarfed by the payoffs to those who wager on their labors, Sayles clearly captures their exploitation by larger economic forces in this carefully crafted sequence of scenes.

Once the Sox arrive in Cincinnati, the suspicions become rampant. As the Series begins, Sayles presents short scenes in sequence, constructing a montage that highlights the tension felt by the compromised players.

Looking at the mob scene building out from his hotel window, Cicotte stares at the money he has taken and realizes that he has been bought. In a pre-game conversation, manager Gleason tells sportswriters Lardner and Fullerton that, as a baseball old timer, he has heard rumors of fixes for years. On the mound to begin game one, Cicotte quickly realizes what the gamblers have known all along, that the task of throwing the series will fall mostly on his shoulders. Back in his hotel room after his shellacking, he lies to Lardner, telling him that despite the game one rout the team's play is on the level.

Game two arrives, and after crossing up his fiery catcher Schalk throughout it, pitcher Lefty Williams becomes the next goat. Between innings, an effigy in a Sox uniform is dropped from a plane circling above. As it lands in front of the Chicago dugout, and Gleason glares at it, his suspicions piqued by his team's poor play. He turns to his struggling lefthander, wondering if the dummy might be willing to throw a few. Later, after their second loss, another dummy, also in a Sox uniform, is burned in effigy outside of the team's hotel in Cincinnati as the fix begins to crack. Gamblers Burns and Maharg come to see that Attell has used them, employing his association with Rothstein to capitalize on their wrangling to advance his own profit. Back for game three in Chicago, the duo seeks to recoup their losses. They bet against Dickie Kerr, who enjoys a career day in beating the Reds on a three-hit shutout. During the game, when a loafing Gandil is forced at third, Lardner observes that the first baseman's acting skills are wanting.

Just as the Sox rebelled against their owner, they chafe against the control exerted on them by the gamblers—who watch the purse strings with a parsimony equal to Comiskey's. As the Series progresses, the responsibility for orchestrating the fix falls increasingly on the pitchers' shoulders, especially after the position players—especially Jackson and Weaver—begin to play on the level. In game four, Cicotte has to foil Jackson's stellar play, cutting off the outfielder's perfect throw home and thus allowing a Cincinnati run. In game five, Williams, though given some help from centerfielder Felsch, must do most of the dirty work himself to throw the game. Facing defeat, the Sox mount an improbable rally, and when Gandil tries to force a game-ending ground out in game six, his batted ball unintentionally finds the hole, plating Weaver with the winning run. In one of the film's more comic moments, Gandil's jubilation is poorly feigned.

After the game, Cicotte and Williams lament their plight as the scandal's most essential operatives. Both realize that their pursuit of a big payoff has helped clarify to them what's really important: their integrity

6. *"You don't play the angles, you're a sap"* (Tormey)   71

to the game, their team, and themselves. When the promised payoffs from the gamblers don't materialize, the seeds of the players' rebellion against the plan are fully sown. During his solid outing in the seventh game, a 4–1 victory, Cicotte exchanges glares with Risberg as the Sox fight back. With their victory, the dour Gandil is again forced into celebration with his teammates, whose commitment to throw the Series is also being subsumed as much by their natural competitive instincts as by Attell's tardy payoffs.

As the ballplayers revolt and narrow the Series gap, the gamblers see their profits wane and begin to exert their muscle. In the hotel lobby, Williams, on the eve of starting the next game, is approached by a hit man, who suggests the pitcher's wife will be in peril if his command over the Reds is too great. As the game begins, Williams, preoccupied by the threat, doesn't get past the first inning. The Sox lose, game and Series. Throughout this montage of quick interludes, Sayles' account of the thrown series underscores the ways in which the ballplayers find themselves "owned" by gamblers, whose hold over the purse strings is as tight as Comiskey's.

Historically, over the winter of 1919 and into the 1920 season, the rumors of the fix continued to circulate. The Grand Jury convened, the writers making accusations were themselves accused of impugning a national institution, and Comiskey summoned attorney Alfred Austrian, who offered a strategy to the Sox owner. While Asinof describes Comiskey's lawyer and confidant in some detail, Sayles portrays him only briefly as a "legal Babe Ruth," capable of manipulating the facts and the press to ensure the health of Comiskey's bottom line. Likewise, forced by the constraints of his medium to condense a year's time into a much shorter narrative, Sayles depicts the Grand Jury investigation as if it followed on the heels of Series and proceeded into the winter months. In so doing, he omits details such as Gandil's retirement, Risberg's holdout, and most importantly, the 1920 season and pennant race (where Williams and Cicotte, still on gamblers' payrolls as the result of blackmail, nevertheless comprise two of the four 20-game winners on a second-place Sox staff).

Though insisting on the guilt of his players, Comiskey is told by lawyer Austrian that to maintain the business of baseball, the game must preserve its image of cleanness, even though it had, in reality, become rotten to the core. The imperative to maintain the profitability of the national pastime underscores the status of the ballplayers as laborers. And the legal proceedings highlight the struggles of the scandal's important laborers, the pitchers who were forced to execute most of its dirty work.

Fittingly, the responsibility to confess also falls on their shoulders. In tearful testimony, Cicotte caves in and admits guilt. And as the proceedings continue, Sayles depicts the moment of his epiphany, his private realization of the forces of ownership that maintain the distance between his wages and his power to generate profits:

> I always figured it was talent made a man big. Like I was the best at something. I mean, we're the guys they come to see. Without us, there ain't a ball game. Lookin' at who's holdin' the money and lookin' at who's facing the jail cell—talent don't mean nothing. And where's Comiskey and Sullivan and Attell? Out in the back room cuttin' up profits, that's where. That's the damn conspiracy.

Sayles adapts this scene from Asinof's account, which describes the pitcher's epiphany in more personal terms. Significantly, however, both accounts portray the pitcher as a disillusioned performer who has, late in his career, finally realized the distance between the wealth he's generated and the wage he'd been paid:

> He had grown up believing it was talent that made a man big. If you were good enough, and dedicated yourself, you could get to the top. Wasn't that enough of a reward? But when he got there, he had found out otherwise. They all fed off him, the men who ran the show and pulled the strings that kept it working. They used him and used him, and when they had used him up, they would dump him. In the few years he had been up, they had always praised him and made him feel like a hero to the people of America. But all the time they paid him peanuts. The newspapermen who came to watch him pitch and wrote stories about him made more money than he did. Meanwhile, Comiskey made a half million dollars a year on Cicotte's right arm.
> Burns knew how to operate. So did Gandil. Cicotte didn't. That was the answer [413–4].

In manager Kid Gleason's testimony, he fields questions about who controls the game. Recalling his experience as a pitcher, he recounts "hearing stories" about games thrown but confidently states that he'd had a clean reputation. But knowing his players' tense relationship with their penny-pinching owner, he reveals that, under certain hypothetical circumstances, he can understand how an embittered and underpaid player can be bought. He then reasserts that the Sox are the greatest club he has ever seen. A former pitcher himself, he hints at an understanding of Cicotte's plight. In this way, his thoughts underscore the significance of the role of the pitchers in the scandal, within the larger themes of labor and exploitation.

Immediately following the trial, the film then cuts to the Sox celebrating their "not guilty" verdict, which Lardner, commenting to Fullerton, describes as "a bigger fix than the Series." However, in order to restore public confidence in baseball, Judge Landis is summoned to serve as Baseball's first commissioner. Insisting on absolute power and a lifetime appointment, he is introduced to the public by Comiskey himself, who justifies the appointee for reasons of patriotism, alluding to the judge's "anti-red" record. This detail refers, of course, to Landis' anti-labor and anti-union record, and the Sox owner conveniently omits mention of the judge's anti–Federal League stance four years earlier. Nevertheless, with this pro-business judge tabbed as the one capable of bringing baseball labor into line, Sayles seeks to portray what was true in real life: eventually, Comiskey came to understand his players' sellout as a labor grievance and the overall culture of gambling that had become a fixture in the national game. With a strong figure in place who could simultaneously stand against baseball's culture of gambling as well as its unionizing impulses, Comiskey knew to raise the salaries of his remaining players so that as the 1920's began they would be less tempted by gamblers' overtures.

By installing as commissioner a figure noted for his anti-labor record, the owners hold over the players was strengthened, and Sayles deliberately calls attention to these labor-related matters in the film's later stages. Seeking to emphasize Landis' anti-labor record, Sayles deliberately portrays him as the one who maintains baseball's climate of exploitation. And in one of his interviews with Smith, he describes the connection between unionizing Chicago workers, Chicago ballplayers, and Landis' relationship with both of these exploited labor pools:

> One of the ironies for me, of course, is that Landis was the guy who sent the Wobblies either into jail or exile. Whatever the level of judge just below Supreme Court is, he was the Chicago guy. Because of the Haymarket Riot and various organizational things, the Wobblies had a lot of their big guys, like Big Bill Haywood, in his district when the Wobblies not only said, "Don't report to the draft, don't enlist for World War I," but also, "We should commit sabotage against it because this is an antiworker war." Which it pretty much was—they weren't too far off base there. The big Red Scare was in 1920, but they pretty much broke the back of the Wobblies by sending all their leaders to jail, or the ones who didn't want to go to jail went into exile. And Landis was the guy who read the sentences on these guys [154].

With Landis' pronouncement of the Sox banishment, the film moves toward its coda, and its exploration of the labor of baseball is closed. The scene shifts to a picturesque ballpark well removed from Chicago's urban environs. Cinematic details provide the context of an independent league contest taking place in Hoboken, NJ, in 1925. An aging Jackson, making amazing catches and hitting monumental blasts, takes control of the game. Watching from the stands, New Jersey wags disparage him for making a killing on the Series and selling out to gamblers. Sitting close by, a wistful Buck Weaver reminisces to them, saying that his teammate was the best and that they've mistaken this bush-league star for the great Shoeless Joe. This scene parallels Asinof's use of wistful lines from a Nelson Algren poem to close the historical version of the players' story.

Nevertheless, the greatest share of both Asinof's narrative and Sayles's film justifiably focus on the economics of the ballplayers as laborers. In the later stages of Asinof's narrative, he details the organizing efforts of lawyer Raymond J. Cannon, whose efforts to clear the name and secure the back pay of Jackson, represent an early challenge to the supremacy of the game's owners. In Sayles' labor-oriented vision of the 1919 World Series, the Sox pitchers exert a more direct control over the outcome of the game than their conspiring cohorts do, and it is in this regard that *Eight Men Out* is most vivid as an outgrowth of *Matewan*. In Cicotte's case, his exploitation by the labor economics of post World War I links him most closely to the workers across the country, and Sayles magnifies his inner conflicts most greatly as a result. Despite their own struggle to organize, the climate of the day and the media-controlling efforts of the game's magnates lead the fans to see the banished eight as traitors to the national pastime. In both the book and the film, however, they are ultimately depicted as struggling laborers seeking to improve their lot as wage earners in a harsh capitalistic world that was only beginning to confront the reality of organized labor.

WORKS CITED

Asinof, Eliot. *Eight Men Out*. Henry Holt, 1987. Holt, Rinehart, and Winston,1963.

Klempley, Rita. Review of *Eight Men Out*. *Washington Post*, 23 September 1988. 3 Jan. 2002 <http://www.washingtonpost.com/wpsrv/style/longterm/m.../eightmenoutpgkempley_a0c9ed.ht>.

Sayles, John, Dir.and screenwriter. *Eight Men Out*. Perf. John Cusack and D. B. Sweeney, Orion Pictures, 1988.

_____. Dir, screenwriter and director. *Matewan*. Perf. Chris Cooper and James Earl Jones, Orion Pictures, 1987.
Smith, Gavin, Ed. *Sayles on Sayles*. London: Faber and Faber, 1998.
Taft, Philip. *Organized Labor in American History*. New York: Harper & Row, 1964.

7

"The proper distance for worship": Art Worlds and Assimilation Narratives in *The Celebrant*

Ronald Kates

Throughout Eric Rolfe Greenberg's *The Celebrant*, brothers Jackie and Eli Kapinski create an assimilation narrative that, at its root, mirrors the melting pot ethos. During their first spring in New York—their first spring in America—the two Jewish immigrant boys find baseball everywhere, in the consciousness of fans and on the streets and sandlots of the city, where they adopt the language and behavior of the other boys, cocking their caps at a particular angle and losing their European accents in the "curses and intonations of the game" (12). Both brothers approach baseball as an avenue to assimilation, yet Jackie and Eli each create a world that defines their respective relation to the game and the dominant culture to which they wish to assimilate.

Jackie, a talented pitcher as a boy, embraces baseball—more specifically star Giant hurler Christy Mathewson—as his means of artistic inspiration in designing commemorative rings for the family business that celebrate Mathewson's accomplishments. Eli, in contrast, tries to insinuate himself into friendships and confidences with John McGraw and Giants' players, willingly inhabiting an artificial world rooted in chance encounters, gambling, gossip, and an exorbitantly foolish lifestyle. He fails to recognize the impossibility of his attaining a stature where he could offer something, rather than receive "the same joking dismissal" given him by the Giants following the Merkle's Boner game (146).

Disdaining Eli's artificiality, Jackie creates what art historian Howard Becker refers to as an "art world," which forms when "people who never cooperated before [are brought together] to produce art based on and using conventions previously unknown or not exploited in that way" (310). As a result, when Eli asks Jackie whether he worships Mathweson from "afar," Jackie responds as an artist with respect for his subject: "Isn't that the proper distance for worship? You don't crawl into the ark to worship *torah*" (42). By emphasizing *creation* rather than adulation or emulation, Jackie, with his jewelry designs, can create a world where he and Mathewson can maintain a subtle presence in each other's lives.

While both Kapinski brothers inhabit worlds defined in large part by sport, they maintain differing perceptions of the power of sports to become an all-encompassing factor in a person's life. In his introduction to *Body Language: Writers on Sport*, Gerald Early asserts that "an understanding, not necessarily an appreciation, of sports, is essential in understanding how modern life is structured and how human desire is sublimated" (x); indeed, "with the exception of our politics, nothing comes as close to being recorded almost completely as an epic narrative in our news as our sports" (xi). Eli's largely deluded sense of his place in the game contrasts with Jackie's vision of sport as both inspiration and reflection of reality. Where Eli views baseball and the Giants as a means to financial and social gain, Jackie understands that baseball ultimately enables him to define himself as an artist and as an American.

Becker asserts that while "some art worlds begin with the development of a new concept, a new way of thinking about something," other art worlds "begin with the development of a new audience" (312–3). Eli perceives his efforts to ingratiate himself with John McGraw, other Giants, and eventually notoriously crooked Yankee star Hal Chase as an opportunity to elevate not just his status as a sporting man but the status of the family's jewelry business as well. Eli, however, fails to see that his audiences recognize the artificiality of his business and gaming facades. His fantasies eventually lead to his estrangement from the family and his eventual suicide when he learns too late that the fix was in for the 1919 World Series. Conversely, Jackie forges an emotional association with Mathewson first as a fan, then as an artist, and finally as what celebrated sportswriter Hugh Fullerton calls "the celebrant of [Mathewson's] work" (175).

The worlds Jackie and Eli create, the artistic and the artificial, meet and diverge on July 15, 1901, when Mathewson throws his first of two career no-hitters. The brothers attend the game in St. Louis with several clients, reasoning that the ballpark offers a "so American" (17) alternative to the traditional hotel sales meeting, yet by the game's end, Eli has won a considerable sum from them and feels obligated to rectify matters by treating them to "an evening of splendid debauch" (27). Whereas Eli despairs at taking his clients' money in a series of bets throughout the game, Jackie marvels at Mathewson's ability on the mound and begins observing the game vicariously, returning to the time when he too could retire batters with a mix of guile and power. Jackie's role-playing briefly buoys his self-identity but eventually leads him to reflect on his failure to defy his parent's wishes and pursue an opportunity to play minor league baseball.

When later that evening Jackie watches Mathewson and his teammates through the closed parlor car door on the train to Chicago, he surmises that the pitcher, "was everything I was not," and that "there was a gulf between us that I felt I must not cross" (29). At this moment, Jackie fully, painfully understands his inability to "be like" Mathewson. He is not the All-American hero pitcher but an immigrant Jew with artistic talent and a place awaiting him in the family business. His regret, however, sparks the artistic inspiration that prompts him to design the ring celebrating the no-hitter and transforms him into a "celebrant" and art world creator, rather than a mere instrument of commerce like his brother.

Even though the rings Jackie designs forge an artistic and personal bond with Mathewson, his art world never forms until the pitcher acknowledges his role as subject and motivating force. Becker insists that observers need to "understand, not the genesis of innovations, but rather the process of mobilizing people to join in a cooperative activity on a regular basis," as well as discern that "new art worlds grow up around something that has not been characteristic practice for artists before" (311). Mathewson acknowledges the artistry of the ring Jackie designed as the two men meet at a dinner arranged by Jackie's father-in-law. The pitcher tells the artist: "'when I was giving some considerable thought to whether I'd play again the following year, out of nowhere came this marvelous piece of work. It made the moment [of the no-hitter] real again, and I never wear it but that I feel it anew'" (89). In this moment, when Mathewson grips Jackie by the wrist to affirm his admiration for the emerald and ruby rings, pitcher and artist enter into a creative collaboration, or mobilization between icon and iconographer.

Jackie's assimilation narrative differs greatly from the artistic narrative Greenberg creates throughout *The Celebrant*. Once Jackie meets Mathewson and hears the pitcher exclaim, "I think your work is extraordinary" (74), he redefines his self-perception of artistic success. Whereas Jackie the Jewish-baseball-player-turned-jeweler strives to create and maintain an *American* persona, Jackie the artist—the "celebrant" of Mathewson's triumphs—still determines to "worship" the pitcher from a distance, fearing that a closer association with his subject would limit the objectivity an artist must maintain. When Jackie, Eli, and John McGraw surprise the naked Mathewson in his apartment during an impromptu visit, Jackie tempers his embarrassment with an impulsive artistic impression of Matty's powerful body as cast "in marble" (71), a prevailing image that enables him to maintain a certain detachment from his subject.

Unlike Jackie's artistic connection to the game, Eli's artificial sportsman's narrative allows for no detachment; indeed, the identity Eli craves necessitates *the appearance of* connection or acceptance. As Eli builds his façade, he gradually transforms himself into what Eric Solomon refers to as the "anti-celebrant, the one who loves the game largely for its cash value" (89). While Jackie gains approval from Mathewson, McGraw, and other Giants based on his artistry and deliberate distance, Eli thrives on the illusion that he has somehow become an indispensable insider to the Giants, as well as on the New York sporting scene.

When Eli and younger brother Arthur ask Jackie to solicit an endorsement from Mathewson to promote the family's new jewelry line, Jackie steadfastly refuses, insisting that to exploit his bond with the pitcher is wrong. Even though Mathewson accepts the endorsement offer, and the new line turns a considerable profit, Jackie sees an irrevocable breach in the art world he has created. By allowing his family and business to infringe upon and even dictate his artistry, Jackie begins to understand that art worlds, too, have illusory natures that bring about often unwanted change. Becker suggests that "art worlds decline when some groups that knew and used the conventions which inform their characteristic works lose that knowledge, or when new personnel cannot be recruited to maintain the world's activities" (349). Even before Arthur, Eli, and his Uncle Sid ask Jackie to approach Mathewson with the endorsement offer, Jackie confronts an artistic crisis that affects his roles in both the art world he creates and the outside world into which he wishes to assimilate.

After designing the first no-hitter ring in 1901 and presenting it to Mathewson, Jackie subsequently creates three other rings to commemorate another no-hitter, the Giants 1904 National League championship, and their 1905 World Series victory; however, by 1908, "designing the company line had become as routine as the ride to work on the 'el'" (118). Jackie ultimately resolves this conflict between his art world and assimilation narrative after reading a ghostwritten autobiography of Mathewson. Upon finishing the book, Jackie turns to look at the drawings of the rings he created for Mathewson, "envying their youthful energy and clean direction," yet simultaneously understanding that like the autobiography's writer, he had spent the last few years "exploiting rather than glorifying the hero" (175). After looking over his current work, Jackie feels "ashamed" while realizing that he "needed new inspiration and could not look to Mathewson" (175).

Jackie's art world declines, not because he loses knowledge or cannot recruit other artists or subjects to it but because he perceives that combining art and business often leads to artificial rather than purely artistic products. Jackie creates the first ring based on the inspiration he receives from watching the no-hitter and then observing Mathewson in the rail car "through [his] own mirrored image in the glass" (29), ultimately deciding to replace the emerald center stone with "a polished ruby, red with fire" (30). However, when Arthur later asks him to create rings for young Giant hurlers Rube Marquard and Jeff Tesreau, Jackie refuses insisting that the rings he designed for Mathewson "were done on impulse" (178). Arthur, who values business over art or sport, cannot understand the intricacies of this "art world" and rejects Jackie's concerns by emphasizing, "this is a business concern" (178).

Throughout the last half of *The Celebrant*, these "business concerns" continually threaten the "art world" Mathewson and Jackie have created. Indeed, without Arthur's insistence that Mathewson appear at the grand opening of the family's Boston store—on the day he will pitch the deciding game of the 1912 World Series—Jackie would never have had his "celebrant" role defined for him by noted sportswriter Hugh Fullerton. Fullerton delivers a plea from the pitcher asking to skip the ceremony, and in the ensuing conversation, he imparts to Jackie that Mathewson perceives him as "the celebrant of his works" (195). When Fullerton explains the "celebrant" concept, he furnishes Jackie with a link that enables him to reconcile his artistic and assimilation narratives. "You and me and my brethren of the press corps, more than anyone," Fullerton tells Jackie,

> All the celebrants of his works. We make the greatest demands. Every time he pitches I find myself hoping for the most extraordinary achievement, for my immortality lies in his ... you're the high priest, Kapp, the celebrant-in-chief. He demands that you equal in fashioned stone anything he may do on the field ... I suspect that your work is infused with the wish that you were he. You're not alone. Inside every sportswriter, there's a frustrated athlete ... the same thing is inside every fan, or anyone who ever picked up a bat and ball [196–7].

Fullerton, of course, tells Jackie what he already understands—that the frustrated boy whose parents forbade him from pursuing a baseball career drives the artist who derives artistic impulse and ambition from his foremost subject. Mathewson's admission during the dinner they share that "it wasn't easy to sign a major league contract, you know. My parents were against it. It wasn't a fit career for a gentleman" (89) does not mock Jackie's inability to define his own wishes; in a sense, Mathewson approves of Jackie's decision to place art before baseball in his art world hierarchy. Years later, during a party prior to the 1919 World Series, an inebriated Jackie reflects back on the possible baseball career he foresook for his position in the family jewelry business, but ultimately he reasons that choosing baseball would have diverted him from the things he holds in the highest esteem: his family, work, and home (235). As an artist, Jackie has the opportunity to create enduring pieces that can transcend a ballplayer's singular career achievements, yet his intimate baseball knowledge enables him to infuse his art with an intricacy and vigor a non-athlete could never produce. As Becker insists, "the conventional way of doing things in any art utilizes an existing cooperative network, which rewards those who manipulate the existing conventions appropriately in light of the associated aesthetic" (306).

In a paper at the 2002 Indiana State Baseball in Literature and Culture Conference, Pete Peterson referred to *The Celebrant* as a "novel that elevated baseball fiction to the level of tragedy." While the novel possesses decidedly tragic elements, one could argue that the culmination of Jackie's assimilation narrative bears a resemblance to Northrop Frye's concept of traditional comedic action, whereby barriers placed before a young man "are eventually circumvented and the comedy ends at a point when a new society is crystallized" (72), and audience members are encouraged to participate in "the festive mood [the celebration] generates" (92). This crystallization occurs within an art world as well, yet Becker concludes, "the artists who work in [art worlds] have different problems depending on the state of their world. The kind of work one can make and the fate it will have will differ, too. Artistic work lasts when it has an organizational basis that preserves and protects it" (350).

Jackie, therefore, strives to protect his artistic integrity by creating a new, crystallized art world based on cooperation rather than worship. By creating works "on impulse" (178), Jackie captures an essence usually deleted when people create their own narratives through an expressive or artistic form. Whereas Arthur and Eli suppress the boyish joy of embracing or living vicariously through a hero, Jackie remains truthful to his emotions when he admires Mathewson as he would the *torah*. In creating his art world, Jackie invites his audience, specifically Mathewson, into what theatre scholar Richard Hornby refers to as "a kind of identity laboratory in which social roles can be examined vicariously" (71).

Within this "identity laboratory," Jackie can present an assimilated image as an artist, baseball fan, and American. As Early asserts, sport has the power to transform a game to a cultural indicator, part of an ongoing popular narrative, and while all three Kapinski brothers participate in this narrative as immigrant Jews attempting to assimilate into the larger American culture, only Jackie, the "celebrant" of the decidedly non–Jewish Christy Mathewson, can transcend stereotype and create a unique narrative that compliments his assimilation process. Indeed, long before this final meeting with Mathewson, back when Jackie draws the worshipping *torah* analogy to describe his pre-art world relationship with the pitcher, Eli insists that worshipping an athlete would connote a sort of heresy. After briefly considering Eli's insinuation, Jackie responds, "a very American heresy, Mister Kapp," deliberately using the shortened version of the family name, the name they use for business purposes when they want to conceal their Jewish identity (42). Throughout *The Celebrant*, Jackie never climbs over others to touch or acknowledge Mathewson, nor does he enter the clubhouse or develop a relationship outside baseball, choosing instead the subtle commonality his carefully crafted art world provides.

WORKS CITED

Becker, Howard. *Art Worlds*. Berkeley: U of California P, 1982.

Early, Gerald. "Introduction" *Body Language: Writers on Sport* Ed. Gerald Early. Saint Paul: Graywolf Press, 1998. vii–xiii.

Greenberg, Eric R. *The Celebrant*. Lincoln: U of Nebraska P, 1983.

Hornby, Richard. *Drama, Metadrama, and Perception*. Lewisburg: Bucknell UP, 1986.

Peterson, Pete. Keynote Address. Seventh Annual ISU Conference on Baseball in Literature and Culture. Indiana State University, Terre Haute. 22 March 2002.

Solomon, Eric. "'Memories of Days Past' or Why Eric Rolfe Greenberg's *The Celebrant* is the Greatest (Jewish) American Baseball Novel." *American Jewish History* 83 (1995): 83–107.

8

Nine Assists and No Errors: Rediscovering the Baseball Fiction of Charles Van Loan

TREY STRECKER

Any serious study of the development of sports fiction at the beginning of the twentieth-century must acknowledge the short stories of Charles Van Loan (1876–1919). Between 1909 and 1919, Charles Emmett Van Loan established himself as "the *prose* laureate of the golf-course, the prize-ring, the diamond, and the race-track" (Davis 282). At the time of his death, the *Philadelphia Public Ledger* estimated that Van Loan had "the largest following of men readers of any magazine fiction writer" in the nation (Brignano 339). During a prolific decade in which he published nine collections of short stories, including four baseball books—*The Big League* (1909), *The Ten-Thousand-Dollar Arm* (1912), *The Lucky Seventh* (1913), and *Score By Innings* (1919)—Van Loan was celebrated as "sport's greatest fiction writer and soul (*sic*) historian" (Rice vii) and as "baseball fiction's comic genius" (Solomon 97). Indeed, his friend Grantland Rice reserved special praise for Van Loan's baseball stories, claiming that "no other man has ever unfolded the romance and humor of baseball half as well" (x).

Yet while Van Loan remains best known for drawing the attention of *The Saturday Evening Post*'s editor, George Horace Lorimer, to Ring Lardner's "A Busher's Letters Home," his own stories decisively capture the feel and texture of the World War I-era game and its characters. As his longtime friend and editor Robert H. Davis explains, Van Loan "possessed the peculiar gift of characterization developed to a high degree and could cover a baseball game, a horse-race, a prize-fight, or any sporting event with fine grace and distinction. In his hands the brawn of life, the animated, playful mob, the lusty-throated fans, the vikings of the diamond, became personalities in literature" (280).

Whether writing about baseball or boxing, Van Loan's popularity derived from his humorous, character-driven stories, where justice prevails, "even if the heroes must resort to tricks and schemes that rival the chicaneries of their antagonists" (Brignano 339). Although many of his stories rely on humor or the sentimentalism demanded by the conventions of magazine fiction, they often deal with serious topics, including race, alcoholism, and gambling. But Van Loan's stories succeed, Rice argues, because the author "made it his business not only to know the game, but to study at close range the human emotions of the players as well ... their habits, their eccentricities, their superstitions, their likes and dislikes" (ix).

Like Lardner, Van Loan examines the ballplayer's lot off of the diamond, and many of his tales unfold in the Pullman cars and hotel lobbies of leagues across the country. Recall how Mark Harris's southpaw Henry Wiggen criticizes Lardner's fiction because it does not appear to really be *about* baseball:

> Lardner did not seem to me to amount to much, half of his stories containing women in them and the other half less about baseball then what was going on in the hotels and trains. He never seemed to care how the games come out. He wouldn't tell you much about the stars but only the bums and punks and second-raters that never had the stuff to begin with [34].

Wiggen would likely say the same of Van Loan's stories, for they are about this baseball life on and off the field—the poker games, practical jokes, and superstitions—in fact, several stories consider whether bridegrooms or bachelors make the best ball players. Van Loan manages a motley roster of ball players sporting clever nicknames like Walrus Potter, Squirrel Wicks, Mixed-Ale Mulligan, The Dayton Adonis, Smokeless Solly Jones, and Shameless Shamus Kehoe. These characters are the stars and the dubs, the team boosters and the newspapers' "war correspondents," the scouts, umpires, managers, and magnates of big city first-division clubs, bush-league tail-enders, and barnstorming aggregations.

A native Californian, Van Loan's stories set much of his fiction in the Western United States, where town teams battle far away from the big league action. Van Loan writes:

> Baseball, as played by a small town team, is a very intimate and personal affair.... Everybody in the town knows everybody else, speaks to everybody else; every joy is a common joy, every grief is common property. The crack of the bat which drives the ball screaming to the fence thrills every local heart. Big league baseball is a wonderful institution, but to see the great American game in its most interesting phase, follow the small town team [39].

In "The Phantom League," Van Loan recounts the story of a scout who cannot believe his good fortune when he stumbles across newspaper reports of an independent league whose players seem too good to be true. He makes an arduous trip to New Mexico to inspect these prospects, but he discovers a fictional league and a baseball dice game that foreshadows Robert Coover's J. Henry Waugh. Life in the west, it seems, is intolerably dull without baseball, so some transplanted baseball bugs have created their own dice league and started a local newspaper to report their games. With "The Phantom League," Van Loan offers an intriguing commentary on the Western experience of Major League Baseball played far away.

Whether his stories depict the Major Leagues or the lowly minors, Van Loan deftly represents the deadball era strategy of inside baseball. Hitters choked up on the bat and tried to punch the ball through the infield, and games turned on a combination of grace, guts, guile, and ginger. The hit and run, the sacrifice bunt, and the stolen base were popular plays, and home runs were almost always of the inside-the-park variety. While many pitchers relied on fast ones and curves, some mastered trick deliveries like the spitball. The ball itself, often misshapen and discolored by grass stains and tobacco juice, was heavy and dead. Big league diamonds were populated with stars like Christy Mathewson and Ty Cobb, Walter Johnson and Hans Wagner, and the diametrically opposed personalities of John McGraw and Connie Mack commanded the action between the foul lines.

As Americans migrated to urban industrial centers during the late-nineteenth century, baseball and other spectator sports thrived. Popular in city sandlots and in rural fields across the United States, baseball was securely established as America's pastime by the early twentieth century. And, as I note in *Dead Balls and Double Curves: An Anthology of Early Baseball Fiction*, sportswriters and other literary professionals, such as Van Loan, Lardner, and Hugh Fullerton, began to produce fiction to satisfy the baseball bug's growing desire for baseball stories.

Born on June 29, 1876, in San Jose, California, Charles Van Loan began writing about sports while working as a secretary for a meat-packing house. Attending minor league ballgames around Los Angeles with his boss, Van Loan took detailed notes on the games, as well as "odd happenings or humorous events on the field or in the grandstand" (Brignano 338). After work, he developed these notes into newspaper articles, several of which were published in the *Los Angeles Examiner.*

In 1904, Van Loan was offered a position as a full-time sports reporter with the *Los Angeles Morning Herald.* In "How I Broke into the Magazines," he recounts his first foray into the newspaper business. Beset by "the author's itch," he composed "a cheerful little story on seventeen pages of yellow foolscap"—"it was full of Chinamen, detectives, gambling hells, opium joints, love's young dream, comedy relief and sudden death" (40). Although this lurid story was unsuccessful, Van Loan was undeterred, and he turned his energies to the newspapers, "where editors are in so much of a hurry that they haven't time to be too critical" (119). One day in 1904, the city editor of the *Los Angeles Morning Herald* offered him a job. "I guess he did it to get rid of me," Van Loan said, "but I fooled him. I accepted it" (119). What the young reporter did not know at the time was that the sporting editor had recently resigned, and the *Herald* was "in the market for an expert on horse racing, baseball, prize fighting, dog shows, billiard matches, yachting, track and field events, three kinds of football—soccer, Rugby and roughhouse—bowling, lawn tennis, golf, basketball and whatever else was loose" (119). When he successfully filed his first story, an interview with English Derby winner Lester Reiff, Van Loan was promptly promoted to sports editor.

After a short stint in Denver, where he met Damon Runyon at the *Post,* Van Loan moved to New York City, where he hoped to sell some of his fiction. By the time Van Loan became a sports reporter for the *New York American* in 1909, he had already achieved a national reputation as a sportswriter, but he was still trying to break into writing magazine fiction. As Van Loan told the story, when he was sent to Philadelphia on an assignment to cover the middleweight bout between Stanley Ketchell and Jack O'Brien, he was bowled out of his seat by an enthusiastic fan. The man in the next seat, who belted Van Loan with his wild imitation of Ketchell's left hook, turned out to be Robert Davis, editor of *Munsey's Magazine.* With Davis's assistance, Van Loan sold his first piece of fiction—"The Drug Store Derby," a racing yarn—to *All-Story Magazine,* and in June 1909, Davis bought "The Golden Ball of the Argonauts," Van Loan's first baseball tale, for *Munsey's.* This break was all he needed. By 1911, Van Loan was successful enough as a short story writer to leave the security of his newspaper job. Thus began "the most concentrated period of sports fiction writing by any figure in American literature" (Brignano 338). From this point on, Van Loan turned out a steady stream of fiction on baseball, boxing, track, golf, and even Hollywood.

Near the end of 1913, Van Loan returned to Los Angeles, where he could play golf twelve months a year. He lived on the West Coast for the remainder of his life, returning East only for a few months' service as an editor for *The Saturday Evening Post*, where he championed a Chicago sportswriter's epistolary short story about a brash young ballplayer. Back in California in 1914, Van Loan suffered a debilitating accident when his car went out of control and careened down a thirty-foot embankment near San Bernardino. Thrown from the wreck, his skull was fractured, and he suffered several broken ribs as well as a compound fracture of the left wrist. His bones were set, but the wrist never healed properly. Van Loan never regained the use of his left arm and hand despite two painful bonegraft operations in 1917 and 1918, which left his arm in a leather sheath. Nevertheless, he continued to play golf, frequently shooting in the eighties using only his right hand, and he continued to write until his death on March 2, 1919 (340).

While his writing often engages the sentimental style of popular magazines of the day, Van Loan "carefully eschews any romantic view of the game," preferring to display "self-mockery of the form of baseball fiction already established" (Solomon 100). In the tall tale of "Mathewson, Incog.," Manager McGuirk finds the star hurler for his crack Colorado club soused on "the orneriest red liquor sold in the state" only hours before the championship game. A mysterious bearded stranger—Slanting Al of Albuquerue—appears and convinces the skeptical manager that he is Christy Mathewson of the New York Giants, on a Western fishing trip, "travelling incog." "Shave him and he'd have Amos Rusie cheated for smoke," a big-league scout tells the manager. Only after "the whiskered wonder" demolishes the competition, as he dodges a herd of well-wishers, does Van Loan reveal that Slanting Al is an escapee from the State Asylum and "a baseball bug of the worst kind": "He thinks he's a fellow named Christy Mathewson."

Throughout his career, Van Loan frequently returns to the tale of the aging player struggling to cope with the loss of his physical prowess. In a nonfiction essay on "Making Good in the Big League," he describes the professional leagues as "a hungry machine": "The survival of the fittest rules in big league ball," he explains, " and the player must 'deliver the goods' or make way for the man who can." Pitcher Stanley Coveleski echoes this lament: "There's always somebody sitting on the bench just itching to get in there in your place. Thinks he can do it better. Wants your job in the worst way: back to the coal mines for you, pal!" (Ritter 123). In 'The Good Old Wagon," Van Loan describes the tragic plight of Jimmy Bowman, a second baseman who has "done broke down":

> Any one of a dozen causes may drop a diamond star toward the horizon. The throwing arm wears out; the leg muscles harden and kink into knots; the batting eye loses its keenness; the overstrained nerves break into a jangling chorus, and your ball player, though he has been more popular than a president, picks up his ragged old glove and moves on into the shadow. There is always some youngster waiting on the bench to take his place. Youth will be served, and who gives a thought to the older men whom it thrusts aside? And baseball is a young man's game.
>
> The big league is a merciless thing, far more cruel than the ordinary juggernaut of competition. The aged clerk, for instance, in whom years have dulled efficiency, is still valuable because of the things which those years have taught him. The baseball player has no such luck. Experience counts for very little when his arms and legs begin to weaken. He may have every intricate point of the game at the ends of his knotted fingers, but if he is not physically able to execute every play with the snap and dash of a youngster of twenty, his big-league seasons are numbered.

For Van Loan's characters—fresh recruits, washed-up veterans, or stingy magnates—baseball is a business and it is work. One irate owner tells a sympathetic manager, "Your pitchers ought to be pitching hay, and they would be, but they haven't got control enough to heave alfalfa through a barn door."

For readers, however, in Van Loan's writing baseball is fun. These are tales that are at turns inventive and comic, brittle and witty, and always rich in the lore and texture of the deadball diamond. Perhaps the most popular baseball fiction writer during his lifetime, Van Loan's stories demand to be rediscovered and read by an audience who wants to experience the culture of 1910s baseball up close.

WORKS CITED

Brignano, R.C. "Charles E. Van Loan." *The Dictionary of Literary Biography*: *Twentieth-Century American Sportswriters*. Ed. Richard Orodenker. Vol. 171. Detroit: Gale: 1996. 337–341.

Davis, Robert H. "The Late Charles E. Van Loan." *The Bookman* 49 (May 1919): 280–285.

Harris, Mark. *The Southpaw*. Lincoln: U of Nebraska P, 1984.

Rice, Grantland. "Introduction." *Score By Innings,* by Charles Van Loan. New York: Doran, 1919. vii–xii.

Ritter, Lawrence S. *The Glory of Their Times: The Story of the Early Days of Baseball Told by the Men Who Played It.* Enlarged ed. New York: Quill, 1984.

Solomon, Eric. "An Early Baseball Fiction: Charles Van Loan's *Score By Innings.*" *Aethlon* 9.2 (Spring 1992): 97–103.

Strecker, Trey, ed. *Dead Balls and Double Curves: An Anthology of Early Baseball Fiction, 1838–1923.* Foreword by Arnold Hano. Carbondale: Southern Illinois UP, 2004.

Van Loan, Charles E. "How I Broke Into the Magazines." *American Magazine* Dec. 1918: 39+.

All quotations of Charles Van Loan's fiction are taken from *The Baseball Stories of Charles Van Loan.* Compiled and with an introduction by Trey Strecker. Jefferson, NC: McFarland, 2004.

Part II

Baseball in American Culture

9

Baseball, Scholarship, and the "Duty to Justice"

Frank D. Rashid

When I think about my responsibility to confront injustice, I ponder Henry David Thoreau's assertion that he "came into this world, not chiefly to make this a good place to live in, but to live in it, be it good or bad" (25). Nevertheless, had I lived in his time, I hope I would have had the moral sense to recognize the evils of slavery and the courage to speak out against them, as he did. So when I borrow the phrase "duty to justice" and apply it to baseball and scholarship, I must balance my own desire to accept the game of baseball "be it good or bad" with my awareness that injustices are carried out in the name of an institution that has been important in my life. Based on my nearly fifteen years opposing public subsidies for Major League Baseball, in particular for the replacement of Tiger Stadium, I will argue that scholars of baseball have a proper role as critics of the actions of professional baseball's management. In doing so, I will apply Harvard University Professor Elaine Scarry's ideas about the literature scholar's "duty to justice" to my experience opposing public subsidies for Major League Baseball.

In "Beauty and the Scholar's Duty to Justice," Scarry discusses the particular obligations of teachers and scholars of literature to oppose behavior that causes injury and fosters injustice. Her arguments—which she bases on the work of John Rawls—rest on three propositions: 1) Nothing in our profession exempts us from our obligation as citizens to speak out when we recognize an injustice. 2) As teachers and scholars, many of us have not only the communication skills to take public positions but also the scholarly expertise to discover and document information that can support these positions. 3) Because of our backgrounds in aesthetics, scholars of literature have a heightened sensitivity to departures from beauty; she defines such departures as causes of injury and injustice (24–25).

The third proposition is particularly germane to scholars of baseball in literature and culture. We find beauty not only in poetry about baseball but also in the poetry of the game itself. For those of us attuned to baseball's aesthetics, its beauties are measureless. Filled with vivid imagery, colorful language, complex characters, absorbing plots, and riveting climaxes, baseball often seems a self-contained alternative reality that has no connection with the world outside. When I was growing up, a game at Tiger Stadium had this effect on me. It was a beautiful world unto itself, apparently untouched by the poverty and racial and economic injustice that I encountered every day in my inner city Detroit neighborhood. I so wanted to maintain this separation that when my dad took me to Detroit's great sports saloon, the Lindell Athletic Club, I begged him not to approach Norman Cash who stood at the bar. I didn't want to spoil the image I had developed of the great first-baseman. I did not want to connect baseball with real life.

Of course, there is a connection, though we baseball lovers sometimes resent it. A greater problem is baseball's intrusion into the real lives of common people in the cities of the United States and Canada, its unwarranted demands for public resources, and its expectation that ordinary folks owe it something more than loyalty to the team, love of the game, and the purchase of tickets and merchandise. The actions of professional baseball's management undercut the beauty of the game and threaten its future health. If we love this game and celebrate its many contributions to our culture, how can we ignore injustices carried out in its name? Our sensitivity to Major League Baseball's departures from beauty should be strong, and our "duty to justice" compelling.

THE INJUSTICE OF STADIUM SUBSIDIES

What are the departures from beauty in baseball today? Across the United States, the owners of professional baseball teams in recent decades have placed their own short-term financial interests against the welfare of the public and against the long-term interests of the game itself. Acting with the advantages of its antitrust exemption and without the control of a strong, independent commissioner, Major League Baseball increases its revenues by demanding public subsidies while disingenuously pleading poverty. As Baruch College Professor of Public Affairs, Neil J. Sullivan has pointed out, politicians who are tough on welfare for poor people are only too willing to subsidize wealthy team owners (15). The owners and Major League officials use the language of free-market capitalism to defend an arrangement that is corporate welfare.

The construction of a stadium and the negotiation of new lease agreements become opportunities to socialize the costs of doing business while privatizing the profits. The public bears all or most of the costs of the physical plant—built, of course, to the specifications of the owner and the major leagues—while the team and the league take the profits. Through a process that *Elysian Fields Quarterly* editor Tom Goldstein likens to strip mining (3), baseball's management routinely resorts to distortions, threats, and outright blackmail to extract hundreds of millions of public dollars from cities, counties, and states that have difficulty maintaining quality schools, keeping libraries open, paying firefighters and police, collecting garbage, and providing parks and playgrounds for their children.

Probably no other business routinely demands the same level of public investment for so little return. The owners and their representatives make bold promises about the benefits that municipalities and fans can expect for their huge investment, but these promises rarely come true. As Roger Noll and Andrew Zimbalist have written, "The effect of stadiums on the cash flow of teams and cities suggests that new facilities rarely, if ever, are worthwhile. Sometimes, they can be financially catastrophic"(30). No serious academic economist advocates stadium development as a way to bring economic vitality to a city or region. New stadiums for new professional teams do not bring benefits commensurate with their expenses. Replacement stadiums do not create new jobs; they do not stimulate significant new economic spinoff; they do not add to the tax base. Nevertheless, professional sports teams have raided public coffers for billions of dollars in the last decade.

The economic damage from stadium development goes beyond the dollars spent, and the peculiar nature of stadium financing often disguises the true costs. For Comerica Park in Detroit, for example, the official word is that the public contributed "only" $115 million to the stadium project, while Mike Ilitch, the Tigers owner, contributed $185 million. What's overlooked is that collateral for the Tigers' financing came largely from parking revenues which the city of Detroit handed over to Ilitch and that $66 million of "his" money came from naming rights which *he* sold to Comerica Bank, even though the stadium is publicly owned. As *Metro Times Detroit* investigative reporter Curt Guyette has shown, this stadium deal may look better for the public than some others, but it's hardly as good as it looks.

Dollars constitute only part of the stadium damage. Stadium projects also cost heavily in missed opportunities. Stadium boosters touted Oriole Park at Camden Yards as an economic engine, but, as Dennis Zimmerman shows, compared with other projects, such as those undertaken by the State of Maryland's Sunny Day fund for economic development, the stadium is a "poor investment" which will "impose losses on Maryland taxpayers" (123). Analyses of stadium financing and impact in Noll and Zimbalist's *Sports, Jobs, and Taxes: The Economic Impact of Sports Teams and Stadiums,* James Quirk and Rodney Fort's *Hard Ball: The Abuse of Power in Pro Team Sports,* and Joanna Cagan and Neil DeMause's *Field of Schemes: How the Great Stadium Swindle Turns Public Money into Private Profit* lead to one clear conclusion: new Stadiums cost much more and do much less than promised.

In Detroit, which has limited funds and opportunities to stimulate revitalization efforts, stadium projects suck up resources that could be used for schools, police, libraries, parks, and development with potential to produce real and lasting benefits. Detroit needs to encourage downtown residential development. However, new stadiums have used up funds that could have gone to spur development of residential lofts in the central city. Detroit writer Kristin Palm reports that Downtown Development Authority funds have gone toward "big-ticket projects," including new stadiums for the Tigers and NFL Lions. "Consequently," she adds, "those who come knocking these days at the DDA's door asking for money to invest in residential projects are all being told the same thing: No" (par. 24).

Tax abatements given in the mid-nineties to Cleveland's Jacobs Field, Browns Stadium, and Gund Arena cost the city school systems millions in revenues as teachers were being laid off, athletic programs were slashed, and the system was placed in state receivership (Cagan and DeMause 23). Public funding for stadiums often comes from regressive sin taxes or lotteries that disproportionately burden the poor. Moreover, taxes added for stadiums contribute to tax wariness on the part of voters asked to approve school millage and other public expenditures. Massive projects like stadiums absorb civic energy as well as resources, limiting options and channeling an urban vision to expensive strategies

Small businesses contribute more to a local economy than one large recipient of abatements and direct subsidies, but replacement stadiums, designed to absorb all ancillary revenue-generating activity, also eliminate small businesses—independent parking lots, souvenir stands, bars, and restaurants—with no track record of achieving what they promise. Proven redevelopment strategies are ignored while the powerful stadium lobby, possessed of limitless resources, directs the visions of politicians and the general public to stadiums as the solution to a vast array of social and economic problems. According to urban development scholars, Roberta Brandes Gratz and Norman Mintz, after a city surrenders to a team's demands, "projects that could directly benefit the city and add momentum to genuine city rebuilding are either ignored or given crumbs." Such "small investments," they argue, "mean real economic development, real entrepreneur generation, real community building, real people building" (336). But projects like stadiums effectively block them.

In short, new stadiums contribute little or nothing to the quality of life of the majority of taxpayers who fund them, and their hidden costs amount to much more than the actual dollars expended on them. Stadiums have become a cynical way for politicians to appear to do something for a community, while ignoring its real needs. An official from the office of Michigan Governor John Engler admitted as much to a delegation of Tiger Stadium Fan club representatives. He said that outstate Republicans would not stand for doing what really needed to be done for the city of Detroit, but that supporting a stadium was a way for the administration to placate critics with the appearance of responsiveness to the city's needs.

New Stadiums and the Future of the Game

In addition to the damage publicly financed stadiums do to their home communities, they also cause long-term injury to the game of baseball itself. While radically increasing franchise value for the owner who wants to cash out quickly and generating increased revenues for the team in the short-term, new stadiums cut baseball's traditional fan base. Baseball was once affordable entertainment for young people and families. Generations of fans learned to love the game in older stadiums with plenty of cheap outfield seats. New stadiums dramatically cut down on these seats, restricting opportunities for inexpensive family entertainment and sending the message that these fans are not as welcome as corporate clients and affluent patrons who can afford luxury suites or club seats. If the Commissioner of Major League Baseball were truly interested in the game's future, he would insist that new stadiums provide more affordable seating for young people and families.

He would also recognize that using so much public money on professional stadiums actually limits the public subsidy that has always been most important to the game of baseball. Detroit now has a gaudy baseball palace, but throughout the city, hundreds of public baseball diamonds are in various stages of ruin. The city's Department of Parks and Recreation maintains very few places where kids can engage in pick-up games, which, as David Ogden has pointed out, are so important to building skills and affinities that lead not only to future players but, more importantly, to future fans. Anyone concerned about baseball's future would do well to study Ogden's research into declines in funding of city baseball venues and programs for youth, especially for African-Americans. Ogden feels that the decline of pick-up baseball among all youth and the declining numbers of African-American kids playing ball both indicate "a changing relationship between baseball and society" (205). He warns, "The infrequency of pick-up ball may mean that baseball is losing its place among youngsters as a vehicle for building interpersonal relationships. This may be particularly true for African-American youth, few of whom play baseball either formally or informally or attend professional games with family." Finally, Ogden observes that "those adults who played the game as children, as compared to those who did not, attend more professional games and are less likely to find those games 'boring' or 'slow'" (206).

I don't see many city kids playing baseball any more. I don't see them playing catch. I don't see them playing pick-up games in parks, and I see very few organized leagues. I see more organized baseball in the suburbs, but I see still more soccer. The question of how best to build a future generation of baseball lovers is complex. But it is clear that Major League Baseball now focuses its energies on the short-term profits of its present owners, not on the future of the game.

An Appeal to Scholars of Baseball and Culture

These issues may seem to be the province of the social scientist rather than of the scholar of language, literature, and culture. I maintain, however, that those who study baseball's contributions to American culture must take notice when the sport diminishes that culture. We rely on the research of our colleagues in the social sciences, but we have a very important function of our own. We have particular critical thinking, research, and writing skills; sensitivity to language and beauty; and memory of cultural narrative. Many of us are, by training and disposition, intellectual generalists, capable of combining different kinds of information into interpretations, judgments, and conclusions. We can translate the studies of the social scientists into the layperson's language; we can participate in the public debate; and we can express what the culture loses when those who have charge of baseball abuse that privilege, exploit its beauty, and enrich themselves at public expense.

In order to be effective, we must be willing to cross the chasm that separates the academy from the world of the working journalist. One great frustration in the ten-year Detroit stadium battle was my observation of how little of the vast amount of academic research on the issue ever made it into newspaper, radio, and television coverage. Consequently, I was forced to recognize what a small impact scholarship has on public policy. As Elaine Scarry points out, journalists become impatient with the scholar's insistence on depth and documentation ("Beauty" 29–30), and academics often regard with disdain the superficial treatment given to complex issues in the popular media.

Learning to convey the complexity of an academic article or book in a sound bite is quite a skill, one which, I must confess, I never mastered. However, the Tiger Stadium Fan Club kept the Detroit stadium issue alive for nearly a decade by adjusting when we could to journalists and their needs. At the suggestion of a supportive local politician who was probably tired of our well-developed, thoroughly documented, and, no doubt, deadly dull presentations, we developed a series of fact sheets which boiled down the conclusions of stadium experts into clear, concise, and occasionally, even pithy statements. We made good use of bold type and bullets, and we always provided a complete bibliography. We saw informing the public as a chief responsibility, and all of our printed materials— newsletters, leaflets, and news releases, as well as fact sheets—included depth and documentation in economical, readable prose. New stadium opponents in Boston, Minnesota, and St. Louis have since improved on these methods, and they have effectively waged their battles on the Internet.

It helped that our group included a few journalists. That's another lesson I learned in the stadium wars: an effective opposition must be interdisciplinary and diverse. In addition to relying on the work of stadium experts from many fields, our group had academics from different disciplines, as well as architects, office workers, lawyers, artists, secretaries, clergymen, stockbrokers, grant writers, postal workers, and political aides. We learned to listen to each other and accept criticism from one another. I had to learn that my letters to the editor could be strengthened if people who didn't major in English proofread them. Nevertheless, I knew that my background as a scholar of language and literature contributed to the effort. I was trained to see one thing in terms of another. I could interpret the signs in the different kinds of texts that we encountered. More important, I had the passion born of an understanding of beauty. I recognized the poetry in the game, and I saw the owners' machinations as antipoetic acts, betrayals of the game itself as well as of my city and its people. I knew that my discipline imposed a "duty to justice"—although I didn't call it that—long before I heard Elaine Scarry speak in 1999.

Whether working as individuals or members of a group, those with a similar passion have much to contribute to the future of baseball and its relationship with society. Stadium battles continue in several cities, threatening some of the game's remaining historic sites; the issues of baseball's antitrust exemption and the law governing tax-exempt bonds must be addressed; the need for strong, independent leadership of Major League Baseball remains; the question of what the game gives back to its communities receives too little attention, as do the ways in which the game neglects its own future. Although experts like Quirk and Fort (175–6) and Zimmerman (119–145) may differ over the best ways to address the specific injustices of sports, the need to raise public awareness is fundamental to any effective strategy. On such issues, scholars of baseball in literature and culture have already made concrete contributions. Among the most consistent and stalwart critics of professional baseball's injustices have been editors Steve Lehman and Tom Goldstein of *The Elysian Fields Quarterly, The Baseball Review.*

These contributions are badly needed. In every city with a new stadium, a public record of promises exists. Too often, the media and the public forget these promises as the project moves ahead. Researchers can unearth the promises, analyze them in terms of actual performance, and use them as the basis of scholarly publications evaluating the major media's coverage of the issue. Since the same promises get made in almost every city, documenting the outcomes is important. These concrete instances can be applied persuasively to the situations of cities still embroiled in stadium battles.

Scholars of literature need not only analyze print texts. Political issues cry out for interpretation in every city. Major League Baseball's demands for stadium subsidies should be juxtaposed with the need for city parks and playgrounds, schools and libraries, human service agencies and homeless shelters. But scholars and writers must make sure their work gets to the public. Too often, the excellent work done on stadiums and other issues remains in academic journals and books. We scholars get our publications (and promotions and tenure) but neglect to contact reporters and editorial writers to make sure our work reaches a broader audience; we don't write that important letter to the editor to complain about misleading coverage that ignores our research and that of others; we hesitate to call the radio talk show to provide a clarification or an insight; we don't always see to it that the activists in specific stadium battles become acquainted with our work; we often refuse to translate our academic prose into language intended for a general audience. It is difficult to leave the academic world's protective complexity for the often simplistic and wrongheadedly judgmental world of the popular media. For understandable reasons, academics become frustrated when they attempt to cross the chasm between the scholarly and public worlds, but when we do make the effort, responsible journalists start to call back.

"IMPEDIMENTS" TO ACTION

The difficulty of making the connection with the media and through them the public is but one of the "impediments" that, Scarry says, can inhibit academics from acting to address injustice. Three other impediments are 1) the difficulty of perceiving an injustice and of helping others to see it 2) the recognition of one's powerlessness in the face of potent opposition, and 3) the embarrassment that can result from lifting one's voice ("Beauty" 26–29). Scarry argues that none of these impediments absolves us from the duty to justice. During our group's long struggle to save Tiger Stadium and block public financing of a new stadium, we experienced each of these impediments in different ways.

We became very familiar with the first impediment: the difficulty of perceiving an injustice and of helping others to see it. For example, it's difficult to overcome the entrenched American assumptions that old means obsolete and new represents progress. Certainly this is a habit of mind in Detroit; Henry Ford II praised "obsolescence" as "the very hallmark of progress" (qtd. in Sugrue 133–34). Even though several respected structural engineers testified to Tiger Stadium's soundness, politicians and team officials continued to make ominous pronouncements about the building's condition. Longtime Detroit Mayor Coleman Young asserted that "the damned thing is falling down" (qtd. in Betzold and Casey 133), and a Detroit Tigers official concocted an elaborate explanation for the stadium's alleged weakness: salt used to melt ice on the ramps during Detroit Lions football games had seeped into the stadium's decking, rotting it away. Although we successfully refuted these claims and the exaggerated estimates for the cost of repair and renovation associated with them, doing so took considerable time and effort, and we could never erase them entirely from the minds of the public or the media. (Anyone interested in the details should read *Queen of Diamonds: The Tiger Stadium Story* by Michael Betzold and Ethan Casey.)

Similarly, despite mounds of contrary evidence, new stadium advocates get away with projections that public stadium subsidies will generate growth. A Web site for the Ballpark Partnership in St. Louis says that the proposed new Cardinals stadium will create 7,000 jobs and that the State of Missouri will receive a 4–1 return on its investment. Such groundless projections get serious attention, not only because they are attractively easy answers to complex problems but also because an entire network of interests—team owners, players, builders, contractors, bond attorneys, bankers, and politicians—profits from promoting them. As Scarry points out, it is much easier to recognize a past injustice that has been reversed, like slavery or segregation in baseball, than it is to recognize injustice, like the corporate welfare of stadium finance, that exists in the present. Once an existing injustice has broken through one's own consciousness, its persistence can be the source of tremendous frustration, especially for teachers who spend their careers confronting ignorance. That may be one reason that teachers from all disciplines are among the strongest voices and most dedicated volunteers in any stadium fight.

It is very common also to experience the futility of one's efforts in a stadium fight. The pro-stadium opponents are among the most powerful members of society. In a stadium battle, one suddenly finds oneself confronting the entire political and corporate leadership of a community and state in addition to the forces behind Major League Baseball. As a matter of fact, President George W. Bush launched his political career with the millions he made from a killing on a stadium deal. In most referendums, the opponents of public subsidies for stadiums are greatly outspent, and even when proposals are voted down, pro-stadium forces lobby legislative bodies to get what they want (Quirk and Fort 160). So why bother? It would be easier to surrender to the lost-cause argument were it not for the amazing circumstance that, despite the power of the pro-stadium forces, opponents have still won a few.

Although we ultimately lost the Detroit stadium fight, we kept it going strong for nearly nine years by taking the pro-stadium forces by surprise and capitalizing on their mistakes. In 1992, we won one ballot initiative prohibiting the use of public funds by a 63–37 percent margin, before getting outspent 20–1, and blown out on the same question in 1996.

Our efforts did not result in a better stadium deal for Detroiters (only a better-looking one), and the construction of a pro-football stadium next to Comerica Park is to me a depressing sign of absolute defeat. However, the many times that San Franciscans and residents of surrounding communities turned down stadium proposals did lead to a much more satisfactory financing arrangement, and—at this writing at least—new stadium proposals appear to be losing momentum in Boston and St. Louis.

Pro-stadium forces usually must go to extreme measures in order to get public funding. Despite limitless funds for campaigns, they still usually win by very narrow margins or, once defeated in referendums, manipulate the executive and legislative branches into giving in to their demands. Major League Baseball's contraction threat a couple of years ago was partly a desperate attempt to extract public funds from habitually reluctant citizens and legislators of Minnesota. In my experience, most people who oppose publicly funded stadiums are realistic about their chances of success; they understand the power of the opposition when they get into the battle, but they fight it anyway. As Scarry points out, even certainty that we will not be effective does not release us from the duty to justice.

Scarry's third impediment to this duty is the fear of embarrassment that attends any public act, especially one that threatens the rich and powerful. Embarrassment is definitely a factor in the stadium game. Anyone opposing funding for a replacement stadium runs the risk of being disparaged as a sentimentalist, a nostalgia freak, a naysayer, an obstructionist, a zealot, a nut. New stadium advocates who would benefit from the project will be treated as responsible, public-spirited philanthropists or tough negotiators who are trying to get a job done. Corporate and political leaders have little tolerance for grass roots groups made up of people who put so much energy and time into something that brings them no financial gain. The more effective the opponents to a new stadium become, the more their motives are questioned. They hear insinuations that they have some financial interest in preserving the old stadium. Or they are treated as having no legitimate stake: pro-stadium forces question their rights as citizens to speak out on an issue in which they have no direct financial interest. They are asked what they as ordinary people with few dollars to invest in development projects have contributed to their communities. Politicians asked me more than once what right I had to try to influence the stadium decision. In one debate, Detroit's Mayor, Dennis Archer, asked me what I had "invested in the city." Pro stadium forces are adept at marginalizing their opponents, and their friends in the media will do their work for them. Local journalists, in attempting to marginalize us, completely ignored the information we provided them and repeatedly invented ulterior motives for our behavior. They simply did not—or pretended that they did not—understand that we sincerely believed that refusing to finance Tiger Stadium's replacement was best for the city, the fans, and the game of baseball.

Baseball's Beauty and Stadium Activism

Of course, despite these impediments, concerned citizens come together to oppose stadium deals in almost every city in which they are proposed. They do so for many reasons, but in coming to know the many individuals whom I met in the Detroit stadium battle, I think that experience of beauty has plenty to do with it. I was amazed at how often I heard stories of the first visit to Tiger Stadium from my friends in the Tiger Stadium Fan Club. The stories were almost archetypal in their common details—the walk up a ramp, across a catwalk, under the stands, and out to encounter that marvelous green space in the midst of the city. There were those who spoke of the beauty of relationships formed or strengthened at the ballpark. Others recalled the amazing, community-building moments in the world championship year of 1968—one year after the riots exposed Detroit's dysfunction and injustice—when it seemed that baseball could actually have a beneficial impact on our riot-torn but resilient city. Others were not baseball fans but social visionaries who saw the possibility that the city might stop putting powerful interests first and began to base its planning on real human needs. Our different experiences and visions of beauty drew us together.

Elaine Scarry says that one of beauty's properties is to inspire "a deeply beneficent momentum toward replication" (*On Beauty* 6–7). Beauty inspires beauty in new forms and media. The people who come together to oppose baseball's injustices cannot replicate the beauty of a perfectly executed double-play, and they may not create poetry from the experience of the game, but they do replicate the beauty of their experiences and visions in responding to the duty to justice. Scholars of beauty in baseball and literature have much to contribute to this replication.

Works Cited

Betzold, Mike and Ethan Casey. *Queen of Diamonds: The Tiger Stadium Story.* West Bloomfield, MI: A&M, 1992.

Cagan, Joanna and Neil DeMause. *Field of Schemes: How the Great Stadium Swindle Turns Public Money into Private Profit.* Monroe, ME: Common Courage, 1998.

Gratz, Roberta Brandes and Norman Mintz. *Cities Back from the Edge: New Life for Downtown.* New York: Wiley, 1998.

Goldstein, Tom. "Notes from the Dugout: The New Politics of Baseball." *Elysian Fields Quarterly: The Baseball Review.* 15.4 (1998): 2–5.

Guyette, Curt. "Render unto Caesar: The Devil's in the Details and Pizza Man Mike Ilitch Got One Hell of a Deal." *Metro Times Detroit* 23 April 1997. http://www.metrotimes.com/news/stories/news/17/43/render.html.

Noll, Roger G. and Andrew Zimbalist. "Build the Stadium—Create the Jobs!" *Sports, Jobs and Taxes: The Economic Impact of Sports Teams and Stadiums.* Eds. Roger G. Noll and Andrew Zimbalist. Washington, DC: Brookings Institute, 1997. 1–54.

Ogden, David C. "African-Americans and Pick-up Ball: The Loss of Diversity and Recreational Diversion in Midwestern Youth Baseball." *Nine* 9 (2001): 200–207.

Palm, Kristin. "Lofty Words: Bringing Residents Downtown the Slow Way." *Metro Times Detroit* 17 Feb. 1990. http://www.metrotimes.com/19/20/Features/newLofty.html.

Quirk, James and Rodney Fort. *Hard Ball: The Abuse of Power in Pro Team Sports.* Princeton: Princeton UP, 1999.

Scarry, Elaine. "Beauty and the Scholar's Duty to Justice." *Profession* (2000): 24–25.

_____. *On Beauty and Being Just.* Princeton: Princeton UP, 1999.

Sugrue, Thomas J. *Origins of the Urban Crisis: Race and Inequality in Postwar Detroit.* Princeton: Princeton UP, 1996.

Sullivan, Neil J. "Big League Welfare." *New York Times* 4 Nov. 1995: 15.

Thoreau, Henry David. "Civil Disobedience." *Walden and Civil Disobedience.* Ed. Paul Lauter. New York: Houghton 2000. 16–36.

Zimmerman, Dennis. "Subsidizing Stadiums: Who Benefits, Who Pays?" *Sports, Jobs and Taxes: The Economic Impact of Sports Teams and Stadiums.* Eds. Roger G. Noll and Andrew Zimbalist. Washington, DC: Brookings Institution, 1997. 119–145.

10

Is Baseball an American Religion? A Sociological Analysis

Toby Ziglar

> I believe in the church of baseball. I've tried all the major religions, and most of the minor ones.... I've tried 'em all, I really have, and the only church that truly feeds the soul, day in day out, is the church of baseball.
> —Annie Savoy, *Bull Durham*

I love baseball. As a child, I played the game in my yard, the neighbor's yard, the Little League field—anywhere my friends and I could find enough room to put down bases. My love for baseball has continued through the years as a fan, not the kind of fan who has memorized the history of the game or the stats of every player but one who has kept an affiliation with one team throughout his thirty-eight years of living. In 1969 at the age of five, growing up in a small city in Alabama, I became aware of the Atlanta Braves through the gift of a baseball card. My fascination with the team, fueled by the discovery of baseball cards, eventually led to our family taking annual trips to Atlanta to see the Braves play. It was at this same time that my Little League career began as I played second base in the "farm league" in my local community. As five-year olds, we played with a real baseball. We also had pitchers who actually pitched, six balls for a walk and three strikes for a strikeout—no stinking T-ball for us. We were playing the real game with real equipment, just like the big leaguers. My career ended when I was twelve. I was a burned-out ballplayer who needed a break from the excessive practices and elongated seasons. The ending of my career, however, did not end my love for the game.

In the spring of 2001, I found myself teaching religion at Carson-Newman College in Jefferson City, Tennessee when I received an email from a friend inviting me to join a fantasy baseball league. I consented, and thus my ascent to heaven, or some might say my descent into hell, or at the very least, my baptism into the religion of baseball. If I could total the hours I have spent on fantasy baseball over the past two seasons and apply them to my career, I might be at the top of my field. Instead? I have an addiction to fantasy league baseball and little scholarly work to show for it. My own personal obsession with fantasy league baseball, an obsession shared by thousands of others, has led me to my office on Sunday mornings to post messages on the league message board for other "owners" to read, messages touting my devotion to the league while others either slept or attended their local church. At one point, I appointed myself chaplain to the fantasy league and declared that I would hold services on Sunday mornings at 11 a.m. for those who wanted to join me online.

When that first fantasy season ended, I was left with an empty feeling. I was saddened that there would be no more baseball, but even sadder that the banter on the message board would end. In seven months of fantasy league baseball, we had created a community that went well beyond the actual game. As I analyzed what had taken place over those seven months, my mind turned to the relationship of baseball and religion. Is it possible that a religious-type community could form around the game of baseball? Does baseball have the power to serve a religious function in American society?

IS BASEBALL A RELIGION?

In *The Faith of Fifty Million: Baseball, Religion and American Culture*, editors Christopher Evans and William Herzog II suggest that baseball has a sacred meaning for many who follow the game (3). They even suggest that baseball is a transcendent symbol that "will turn our hearts away from the world's despair, in order that we may glimpse a vision of a world better than our current one" (7). Is the game of baseball so powerful that it can serve as a source of ultimate meaning for its followers? Evans and Herzog seem to posit as much in their introduction to the collection of essays.

Before one can analyze baseball in terms of religion, it is necessary to determine how religion should be defined. Since baseball is a part of American culture, a sociological definition of religion seems appropriate for this comparison. Sociologists, however, vary as to how they define religion, basically defining it in three main ways: substantively, functionally, and symbolically. By examining each of these definitions, it will be possible to see if baseball can be categorized as a religion according to any one of them. Any attempt to define religion is to establish a set of arbitrary boundaries around various phenomena. Thus, certain ways of defining religion are more restrictive than others.

BASEBALL AND THE SUBSTANTIVE DEFINITION OF RELIGION

Religions are systems of beliefs. Those beliefs change according to the religion, but concrete beliefs are something important to almost every religious system. The attempt to define a religion based on its beliefs is an attempt to define a religion by its substance. This sort of definition does not seek to pass judgment on the religious beliefs but rather to simply state what a religion *is*. Substantive definitions have tremendous value because they allow sociologists to compare and contrast beliefs that are specifically stated by the various religions. Substantive definitions are limited, however, because they tend to define best those stable religions that exist in established societies: Christianity in the West or Islam in the Middle East, for instance. The danger of a substantive definition of religion is that sectarian movements within a larger religion are rarely acknowledged, and new religious movements are often ignored.

Ronald Johnstone defines religion as "a system of beliefs and practices by which a group of people interprets and responds to what they feel is sacred and, usually, supernatural as well" (13). Johnstone's definition is an excellent example of a substantive definition of religion because it includes the concepts of sacred and supernatural. In *The Elementary Forms of Religious Life*, Emile Durkheim states, "One idea which generally passes as characteristic of all that is religious, is that of the supernatural. By this is understood all sorts of things which surpass the limits of our knowledge; the supernatural is the world of the mysterious, of the unknowable, of the un-understandable" (39).

A substantive definition of baseball seems to exclude baseball from the realm of the religious. Though governed by a system of beliefs and practices such as rules, baseball does not have at its core a belief in the supernatural. According to Buck O'Neil, the first baseman of the Kansas City Monarchs, baseball was like religion to him because, as he put it, "it taught me and it teaches everyone else to live by the rules, to abide by the rules" (qtd. in Ward and Burns 231). O'Neil's idea of baseball as religion shows the danger of defining religion simply as set of rules. If religion is simply defined as a system by which one is taught to follow an arbitrary set of norms or a codified set of rules, then any type of game would satisfy this definition of religion, be it baseball or backgammon. Unless, like Red Sox fans, one believes in the Curse of the Bambino or accounts for the '69 Mets's World Championship as proof of divine intervention in earthly affairs, substantive definitions of religion seem to eliminate baseball from the category of religion because the game does not assume the presence of the supernatural.

BASEBALL AND THE FUNCTIONAL DEFINITION OF RELIGION

Whereas a substantive definition of religion focuses on what a religion *is,* a functional definition of religion focuses on what a religion *does* for the individual or group. This type of definition is less concerned with the beliefs and practices of the religion and instead more concerned with the value of the religious belief within society. Milton Yinger defines religion as "a system of beliefs and practices by means of which a group of people struggles with the ultimate problems of human life"(7). Yinger's functional definition sounds similar to the substantive definition of Johnstone. The difference, however, is that Yinger's definition focuses on the function of religion as a means to help a group of people struggle with the ultimate problems in living, individually and communally.

Such a definition of religion expands the phenomena that can be considered religion. Yinger does not mention the sacred or supernatural in his definition. Science, then, could serve a religious purpose for those who believe that science will eventually answer all the ultimate questions of life. Keith Roberts notes that a functional definition of religion could allow those who have an intense faith in nationalism or capitalism to be considered religious (7). It could be argued that if the concept of the supernatural is removed from religion, then almost anything to which one is devoted could be considered a religion. Sociologists of religion have debated this point at great lengths and will continue to do so. What is clear is that a functional definition of religion opens up the possibility of examining many more beliefs and practices as religious in nature.

The shift from defining religion by *what it is* to defining it by *what it does* makes it possible to explore baseball in terms of religion. How, then, does "a system of beliefs and practices by means of which a group of people struggles with these ultimate problems of human life" describe baseball?

First, baseball provides a sense of community. David Chidester has noted that baseball can create a sense of community in the midst of an ever changing world. According to Chidester, baseball's ability to capture the sacred memory of the past and link it to the future provides both a sense of security and community for those who need to create sacred time and space in their lives (745). Robert Bellah et al believe that when individuals have difficulty making sense of the complex world in which they live, they grasp for contexts that are more easily understandable. Instead of attempting to understand the complex systems that have developed in the world, they seek to return to more familiar systems such as a family or sports. Bellah notes the odd attraction that Americans have to baseball. Despite the decline of the popularity of institutions in America, baseball has somehow has found a way to draw people into its grasp (39).

It is easy to see how baseball fosters a sense of community around Little League, for example. Families are drawn together to support young players as they learn the basics of the game, socialize among their peers, and wear uniforms just like the professional players. Parents of players get to know one another as they sit in the stands and share stories of their children's great abilities or as they sit and watch their children practice. Younger children run and play while the game is being played, often starting their own unofficial game of ball outside the playing field. The concession stand provides the food as these families sit down together to share a meal, a game, and good fellowship.

What about professional baseball? How can a sense of community be established when the players are professionals who are usually from other communities, even other countries? How can sitting in a ballpark that seats fifty thousand people foster a sense of community? How can paying twenty-five dollars for a ticket and nine dollars for a sack of peanuts and a beer help people make sense of the world? Many fans of Major League teams do, however, feel a sense of community through supporting their team, attending games, tailgating, and wearing their team's garb.

Besides a sense of community, baseball presents a sense of order. Instead of presenting to us theories of the unknown or mysteries of the divine, baseball is played on the field in front of everyone, following rules that have remained mostly unchanged for years. From season to season baseball presents to its fans something steadfast and certain—a game that is played by the rules—relatively simple rules. Teams may change uniform styles, ballparks, even cities. Managers may have strategies, players may have superstitions, but the game comes down to the basics of hitting, fielding, and pitching. The game indeed provides stability through changing times. In the midst of a war, as serious as it is, the fact that baseball is being played provides a sense of comfort and order, as is evidenced by the decision that teams play during both world wars and various subsequent international conflicts.

Finally, baseball provides a sense of time. My first daughter, Rachel, was born October 3, 1993. It was a Sunday afternoon, the last day of the season. The Braves beat the Padres and then waited to see what would happen between the Dodgers and the Giants. The Giants needed a win for a tie in what was then the National League's Western Division—a win they did not get. The Braves had won another division title. I was able to watch both games, then watch the birth of our first child. Such stories are common among baseball fans. They can remember specific times, places, and events because of some spectacular moment that took place on a baseball field.

A functional definition, then, would allow for baseball to be classified as a religion because the game does provide a sense of community, order, and time. There is, however, another way in which the religious nature of baseball can be explained. That is through a symbolic definition of religion.

BASEBALL AND THE SYMBOLIC DEFINITION OF RELIGION

Clifford Geertz has developed a definition of religion that is symbolic in nature. Geertz also believes that religion is important because of what it does. Geertz defines religion as a system of symbols which acts to establish powerful, pervasive, and long lasting moods and motivations in [people] by formulating conceptions of a general order of existence and clothing these conceptions with such an aura of factuality that the moods and motivations seem uniquely realistic (4). Geertz seems to suggest that the dominant symbols of society somehow serve the purpose of religion. This is in line with Durkheim's understanding of religion—that it is social in nature and that it is simply the sanctification of society essential to social maintenance. If a certain religion dominates a society, then that religion can provide the common meaning that orders life for the individual. If, however, the society is more heterogeneous with regard to religion, then a need arises for macrosymbols that can unite people of various religious backgrounds. The combination of these symbols into national religions is referred to as civil religion. Keith Roberts defines civil religion as "the set of beliefs, rites, and symbols that sacralize the values of the society and place the nation in the context of an ultimate system of meaning" (381). Roberts notes that all symbols in life are not religious in nature. It is the macrosymbols, those symbols that help interpret the meaning of life that involve a cosmology or world view, that function as religious symbols.

A symbolic definition of religion fits well within a functional definition of religion. The functional definition of religion focuses on *what* a religion does. The symbolic definition takes the next step and describes *how* religion functions within society, using these macrosymbols to appropriate meanings and values to individuals within the society.

The symbolic definition of religion also allows for baseball to be classified as a religion if, and only if, the symbols serve to aid in the understanding of a particular view of the world that helps interpret life and give it meaning. Geertz adds that the practice aspiring to be religion must symbolize "some transcendent truth" (13), noting that we may say a man who golfs passionately every Sunday is religious about the game, but for the game to be religion the man must see it as embodying this transcendent truth. What, then, is the truth that baseball conveys? How does a relationship to the game of baseball help interpret life and give it meaning?

In *The Faith of Fifty Million*, Christopher Evans and William Herzog begin by offering to the reader the idea that baseball is sacred and the "faith of fifty million." They also point out, however, that baseball doesn't always seem fair. In examining the 1956 World Series, Evans and Herzog describe the Dodgers as a culturally diverse team that represented the future of baseball and America, while they describe the Yankees as a symbol of white middle-class America's resistance to change. In the end, however, the Yankees won the Series over the Dodgers, as they did also in 1941, 1947, 1949, 1952, and 1953. Evans and Herzog also recall Game Six of the 1975 World Series. Baseball fans were given a moment to remember when, in the bottom of the twelfth inning, Carlton Fisk hit a game-winning home run. The image of Fisk waving the ball fair has led many baseball fans to forget the final outcome of the Series, that the Red Sox lost the seventh game—that the moment of transcendence in this life is momentary, if not illusory. Evans and Herzog conclude that much of what happens in baseball does not seem fair: "What this book shows is that baseball in American culture, both individually and socially, is often about losing—a fact that cannot be overturned by faith in a just God.... In baseball, as in life, faith that our good words (and our suffering) somehow will offer the promise of a better future guarantees us nothing but disappointment" (2).

Why, then, is baseball so popular? Perhaps because baseball mirrors life in providing hope in the face of inevitable disappointment. In life, there always is the need for hope, a concept that is intrinsic to the game of baseball. The lack of transcendence in baseball is easily offset by the hope that the game provides, the hope that every new season brings. So what if the Red Sox haven't won the World Series since 1918? This year could be the year! Christopher Evans notes that baseball has been a means of holding out hope that Americans, regardless of class, race, or gender, could understand the fuller meaning of "liberty and justice for all"(33). It would be easy to single out the failures of baseball to achieve the equality that our nation needs. Yet in comparison to the institutional church, baseball has led the way in many of these areas, especially in the area of race.

Unlike life, which permanently places upon us the mistakes and failures of the past, each baseball season offers a new sense of hope for so many in America who have little hope in their own lives. For the diehard fans of the Atlanta Braves who stood by the underwhelming teams of the 1970s and '80s, the hope of next year finally paid off throughout the 1990s. For every hope that is fulfilled, many others are not, as the Braves postseason performances usually attest. Baseball fans are able to defer hope until next year. Perhaps this is possible because many fans deal with defeat and disappointment too often in their everyday lives.

Baseball offers truth that, if not transcendent, is at least comforting. In addition, the symbols of baseball show the religious value of the game within the larger context of civil religion. When entering a baseball stadium, not only does one enter into the place where the game is played, fans also enter into a field of symbols. The newest ballparks have incorporated the latest architectural achievements while at the same time moving back in time to attempt to replicate parks as they existed generations ago. This attempt to connect baseball to its past is not lost on those who have visited the new parks while reminiscing about the old ones. Old or new, the stadium itself, a made structure, gives way, to the natural green of the field, and together the structure and field constitute the park. The "park" theme fits right in with the presence of food and a friendly game of baseball. What could be more American?

The importance of team memorabilia like jerseys and caps helps connect fans to their favorite team, creating the sense of community important to functional definitions of religion. The number of items that can be purchased with the team logo on it is infinitesimal. Replica jerseys allow fans to wear the jersey of their favorite team of the past, symbolically evoking sacred memories for many and working like religious relics to bridge time. Not unlike the Papal indulgences of medieval times, however, these symbolic items come with a price that deflates their religious power for many. It is not uncommon for throwback jerseys to sell for hundreds of dollars, and ultimately they are replicas, not the real thing. Team symbols also can be worn by individuals who are not actual fans, allowing non-believers to pretend.

It is interesting to note that, with few exceptions, the teams that are winning sell the most memorabilia. Individuals enjoy wearing the symbols of the World Series champions. This attempt at status by association is important to consider because it shows a desire by many individuals to associate with a winner. Team symbols, then, become symbols of success and are often worn by people who have not had much success in their own personal lives but wish to be seen as a winner. Associating with a winning team brings to these individuals a sense of self-confidence, perhaps even some measure of hope that one day soon they too will transcend their difficulties and be a winner. In this sense, success itself becomes the religion, and a very American one at that.

Another symbol at the ballpark is the presence of the national flag and the kind of patriotism it connotes. The playing of national anthems as part of the pre-game ceremonies is important to the fans, especially in the United States. In Japan, the Pacific League plays the Japanese anthem before games, but the Central League does not. Nor are anthems played before regular season games in most major soccer leagues around the world. Going beyond the anthem, post 9/11 and during the Iraqi War, many clubs also played "God Bless America" before games or during the seventh inning stretch. The melding of baseball and the flag of the United States seems to suggest that the game is part of a larger religion—a civil religion that uses various symbols to help to sacralize the values of a society or nation.

It appears that there is something religious about baseball. David Chidester notes, "Like a church, with its orthodoxy and heresies, its canonical myths and professions of faith, its rites of communion and excommunication, baseball appears in these terms as the functional religion of America" (748). On the other hand, it may be more accurate to view baseball as a part of civil religion in America—a religion that takes in success and patriotism as well as baseball and whose function is to unite society through various symbols and practices. On its own, baseball may very well function as a religion to some—especially to those who spend their lives being ordered by its rites, rhythms, rituals, and rules. I suspect, however, that it is part of a larger religion for most—a religion that is American in nature.

There are those who have "given up the faith." Many fans were disillusioned by the abomination of all abominations—the strike of 1994. A colleague with whom I teach has not been to a game since the strike. He has given up on the religion of Major League Baseball, but I cannot tell if it was because of the strike or that he was a Cubs fan and simply tired of waiting until next year. Such shattered faith can be found both in baseball and religion. Much more could be said about the relationship between baseball and religion, and also much less. After all the game is hardly as important as religion or even politics, health, economics, war, and so on. Perhaps Thomas Boswell is right. Baseball is religion without the mischief.

WORKS CITED

Bellah, Robert, et al. *The Good Society*. New York: Vintage. 1992.
Chidester, David. "The Church of Baseball, the Fetish of Coca-Cola, and the Potlach of Rock 'n Roll: Theoretical Models for the Study of Religion in American Popular Culture." *Journal of the American Academy of Religion* 59 (1996): 743–65.
Durkheim, Emile. *The Elementary Forms of Religious Life*. New York: The Free Press, 1965.
Evans, Christopher H. and William R. Herzog II, Eds. *The Faith of Fifty Million: Baseball, Religion, and American Culture*. Louisville: John Knox, 2002.
Evans, Christopher H. "Baseball as Civil Religion: The Genesis of the American Creation Story." Evans and Herzog II, 35–48.
Geertz, Clifford. "Religion as a Cultural System." *Anthropological Approaches to the Study of Religion*. Michael Banton, Ed. London: Tavistock, 1966, 1–40.
Johnstone, Ronald. *Religion in Society: A Sociology of Religion*. 5th ed. Upper Saddle River, NJ: Prentice Hall, 1997.
Roberts, Keith. *Religion in Sociological Perspective*. 3rd ed. Belmont, CA: Wadsworth, 1995.
Yinger, J. Milton. *The Scientific Study of Religion*. New York, NY: MacMillan, 1970.
Ward, Geoffrey C. and Ken Burns, Eds. *Baseball: An Illustrated History*. New York: Albert A. Knopf, 1994.

11

Home Run Derby Versus the Pitchers' Duel: Could the Need for Instant Gratification Ruin Baseball?

Joan M. Thomas

As a preface, I would like to share a true event in my life that served as an inspiration to write this paper. A few years ago I spent a "girls' night out" with some long time friends. We had dinner and took in a movie, *For Love of the Game*. I got a lift home with several of the girls, and on the way we discussed the film. I made the comment that I had never had the opportunity to attend a World Series game, but given a choice, I would much prefer to witness a perfect game. To which the woman driving—who professed to be a big baseball fan—replied "Well, a perfect game is boring." Before I had a chance to think I blurted out "Maryanne (not her real name), you're an idiot!" I don't see much of that circle of friends anymore. I regretted my insensitive remark, but I still think that Maryanne's statement was idiotic. Yet I do have her to thank for providing me with a topic for this paper.

Twenty-first century American society dwells on fast-paced, quick-fix, push-button solutions to every facet of life. Everything in our work and leisure time is geared to be time-sensitive and capsulized. Even our language suffers from this tendency to abbreviate in order to avert boredom. What was once Avenue is now Av. In the past when we wanted to ease our way into a pleasant dinner, we leisurely took delight in appetizers—now we "grab some aps." As for eating itself, fast foods and microwave dinners dominate the nation's palate.

Shortening a baseball team's name is nothing new, and the fans seem to enjoy it. But for those who for many years called the Astros, it was a bit disconcerting to hear them referred to as the 'Stros. If one really wants to be in the know, it is imperative to master the most current acronyms. Entire words are sheared to one letter. In baseball, Alex Rodriguez became A-Rod, and Angels' strikeout artist Emmanuel Rodriguez was quickly dubbed K-Rod when he came out of nowhere to whiff several Yankee batters during the 2001 playoffs. This year, Phillies' broadcasters have taken to calling Jimmy Rollins J-Ro. While baseball has always had nicknames, these mimic those of popular NBA Players T-Mack (Tracy McGrady) and K-Mart (Kenyon Martin), stars in a game with no room for leisure moments or intellectual reflection. The very nature of baseball diametrically opposes this modern trend toward brevity. A game that places no limits on foul balls and has no time restrictions on extra-inning play just does not seem to fit in a world that demands instant results.

To a degree, home runs satisfy the lust for rapidly produced thrills. Yet the evolution of baseball—from the early multi-score games, to the dead ball era, to the age of the juiced ball—has not altered the basic format of the game. Home runs are fun and dramatic, but they do not necessarily win games. If that were always true, there would be no need to field nine players. There would be no need for speed or skillful fielding. But a pitcher would always be necessary, even if it came down to the human being replaced by a robotic counterpart. Undoubtedly such an oversimplified version of the National Game would soon prove a terrific bore, especially if the pitchers kept recording strikes. Either baseball will survive in its basic form, and society will rediscover the virtues and complexities of this "simple" summer pastime, or it will mutate into something beyond recognition to lovers of the sport.

Baseball has outlived rule changes, scandals, strikes and loss of interest. Attendance was on a downward spiral until Mark McGwire and Sammy Sosa regenerated the sport's appeal with their 1998 race to smash the home run record. Since then, the number of home runs seems suspiciously phenomenal, suspiciously given whisperings of steroid use and Sosa's bat corking. Fans became desensitized when Barry Bonds so quickly surpassed McGwire's record. Still, a home run record is something that can be anticipated, lending the media a tool to promote certain games. An outstanding pitching performance, however, such as a no-hitter or the even more rare perfect game, is something that could happen on any given day, and be achieved by any given pitcher. Yet many true baseball aficionados may spend a lifetime without ever witnessing either.

Thus arises a discussion on what is more important, hitting or pitching. Baseball pundits never seem to settle on an answer. Perhaps the obvious reason is that it is neither. A pitcher needs a good arm to face good hitting—a batter needs a good eye to face good pitching. Plus, they each need the support of eight teammates.

The authors of "The Changing Game" in the seventh edition of *Total Baseball* admit that "it's plainly obvious that home runs and scoring win the hearts of the fans." (Felber and Gillette 103) That has always been true. The hero has always been portrayed as a hitter. Take, for example, the oft-reprinted "Casey at the Bat." The writer of that timeless American poem paints a vivid picture of a classic confrontation between a steely-faced hurler and the Herculean slugger. Though the pitcher wins, the hitter is portrayed as the tragic hero. It is not likely that the poem would have grown to be the stereotypical portrayal of a baseball contest if the hometown hero had been the pitcher.

Today sports fans are being exposed to seemingly faster-moving herd sports, particularly basketball and football. Many become restless with the pace of baseball and have never picked up on the intricacies of the game. Few come to the game hoping to see a pitchers' duel. One who attends games regularly will comment that more than half of the so-called-fans in attendance arrive late and leave early. And they do so regardless of the score. Lon Simmons argues that "It is interesting about people that leave early from the ballgames. It's almost as if they came out to the ballgame to see if they can beat the traffic home" (qtd. in *Total Baseball* 2472).

As Major League Baseball continues its efforts to boost ticket sales, more and more sidelights are added to accommodate the short attention span of the modern fan. Built in the late 1990s in Arizona, Bank One Ballpark (called BOB—a perfect example of today's penchant for acronyms) is said to be made for baseball. Yet one of its prominent features is a swimming pool in right-center field. Other new parks, like Miller Park in Milwaukee, supply other diversions such as interactive areas or video games in the concourses. Comerica Park offers both a merry-go-round and Ferris wheel. And now the concession stands offer a great deal more than just hot dogs, peanuts and Cracker Jacks. The grudging parent often complains about the expense of taking the family to the baseball game, when most of the money is spent on "diversions" for the kids and stuffing them with food and drink to stifle, or perhaps unknowingly promote, their attention-deficit hyperactivity.

Moreover, the owners' research gurus have influenced the replacement of older, larger stadiums with seemingly smaller capacity retro-style parks. To any fan, it is a plus to have a seat closer to the action, if the new park actually provides one. The last row of the upper deck in old Comiskey Park was closer to the field than the first row of the upper deck in its retro replacement. Even granting the possible fan comfort of new ballparks, the unsettling aspect of what is happening is that there appears to be an attempt to create a theme park atmosphere. Wrigley Field is genuine. A park built just for baseball during the dead-ball era, it strangely survived to the point that it has become almost a museum. Now even people who really do not follow the sport will go there just because it is the in thing to do. The new parks designed to recreate that aura could be likened to a sort of Six Flags amusement park. Worse yet, they could be a novel version of the fictional theme park of the 1960s film *West World*. Such a place could be called Baseball World. That is not far from reality, as St. Louis plans to replace time-honored Busch Stadium with a "Ballpark Village," whatever that might be. While some would see the passing of Busch as the demise of the last of the cookie-cutters, renovations in the last few years—a grass field, hand-operated scoreboard, new bullpens, and bronze sculptures of Cardinal greats along the outside concourse—have made it a comfortable and fan friendly venue, as well as a historical marker of baseball in the era it was built.

There is no doubt that how we spend our money and spare time is influenced by the media, particularly television. We buy what is especially appealing in the advertisements. Worse, we tend to take as gospel anything told to us by newscasters and sports announcers if they merely sound believable and have an appealing personality. Television is presented in time slots, which are not conducive to baseball. Baseball does not allow for TV timeouts. If an inning runs long, sponsors must wait for the airing of their commercial. One has to wonder if we have become a nation of attention-deficit hyperactive disorder (AD/HD) affected sheep who can relate with only that presented by the media.

Clinical psychologist Dr. David B. Stein, author of *Ritalin Is Not the Answer* gives us some leads. Though admittedly not a baseball fan, he mentioned in a telephone interview with me that he cannot seem to get interested in watching a game on TV. However, he said that he truly enjoys taking in a game at the ballpark. The clue here is that while seeing a game on TV we rely on the commentator to complete the picture, and tell us what is important. We can only see what the cameramen show us. Witnessing the same game at the ballpark is an entirely different experience. Although there we often look to the video screen for instant replays of what we just saw, or to see ourselves acting like fools, we must rely on ourselves to frame the action and decide what is important. This requires us to pay attention.

Regarding AD/HD as a condition, there are widely divergent opinions offered by the experts. In his book, Stein says that children diagnosed with the supposed illness just have not been taught to identify values. That is obviously an oversimplified version of his clearly outlined detailed explanation of what he believes to be the causes of AD/HD. However, it leads us to surmise that perhaps we have lost our ability to discern our own values. And if we cannot, neither will our children. Stein says, "As children internalize proper values, they become more motivated and their ability to focus improves. Concentrating is a learned skill, which requires children to be enthusiastic and motivated" (48). What kind of value could there possibly be in attending a ballgame just for the home runs? They do not occur in every inning and sometimes not at all. Fans who learn to fully appreciate the skill it takes to outfox a hitter, as well as base runners, are not likely to consider leaving their seat during play.

Motion pictures, as well as TV, can distort our perception of reality and manipulate our judgment of importance, or value. Baseball has been the venue for Hollywood films more than any other sport. The stories, wrapped in neat little vignettes, deceive our sense of time. For the sake of drama, the home run frequently serves as a climax to the tale. If the main character is a ballplayer, he is usually a hitter. That makes for box office hits like *The Natural*. Even the film *Bull Durham*—with Kevin Costner in the starring role as a veteran minor league catcher—ends with Costner finalizing his playing career by hitting a "dinger."

Costner did play Billy Chapel, a fictional Major League pitcher in a later film *For Love of The Game*. In the story, Chapel shuts out the Yankees in nine innings. Not one Yankee reaches first base. Billed as a drama/romance, the movie received less than complimentary reviews. Unlike their appreciation for *Bull Durham*, the critics did not discern the talent required to produce a believable enactment of a human being achieving the ultimate in his trade. Movie reviewer Lisa Schwarzbaum, in *Entertainment Weekly's EW.com* wrote, "Costner's determination to avoid change keeps this baseball movie at a low line drive when it might have knocked one into the bleachers." It is curious to note Schwarzbaum's use of a baseball metaphor that references hitting—home run hitting—when the film's story centered on a skill of a pitcher! One must consider whether the fact that the very subject portrayed was not spectacular hitting, but rather pitching, could be the reason for the critics' disdain. Accurately depicting a player earning a perfect game would by definition necessitate using up nearly half of the time allotted for the film. Yes the movie's story does qualify as a romance, and it is unquestionably dramatic to those who do not find outstanding pitching exhibitions boring. In addition to Chapel's girlfriend, played by Kelly Preston, his love for baseball, and gritty performance against the vaunted Yankees touched the hearts of the few moviegoers who got the point.

We are living in a time that fosters a need for instant gratification. To the AD/HD fans at the ballpark, the home run is the Ritalin that satiates that incessant craving. But its effects are ephemeral. And the long-range consequences are questionable. Where will it lead us from here?

There are signs that at least some of the youth of our nation have already begun to grasp baseball's significance to their heritage. After many of the game's followers became disenchanted around the time of the 1994 Major League players' strike, an organization calling itself the Vintage Base Ball Association (VBBA) captured the enthusiasm of a number of young adults. Now with some 120 teams around the country, they play the game by the rules and customs of earlier periods. Most try to duplicate the game played in the late 1850s, 1860s and 1880s. That of course, means playing without gloves. The VBBA's web site says "There are numerous other differences, but modern spectators would still recognize our game as base ball." To further the vintage motif, the players, or "ballists," wear period uniforms. The group touts its purpose as to play the game "as it was meant to be played."

One might be tempted to dismiss this group's efforts as merely a summer activity like joining the local softball league. But a survey answered by members of a St. Louis club calling themselves the Perfectos—a name adopted from the early St. Louis Major League Club that became the Cardinals—reveals that they are quite serious about baseball. And they value the sport as much as anyone who professes to be a true fan. They all expressed a passion for the game and chagrin at what it has become. Most learned about the VBBA through an article in the *Smithsonian*. Their answers to the survey question "Who is your favorite player?" were split between hitters and pitchers. But the players they named covered the gamut of eras, from the nineteenth century to present day, only one of which was depicted in a motion picture. This is a good indication that they have studied the game's history. And one can not do that without gaining some appreciation for the sport.

Of the six respondents, they all answered that if given a choice they would rather witness a perfect game than a home run record being broken. Incidentally, several of them indicated that they have had enough of home runs. Five rated pitching over hitting in importance to the modern game. The one person who chose hitting explained that "without hitting, no on can win the game." A true statement, admittedly.

The Perfectos offered some valuable insight into why people get bored at the ballgame. Here are several significant answers:

> Respondent #1 "Look at the popularity of basketball and football where the emphasis is on offense and scoring. Baseball is a thinking man's game and is not appreciated as much because it requires thought. The public's attention span is short these days."
>
> Respondent #3 "There is so much emphasis on offense and home runs. I even find my own interest waning if the bullpens become overused in a game I am watching if it is not close. If there is more time spent warming up than playing in the last three innings, that's not a good thing."
>
> Respondent #5 "Because of lack of appreciation for the game."

The last answer cited probably sums up the principal reason for boredom at the ballpark. However, Respondent number three's observation about the many game delays caused by pitching changes in the modern game is worthy of consideration. The **VBBA** certainly does not depend on relief pitchers!

In the final analysis, there is one important aspect of this subject that needs to be addressed—our speed-oriented culture. We are constantly bombarded with promises of faster and faster Internet access, fast acting detergents, even fast-acting pain relief! Every indicator points to the fact that we need to slow down. And smell the ballgame. In his book, Dr. Stein mentions that this is not a new idea. "Philosophers such as Henry David Thoreau, psychoanalyst Carl Jung, and most eastern and western religions have espoused the importance of slower-paced and more simplified lifestyles" (117).

If we hope to preserve and promote the values that built America, like the young men of the Perfectos, we need to reflect on our past and connect it with our future. We need to hone in on what is best about our collective selves and this sport we call our national game. As Billy Chapel responded to his team's owner's disgust with commercialism in baseball: "The game doesn't stink. It's a beautiful game."

WORKS CITED

Felber, Bill and Gary Gillette. "The Changing Game." *Total Baseball*. 7th ed. Kingston, NY: Total Sports, 2001. 108.

Schwarzbaum, Lisa. Rev. of *For Love of the Game*. www.ew.com October 1, 1999.
Stein, David B. *Ritalin Is Not the Answer*. San Francisco: Jossey-Bass, 1999.
Total Baseball. 7th ed. Kingston, NY: Total Sports Publishing, 2001.
Vintage Base Ball Association (VBBA). www.vbba.org.

12

(Caray)³: Baseball as Narrated on Television

GERALD C. WOOD

Like most seasons since 1945, 1983 wasn't a banner year for the Chicago Cubs. They escaped last place again, but primarily because the Mets's players were injured, inept with the bat, or just plain too young. Maybe a few *aficionados* who religiously read the minor league statistics in the *Sporting News* could find some hope for the Mets in 1984. Few could anticipate the revival that would be experienced by the National League teams from New York and Chicago the next year, but in '83 it was still whiff and bobble as usual for the Cubbies and Mets.

Harry Caray, chief announcer and cheerleader for the Cubs, was already beginning to show disgust with the team's play, and second-guessing of manager Lee Elia (which would eventually lead to his being fired) had begun in Cubdom. The burden of thirty-eight years of baseball frustration was showing itself among loyal Cubs fans. So it was a welcome relief during that dismal year when Press Secretary James Brady, wounded in an assassination attempt on President Reagan, came to Wrigley Field one afternoon. When incompetence and failure started to raise their ugly heads on the field, mercifully the television screen could be filled with images of Mr. Brady in his box seat behind the first-base dugout. If the honored fan could survive John Hinckley's violence, maybe the Cubs could endure yet another decade of humiliation in hard ball.

But this day was different. Before Harry could rub his magic lantern and say "Holy Cow" three times, another miracle descended on the friendly confines of Wrigley Field. Not only was Mr. Brady warmly greeted, not only did the weatherman cooperate, but the Cubs gained control of the game and were winning in the ninth inning. Sensing victory, the crowd rose to its feet to celebrate the final pitches of the game. The ghosts of failure and memories of the 1969 "Manila folders" temporarily back in the closet, Cubs fans, at the park and on the WGN telecast on cable systems across the United States, could savor a moment of triumph. As elation spread throughout Wrigley, the cameras pulled back to show the wave of joy flooding the stands. Everyone in the park, from the batboy to Mr. Brady, was sharing in the excitement, Harry assured the viewers.

Then, without warning, the wheels came off the cart again, as they seemingly always do for Cubs fans. But the breakdown wasn't on the field this time. The Cubs didn't rescue defeat from the jaws of victory in their inimitable way. They won smoothly, easily, and even gracefully. This time it was the cameraman's turn to screw up, along with the director, Arne Harris. Just as Harry was declaring that joy had captured every living presence, a quick cut by the technical crew caught a napping Mr. Brady with his mouth as open as the MGM lion's. It was hard for even the most diehard of all cable Cubbies to avoid the incongruity between the excitement the audience was asked to see and the image that tells no lies. Viewers were told of Hubert Humphrey joy, but they got instead James Brady as Rip Van Winkle.

This scene from the 1983 season is a humorous reminder that baseball games on television are experienced as stories told by the station and interpreted by the announcers. The games are given a dramatic background by the statistics and standings, the climactic moments are underlined by the announcers, and the meaning of the game for the players and fans is offered in the post-game show (Chandler 42–44). The text of the telecast has "a kind of rhythm, orienting patois followed by analytical commentary.... Every situation in baseball comes equipped with a dozen situational clichés attached to it, and the television announcer's job is to seize the time between events we see and fill it with sequenced variations" (Seidel 50). In a baseball commentary, the play-by-play man tries to construct a reality and evoke a sense of immediacy that combines with the color man's perspective to make the viewer feel like he is watching the game with the guys in the booth. The goal, and illusion, of such combination is the dissolution of the boundary between those at the ballpark and the television viewer, absorbing the viewer into the actual (Rose and Friedman 6–7). In the process, the commentators establish their personalities and the ambiance of the park while narrating a history and drama of expectation for their teams and opponents. Players' contracts are bought and sold, franchises change hands, managers are hired and fired in hope that these baseball stories will have happy endings, and the announcers' performance influences how fans perceive these endings.

WGN, Chicago and WTBS, Atlanta are excellent examples of the use of television stations as platforms for baseball narration. In both cases, a company owns the team and the station: the *Chicago Tribune* controls WGN and the Cubs; Ted Turner and Turner Enterprises own TBS and the Braves. As a result of this parentage, the teams and their stations have a common interest in the image and ideals of the games. Both stations broadcast on cable systems throughout the United States, and both telecast a number of away games, so that both stations cover many other National League parks and cities across the Continental U.S. and in Canada. Even though WGN has recently offered the White Sox as well as the Cubs, and TBS has merged with Time-Warner, the Cubs and Braves are regularly scheduled "shows" on their stations.

Because of the similarities in corporate structure and programming, the two stations might be expected to be similar interpreters of their games. Baseball is on both stations seen as a major American sport, with a rich history of dramatic series and heroic plays characteristic of the game as a whole and specific to their respective teams. Injuries and batting slumps, current statistics on batting and pitching are a steady diet on both channels. Both assume a predominately male audience and fill the breaks in the action with commercials for automobile dealers, local and national beers, power tools, and the action movies and other sporting events carried by the stations. They both have employed announcers who are ex-players for their respective teams or members of the Caray family. Father Harry worked for WGN, his son Skip does the TBS play-by-play, and Skip's son, Chip, currently provides the play-by-play for Channel 9. But Chicago isn't Atlanta, Wrigley Field isn't Fulton County Stadium or Turner Field, and Dusty Baker isn't Bobby Cox. Baseball doesn't mean the same thing on Channel 9 as it does on Channel 17.

In the days of Harry Caray, baseball was described as a community activity of the neighborhood surrounding Wrigley Field. That area, between the wealthy apartment complexes on the near north side at Lake Michigan and the fancy suburbs of Glencoe and Lake Forest, had long been a lower middle-class, ethnically and racially mixed area for generations. Earlier a dropping off point for East European immigrants, it grew to include many Hispanics, Thais and Vietnamese. It was a place where old Irish Catholic convents bump up against Korean restaurants. Given this background, it seemed quite natural back in the 1980s when Vince Lloyd, one of the broadcasters, introduced the fans to Ron Hassey, a recently acquired utility infielder, as another "Lebanese." Harry Caray easily outstripped Mr. Lloyd as connoisseur of the melting pot, however. He repeatedly called Steve Stone, the commentator, a nice-looking Jewish boy, and named seemingly every restaurant in Chicago by emphasizing whether it was Greek, Italian, or German. With only day games until 1989, Harry became fond of telling the viewers, "It's still early and we're going into extra innings. If you're in the neighborhood, come on over."

The telecast supported the image of baseball played in an old neighborhood. During the seventh inning stretch Harry would man the p.a. system to lead the crowd in singing "Take Me Out to the Ballgame," with "Cubbies" strategically substituted for "home team" by the fans. Meanwhile, the cameras, as instructed by Arne Harris, carefully filled the screen with close-ups of men and women, blacks and whites, the old and the very young, as well as the fans on the rooftops across the street. Further homey touches were added by the search for interesting hats, pretty sun-drenched girls, and Bill Veeck (ex–White Sox owner), who often was discovered in the bleachers among the young fans. The ultimate in the family setting was achieved when Harry broadcast the game from the bleachers or was shown in a commercial catching a flying Budweiser beer with his fishnet while sitting among the "bleacher bums." From there his "Gee Whiz" style was given a personal touch. Identifying with Harry, the viewer became part of the action in Wrigley Field in Wrigleyville, a real ballpark in a real neighborhood in a real city in real time (Rader 29).

This strong sense of place regarding park and neighborhood was maintained when WGN visited other cities on road trips. One of the common topics of conversation between the announcers was the comparison between the city they were visiting and their Wrigley Field home. The Dodgers came off relatively well in the comparisons because their park, the announcers reminded us, was built for baseball and the Dodgers have, they judged, a classy operation. But the fans are too casual and spoiled; they come late and leave early, departing by car onto the freeway, instead of on foot to the many neighborhood taverns of Wrigleyville. In Los Angeles, baseball is consumed, not loved to the point of obsession as it is in Chicago. Other places pale in comparison with the friendly confines. In many parks, Harry would point out that the playing fields were too far away from the fans, lacking the intimacy of Wrigley, because they were designed to be football fields, with Astroturf and moveable bleachers.

According to Harry, and whoever was his broadcast partner at the time, the cities weren't any better. He was anxious to leave New York because it lacked Midwestern proportion; a Turkey sandwich at lunch could cost $8.50 in the Big Apple. It was no better in hostile Philadelphia; as Harry Caray used to like to say, "I don't know why they call this 'The City of Brotherly Love.' They booed Santa Clause." The best place to live, we were assured on Channel 9, is the north side of Chicago, where people are friendly, individual differences are nurtured, and neighborhoods are still respected.

WTBS will have none of the ethnic mixing and class struggle common on WGN. To make a home for the Braves, the slums were knocked down twice, first for Fulton County Stadium and then for Turner Field. For the announcers the game takes place inside the park with references to its immediate surroundings rare. For the fans who know little about the game or are conditioned to see the game on the tube, important plays are replayed on the giant screen in center field. In the new park, no need goes unmet in Atlanta; first-class indulgences are available to anyone who pays the price. On TV, Ernie Johnson and Skip Caray didn't fill the airtime with updates for neighbors who just got off the early shift. While Harry would enjoy saying "Hi" to Chicago fans away from home, for Skip's fans it was better to make an epic journey to the capital of the New South. When the Braves are playing at home, the commercials advertise 2-for-1 fares on flights to Atlanta for upcoming games. And while TBS wants it unmistakably known that the Braves play in Atlanta, the station also wants to extend the city and team's importance, touting the Atlanta Braves as "America's Team."

The style of reporting on the Atlanta station also differed from that on "Chicago's very own Channel 9." Most striking are the long pauses. For example, during an August 7, 1984, contest between the Braves and Dodgers, after a commercial the game resumed with a long shot of the field, including the line score recorded on the outfield wall. Finally, after about ten seconds, a nonchalant voice said, "Skip Caray, along with Ernie Johnson, hope we didn't keep you waiting." In the tradition of previous teams of commentators, like "Dean and Blattner, Kubek and Garagiola, even Phil Rizzuto and Bill White," Skip and Ernie play off each other "the way comic partner routines used to work in vaudeville and comic couple routines still work in situation comedies: The day's plot is modulated by the season's themes and foibles" (Seidel 51). The narration of the Atlanta games has been cool and sophisticated; it is the voice of the evening newscaster—distanced, clipped, with a flash of self-revelation, but no excesses.

While Harry's broadcasts centered on his attempts, often frustrated, to cheer the Cubbies on to win, the emphasis on TBS is on statistics and technique. When an opposing player beats out an infield hit to the right side, Skip Caray might remain quiet, allowing Don Sutton or any other colorman to instruct, to say something like "That's why it is so important that the pitcher cover first on anything hit to his left." Rather than question the abilities of the manager, Skip Caray will explain that the decision to take out the starting pitcher is the responsibility of Bobby Cox; that's his job. On WTBS the commentators sound like professionals. Where Harry would say, "It's the eighth and the good guys are ahead 5 to 4," his son might say "At the end of eight, it's Atlanta 1, Los Angeles 0." If the opposing team tied the score with a home run in the ninth, Harry got nearly apoplectic, screaming "Holy Cow, what a shame!" His son might say, "You got to be thankful for small things. At least no one was on base at the time." If a Cub runner was thrown out in a double play because he was stealing second when the batter lined to the third baseman, Harry would whine that Ron Cey always tries to pull the ball. His son would say, "Sometimes you get the bear; sometimes the bear gets you." The "loud fun-lover" gave way to his son's "laconic, low-key style." Harry would glad hand "friends, old and new alike, plugging his restaurant and his favorite brew, sometimes forgetting there's a game going on" (Hirsley 36). In contrast, "Skip is strictly business, occasionally breaking out his crackling dry wit" (Nidetz par. 20).

The audiences the two stations imagine are just as diverse as the teams they support. Cubs fans are supposed to respect tradition and history; that is why the broadcasters note the players' ethnic background. Followers of the Cubs are the descendants of immigrants who were neither moneyed nor privileged; they bear the burden of this illegitimacy. Like their team, they've never made it big in America; the Cubs even lost the last time they played in the World Series—in 1945. Cubs fans just can't trust happiness, but they can take strength from the solidarity of the old neighborhood, as long as they discipline themselves to grant others their own space and history.

Braves fans have no patience with such anxieties and community responsibilities. Like their Dodger brothers, who went Hollywood when they moved from Brooklyn to L.A., the Braves and their fans gave up those lower middle-class struggles when they left Milwaukee. The Braves are a new team for the New South; they appear on WTBS as the team for anybody who calls himself an American. While Cubs fans struggle for respectability in the face of adversity, Braves fans are reminded by the coolness of the announcers that they have been winners—how long ago, where, and when isn't very important. Time and the burden of history are less important in the New South than the old one. The Braves and their fans are just doing their jobs, successfully as expected.

With the advent of cable and satellite systems, the telecasts of these two teams became available across the United States, in rural as well as all major urban areas. Subsequently, like all national broadcasting, on radio or television, WGN and TBS both "tended to erode local loyalties" (Rader 198). In the case of the Cubs, "Caray's style and WGN's national reach would expand 'Cubdom' from Chicago's North Side to the rest of the United States and much of Canada" (Bellamy and Walker par. 32). But in line with their differing styles of commentary, the methods and effects of the two stations and their audiences diverged. Typically, displaced Northsiders used WGN to stay loyal to both their team and its home place. Until patterns changed with the advent of a second generation, the Cable Cubbies, the Cubs' loyalties tended to advance with their mobile fans. Rather than shift allegiance when they moved from Chicago, they would remain Cubs fans through their television. On the other hand, TBS used the telecasts to convert people across the United States from their traditional affiliations to the Braves. As Ted Turner, their owner, made abundantly clear, "I'm giving Atlanta to the nation—to the world.... When they [the Braves] start to win, and get into some playoffs, they're going to take America by storm" (Rader 198–99). And so it has gone.

Even as the Cubs rose to contend in the 80s and the Braves began their dominance throughout the 90s, the commentaries by Harry and Son illustrated Michael Seidel's prescription that good announcers possess: "either a sense of irony, as do McCarver, Scully, Jim Palmer, or a sense of fun, as do Harry Caray, Phil Rizzuto, or Dizzy Dean" (Seidel 54). Caray and the Cubs offered their fans "a sense of fun" even when the team wasn't competitive. In the worst years, the focus was on one or two exceptional players, such as The Hawk or Ryno, and the excitement at Wrigley and its neighborhood. Winning was preferred and hoped for, but not necessary, in such a vital, though often frustrating place. In Atlanta, anxiety was never a major player, even before the Braves pitching led them to the top, because Skip's "sense of irony" could keep the audience safely from the chaos on the field and the realities of the standings. His manner, and the distance it offered, was always more comforting than the game, and it was especially so when the action turned dull or the sense of drama was momentarily lost. More than once, he added to his preview of the late movie his wish that a bad game would end quickly so fans could enjoy the movie.

Since the death of Harry Caray at the beginning of the 1998 season, the narration of baseball on WGN has substantially changed. Chip Caray has neither the exuberant edginess of his grandfather nor the irony and distance of his father. He looks both more all–American and more made-up than either of his elders. Whether working with Joe Carter or Steve Stone, Chip seems the new kid, the attendant to the stars, who is comfortable and calm on the air. He is a new millennium kind of guy, confident, natural sounding, and calculatedly well trained to be both. More TV personality than fan, he looks upscale in his Dockers, and despite often sporting WGN polo shirts, he is quite capable of "betraying" the Cubs and their fans by doing televised games elsewhere on Saturdays. Thus, while the rhetoric of baseball remains similar—the confines are still friendly, Wrigley is a unique ballpark, the Cubs endlessly struggle for respectability—the scrubbed yuppie image embodied in Chip replaces the friendly neighbor his grandfather portrayed, and Wrigleyville represents gentrification more than ethnicity. The immediacy of the neighborhood is now presented more as a stage for the telecast, which has become sufficient in and of itself.

Because Chip is part and parcel of the sophistication of television, traditionalists mock him in publications outside the park and work fitfully to oust him. One writer says Chip relies on clichés and is often historically inaccurate. Some fans suspect he is a closet Cardinal fan. But the real problem is his "stilted" language which, when wedded to boyish enthusiasm, "resembles a convention of advertising salesmen, keen on slogans and high-decibel presentation" (Rothschild). In letters collected by Steve Rosenbloom, a *Trib* staff reporter, one Cubs' fan complained that Chip "seems to be in love with his own voice"; another agreed, saying "the best broadcast of the season" was "when Chip Caray had laryngitis." Some react to the Caray grandson as a "hysterical, babbling, cheerleader know-it-all"; others feel his initials, C.C., should stand for his attitude, "conceit and condescension" (Rothschild). While defending Chip as "at least serviceable" when paired with Steve Stone, Steve Johnson, the media critic of the *Tribune*, admits that the announcer is "overwrought, a touch juvenile ... and full of himself, especially in using the annoying 'we' formulation about the team" (par. 3).

Chip Caray's personality aside, Channel 9 now airs less talk about ethnicity and more about young people barbecuing on the rooftops and frequenting the many watering holes around the ballpark. Such narration is true to the revised environs of Wrigley Field, which have become more a yuppie heaven than a haven for immigrants. Gentrified in the last 15 years or so, "The Neighborhood of Baseball" (Gifford) now includes renovated buildings for the college and business crowds, who frequent upscale restaurants, bars, and souvenir shops. The improvisational, casual rooftoppers of the past have been replaced by a more commercial class, whose vantage points are rented from entrepreneurs who constructed bleachers, added electronic support, and even offered some protection from sun and rain. Even though these trendy fans have become a focus in the telecasts, the Cubs are building netted obstructions to make viewing more difficult and suing the rooftop owners for lost revenue from those seats ("Cubs sue"). Ironically, Chip looks more like one of those being sued by the Cubs' organization than the bleacher bums he pretends to represent.

No moment better defined this shift than the broadcast of the October 7, 2001, game, on the Sunday following the death of Arne Harris, the producer/director of Cubs' baseball for thirty-eight years. Of course, the focus of the telecast was on Mr. Harris' life and the myth of Arne Harris as created by Harry Caray and Steve Stone. There was talk of his many kindnesses and innovations in the broadcast images, of his eccentric personal habits, and, most of all, of his caring nature. Central to all this homage was Arne's friendship with Sammy Sosa and the story that Sammy had told Arne's wife how much he would like to hit a home run for Arne. As if on cue, the right fielder produced in his last at bat. No matter that the Cubs lost to the lowly Pirates. Eerily reminiscent of Babe Ruth's legendary pointing to center field before he hit a home run in the World Series, Sammy named his action and then made it real. Afterwards, in an interview he even declared, "Arne, that home run was for you, pal."

Beneath the surface, for those who want to read a subtext into the script, is the fact that Sammy is Hispanic and Arne Jewish. But bridging ethnic difference is no longer an explicit theme of the show. Gone are the avuncular persona of Harry and even the detached sophistication of Skip. Chip is a regular guy, neither a dominant personality himself nor a technician of the game. But he is a pal to Joe and Arne and Steve and Arne's widow. What works for the new generation of Cub fans, the teleCubbies, and their electronic TV land is the image of easy friendship. For decades the announcers have been "cast as friends, friends presumably of each other but friends also in the wider sense of all those who tune in on a regular basis" (Seidel 52). But the new Channel 9 uses such implied connections differently. It looks like Harry's world because it supports racial diversity and place-specific behavior. People of color and white people are chumming before our eyes as celebrity blurs all lines. But the audience is not invited back into the world as something real. Virtual reality is necessary and sufficient.

Baseball on Channel 9, now calling itself a superstation, has entered its self-reflexive era (Marc 152–53, Caldwell 23). Like other stations, WGN assumes its audience knows TV history, idolizes electronic heroes (like Oprah Winfrey), and ritualistically revisits its grandest shows on *TV Land* or *Nickelodeon*. The game is still played by the team that never quite makes it, and the ballpark is still more open, accepting, and friendly than any other sporting venue; it still resonates with the sacredness of a religious shrine. But when Chip Caray and Steve Stone sit in the outfield, the audience is asked to join them in a television event, not get out of their cars or apartments to visit the park. It is no longer just a matter of racial and ethnic mixing on the north side of Chicago, the specific place reflected on the old WGN. It has become a cyber world of pals and fellas, of electronic friends. Chip, Joe, Steve and the other members of the WGN "family" offer us not a vibrant, living past and future. Instead they encourage us to imagine a sense of community which is disappearing everywhere but on television. Without intending to do so, they are marketing nostalgia, the most popular product of the post-modern world's "pervasive sense of loss" (Sobchack 178–79).

In the process, baseball's announcers reflect the changing nature of television viewing. As Judith Kegan Gardiner has identified, the medium is inherently "perverse" and "paradoxical" toward intimacy because it uses mostly private contexts to visualize always public events. While "people watch it in intimate settings," TV provides "access to the world at large, ... gives every American stories and characters with which to identify, and ... focuses social discourse" (20). Harry Caray played to the first pole of this dichotomy, assuming the irritable, confused, and "regular" position of the audience members themselves. In Harry's own words, he expressed the "disappointment, the hurt, the anger, the bitterness, the love, the ecstasy" of "an inveterate fan who happens to be behind the mike" (Smith 459–60). His persona encouraged the viewers to make the television transparent in pursuit of the "real" world of Wrigley Field and its environs. Skip takes a middle ground in which the audience is invited to a degree of intimacy but one held in check by the cool, distanced sharing typical of male bonding. In order to become close to him, the spectator must depersonalize the game itself, have other, more sophisticated interests, and admit that he or she is, in fact, a voyeur watching an electronic apparatus from a safe distance.

In Chip's case, meaningful, warm affection is present, but it is realized primarily in the province of professional ballplayers, political figures, and television characters. Its intimacy will not lead to seemingly endless disappointment, like Harry's often did, and it will not turn away from the game itself, like Skip's. And so Chip's world is the most comforting. But it invites us to gaze as we do at game show hosts, talk show interviewees, or ordinary people on reality shows, all of whom give the impression of having "realer" lives than our own (Gardiner 35). While the intimacy is more immediate and melodramatic than that of the past, on WGN or

TBS, it is also more self-contained. There is less emotionally at stake in watching the game itself, win or lose. But the risks now are in our viewing areas themselves. For, since we cannot finally share in the closeness we study, we must return after the final pitch to our smaller, less real places, where we may feel more isolated than when we first heard "batter up."

Baseball as narrated on television over the last 50 years is not just about the changes in the players' salaries, the height of the pitching mound, or free agency. It is more than the record of racial integration and the breaking of home run standards. As WGN and TBS demonstrate, it is also about the changing ways television imagines its relationship with its audience. Like the movies, telebaseball follows a path from transparency to self-reference. In the primitive, innocent period which included broadcasters like Jack Brickhouse, the game was the thing. The high point was an invisible speaker helping us to look through the screen to share the moment when Ernie Banks hit his 500th home run. Eventually the game was not enough, and so the audience developed a taste for the cult of personality, embodied in Harry Caray, or professional expertise, in the person of Don Sutton or Steve Stone. But finally baseball fans didn't want to leave their newly acquired sophistication at the ticket gate. First they were given Skip Caray, who offered the skinny on whether the movie being touted after the game is really worth the time or which restaurant in Philly is the best. Finally, as television moved into its own baroque period, the images from its own past began to be recycled. The subject is no longer baseball-as-baseball. It is electronic versions of the places, heroes, and value systems first seen on Chicago's very own — now reimagined by two cable networks claiming to be America's stations.

WORKS CITED

Bellamy, Robert V., Jr., and James R. Walker, "Baseball and Television Origins: The Case of the Cubs." *Nine* 10 (2001). 6 Jan. 2003 <http://web6.infotrac.galegroup. com/itw/infomark>.
Caldwell, John Thornton. *Televisuality: Style, Crisis, and Authority in American Television*. New Brunswick: Rutgers UP, 1995.
Chandler, Joan. "Baseball." *Television and National Sport*. Urbana: U of Illinois P, 1988. 24–46.
"Cubs Sue Rooftop Owners," *USA Today*. 17 December 2002. 18 Dec. 2002 <http://www.usatoday.com /sports/baseball/nl/cubs/2002-12-17-cubs_x.htm.>.
Gardiner, Judith Kegan. "Television Intimacy: Paradoxes of Trust and Romance." *Meanings of the Medium: Perspective on the Art of Television*. Eds. Katherine

Usher Henderson and Joseph Anthony Mazzeo. New York: Praeger, 1990. 17–36.

Gifford, Barry. *The Neighborhood of Baseball: A Personal History of the Chicago Cubs.* New York: E. P. Dutton, 1981.

Hirsley, Michael, "Another Harry? Not in this Age," *Chicago Tribune* 22 February 1998.9 Feb.2003 <http://pqasb.pqarchiver.com/chicagotribune/doc26535890>.

Johnson, Steve. "Cubs Broadcasters Have Several Strikes Against Them." *Chicago Tribune* 30 August 2001. 9 Feb. 2003 http://pqasb.pqarchiver.com/chicagotribune/doc>.

Marc, David. *Demographic Vistas: Television in American Culture.* Philadelphia: U of Pennsylvania P, 1984.

Nidetz, Steve, "Two of a Kind." *Chicago Tribune.* 27 June 1989 9 Feb. 2003 <http://pqasb.pqarchiver.com/chicagotribune/doc/24541348.html>

Rader, Benjamin G. *In Its Own Image: How Television Has Transformed Sports.* New York: Free P, 1984.

Rose, Ava, and James Friedman, "Television Sports as Mas(s)culine Cult of Distraction." *Out of Bounds: Sports, Media, and the Politics of Identity.* Bloomington: Indiana UP, 1997. 1–15.

Rosenbloom, Steve. "Announcer's Self-defense Static Storm over Carey." *Chicago Tribune* 1 July 2001. 3 Feb. 2003 <http://pqasb.pqarchiver.chicagotribune/doc/748946>.

Rothschild, Richard, "Chip's Not Hip, Among Other Flaws." *Chicago Tribune* 18 June 2000. 9 Feb. 2003 <http://pqasb.pqarchiver.com/chicagotribune/doc/552986'83.html?MAC=d e7dade93fce54194...> .

Seidel, Michael. "Field and Screen: Baseball and Television." *Meanings of the Medium.* 37–55.

Smith, Curt. *Voices of the Game.* Rev. Ed. New York: Simon & Schuster, 1992.

Sobchack, Vivian. "Baseball in the Post-American Cinema, or Life in the Minor Leagues." Rose and Friedman. 175–97.

13

Baseball Immortals: Character and Performance On and Off the Field

RON REMBERT

Consider the following imaginary debate between two fans concerning Pete Rose as a potential candidate for the Hall of Fame:

>Fan 1: There is no doubt in my mind that Pete Rose should be reinstated into baseball and immediately inducted into the Hall of Fame. His *performance* on the field was incredible, full of hustle and high quality play. His statistics are amazing, especially his 4,097 hit total, a record that will never be broken.
>Fan 2: I won't deny his incredible record-setting performance as a player on the field, which places Rose in the ranks of baseball immortals. But we shouldn't overlook the *character* issue connected with his gambling.
>Fan 1: I don't see what that issue has to do with his *performance*. I think it's totally irrelevant to Rose's candidacy. He should be judged only by his performance, just like the other inductees.
>Fan 2: I disagree. The possibility that his gambling had an effect on the game makes it relevant, especially in judging Hall of Fame players. *Character*, not just performance, should be considered as part of "fame," don't you think?"

Debates along these imaginary lines, although perhaps not quite so stilted or civil, have raged since Bart Giamatti banished Pete Rose from baseball, essentially nullifying consideration of Rose for the Hall of Fame. In

Giamatti's judgment, "one of the game's greatest players has engaged in a variety of acts which have stained the game, and he must now live with the consequences of those acts" (117). "Stained the game" is a loaded phrase in Giamatti's claim, generating emotion and drawing attention to important issues at the very center of the Rose controversy—the connection between the character and performance of a player on and off the field and that player's impact on the game. In justifying his final determination and subsequent action regarding Rose's status in organized baseball, Giamatti claimed to "be responsible for protecting the integrity of the game of baseball—that is, the game's authenticity, honesty and coherence" (118). That agenda regarding "the integrity of the game" invites consideration of character and performance in evaluating any player's career, but especially a potential Hall of Fame inductee, as supported by a key entry in *The Dickson Baseball Dictionary*.

In this collection of baseball terminology, the term, "baseball immortal," noted as a synonym for "Hall of Famer," carries the following definition: "One of the greatest and most influential players to play the game, an individual who presumably will never be forgotten. The title is totally subjective and seems to be bestowed on those who have had an effect on the very nature of the game" (Dickson 36). This definition proves intriguing for two reasons—1) the use of the label, baseball immortal, is "totally subjective," implying that the objective criteria for judging baseball immortality, statistical data, is not the only standard, and 2) the label refers to candidates "who have had an effect on the very nature of the game," implying that one's impact on the game as a whole, not just one's accomplishments on the field, holds significance. These parts of Dickson's definition invite questions about two concepts, "character" as well as "performance," in identifying a baseball immortal or Hall of Famer.

Concerns about character and performance arise in another source focusing on baseball immortals, Bill James's *Whatever Happened to the Hall of Fame?*, a somewhat surprising source because of its primary focus on statistical analysis. In questioning what has happened to the Hall of Fame regarding some induction decisions, James develops objective criteria based on a point system for rating all Hall of Fame Players (174–176). His statistical comparisons of players' productivity on the field leads to the conclusion that some stars who have not been inducted should be and others who have been deemed immortal should not be.

Urban "Red" Faber, for example, who spent his entire twenty-year career with the Chicago White Sox, falls into that second category. Faber fails to satisfy James's statistical standards for induction but nevertheless achieves baseball immortality. According to James, this White Sox pitcher reached that pinnacle because of his *character*, not his performance, a result the author appears to regret:

> The Veterans Committee has always been prone to favoritism [166].
>
> Red (Would You Do Me A) Faber was elected to the Hall of Fame by the Veterans Committee in 1964 [117].
>
> Faber was selected, in all likelihood, for the same reason that Ray Shalk was—he was one of the Clean Sox of 1919, and Warren Brown was on the committee [117].

At first glance, it appears that favoritism prompted Faber's selection. However, the reference to Faber being a "Clean Sox" during the Black Sox scandal suggests that character as an issue arose during the election process. It is interesting that James' argument *against* Faber as a Hall of Famer works *for* his consideration as a baseball immortal, according to Dickson's definition. Note that the Veterans Committee's "favoritism" for Faber implies a subjective judgment on their part, and their consideration of his clean status during the scandal appears to take into account Faber's "effect on the very nature of the game." Even in an argument grounded primarily on statistics such as James promotes, character emerges as a controversial issue.

Concluding that character more than performance played a key role in Faber's Hall of Fame induction requires the acceptance of a questionable assumption that Urban "Red" Faber was approached by the gamblers during the Black Sox scandal. There does not appear to be any evidence that he was contacted. Why not, considering that he was a starter for the White Sox that year? Perhaps it was because of Faber's physical challenges throughout the season: "The most severe blow to the White Sox was the sudden and mysterious failure of Red Faber to be a big winner. He came up with a weak arm in spring training. For the season he struggled to win 11 games while absorbing 9 defeats" (Stein 147). That spring training ailment plagued Faber throughout the 1919 season, leading to the decision that Faber wouldn't even attempt to pitch during the Series because of a weak arm" (Stein 153). In view of Faber's pitching demise, the issue of character in regard to the Black Sox scandal appears inconsequential because there was no good reason to approach him with a bribe. On the other hand, perhaps gamblers did not approach Faber because he was known as a player who would not take a bribe. That possibility introduces the issue of character, making his enshrinement as a baseball immortal on that basis, as James suggests, more understandable. James's analysis of Faber's induction into the Hall of Fame points ultimately to the need to distinguish between a broad and narrow use of the concept of character.

In its broadest sense, the term covers the values, attitudes, qualities and concerns displayed in one's everyday interactions, including family relationships, community life, and work experience. Negative character traits expressed through abusive behavior or marital conflict; drug, alcohol, or gambling addiction; or poor work habits reflect a player's character in the broad sense of the term, but such traits need not necessarily have an "effect on the very nature of the game." For example, on October 8, 1956, Don Larsen pitched the first perfect game during a World Series. His performance on the field was unsurpassed, and in regard to the record books, his "effect on the very nature of the game" long lasting. His character off the field was far from stellar, drawing legal attacks from his estranged wife for Larsen's failure to pay child support:

> In his moment of supreme triumph today, pitcher Don Larsen of the Yankees had in his locker a court complaint filed by his estranged wife, Vivian Larsen, which charged him with nonsupport.
> Bronx Supreme Court Justice Sam H. Hofstadter issued Larsen a show cause order returnable October 15. Mrs. Larsen asked the court to show cause why Larsen's World Series proceeds should not be held up.
> She claims that Larsen deserted her and their daughter, Caroline Jean Larsen, and on July 16 of this year in the same court, Justice Henry Greenberg (not related to former Detroit slugger Hank Greenberg, who also is from the Bronx) awarded Mrs. Larsen $60 a week support money from Larsen. However, she said she had received only four of the payments and still had seven weeks, totalling $420 due to her ["Larson Is Sued" 39].

In this example, Larsen's performance on the field, his pitching of a perfect game in a World Series, was not diminished by his character problems, his illegal behavior toward his former wife and daughter, off the field. Not only did his family problems seem irrelevant to his pitching performance during this record-setting game, but Larsen's dealings in court certainly did not have a lasting "effect on the very nature of the game." His familial problems should not be minimized or overlooked in appraising Don Larsen as a person, a husband or a father, but nor should they be emphasized or overrated in judging him as a player, a pitcher, or a teammate. This broad use of the term character allows for clearer demarcation between a player's performance on the field and actions and attitudes off of it.

Another example of separating character from performance in evaluating a player, one with a more positive outcome, involves the recent retirement of a player's jersey by his minor league team. On August 14, 2003, the Ottawa Lynx celebrated the career of "one of the most terrific players and people to wear an Ottawa Lynx uniform" ("Lynx" 1), Jamey Carroll, who was called up to the Montreal Expos. Carroll's statistical credentials, especially his offensive performance on the field, appear solid but not exceptional. During his minor league career, Carroll achieved a career .268 batting average, hitting 7 homeruns during his 665 games.

Figures in the record book, however, did not serve as the primary reason for retiring his jersey. Jamey Carroll's character and contribution to his community generated this special recognition. According to Lynx General Manager Kyle Bostwick, speaking for the Lynx organization during the celebration of Jamey Carroll Day in Ottawa, "Jamey was a tremendous ambassador for the Ottawa Lynx. His contributions went far beyond what we could possibly ask out of any player. He was a great player here, but beyond that, he was even a better person ("Lynx to Retire" 1). Evidence of Carroll's off the field contributions ranges from "giving clinics to young players, visiting schools to promote reading, or doing public relations to promote Lynx baseball in the Ottawa business community" ("Lynx to Retire"1). This lasting tribute by a team for its player, the retirement of one's jersey, illustrates a strong interest in the character of a player as well as his performance. It also indicates that the two issues can be separated when the term *character* is meant in a broad sense.

The narrow use of the term does not allow for such clear distinction between behavior off the field and performance on it. Gambling, for example, as a personal habit might prove worrisome but expands into a serious, ethical concern when it has an impact on the game, a consideration that the Veterans Committee evidently processed as part of Red Faber's Hall of Fame induction and that Bart Giamatti apparently weighed regarding Pete Rose's future status as a Hall of Fame candidate. This narrow view is more difficult to define because the "effect on the very nature of the game" of one's character may not be easy to determine. The impact may not be clear at first but may grow more evident with passing time. Generally speaking, who plays the game and how they play it, who watches the game and why they watch it, and who governs the game and how they govern it become potential issues that affect the judgment of a player's character. Whichever issue arises, the expected effect on the game of one's character should be positive, or at least not negative, for Hall of Fame inductees. It is often easier to recognize a negative effect of one's character; a positive one often draws little notice. Dickson's definition invites us to consider that baseball immortals or Hall of Famers have an effect and should be judged by their impact.

Another source suggesting a narrow view of character emerges from the archives of The All American Girls Baseball League (AAGBL). This enterprise, launched in 1943 by Philip K. Wrigley as a non-profit, "controlled experiment" to test the potential for an all-women's league connecting several small, Midwestern towns, promoted high principles among its personnel (Browne 22). All players under contract to this new league encountered strict standards for behavior on and off the field, spelled out for them in the official AAGBL guidebook :

> You have certain responsibilities because you too are in the limelight. Your actions and appearances on and off the field reflect the whole profession. It is not only your duty to hold up the standard of this profession but to do your best to keep others in line.
>
> The girls in this league are rapidly becoming the heroines of youngsters as well as groups all over the world. People want to be able to respect their heroines at all times ["Guide" 1].

Not only were all players expected to uphold certain standards on and off the field regarding their "actions and appearance" but also to monitor each other's compliance with official guidelines. This additional requirement adds an interesting dimension to the test of a player's character. Another hint at the importance of character in the guidebook arises with the description of players as "heroines" who, by definition, are expected to elicit respect. The implication follows that each player should regard herself as a role model for others, a responsibility not apparently open to personal choice on the part of each individual but simply assumed as integral to one's professional identity.

The emphasis on professionalism in the AAGBL guidebook stands out. Expectations governing "beauty routine," "loosening and circulation exercises," "clothes," "etiquette," "speech" on and off the field, "sportsmanship," and "dealing with the public" at the park are spelled out in great detail. ("Guide" 2–9). One section entitled, "The Baseball Fan," focuses on interaction with fans and implies that concerns about professionalism prevail: "There is an old saying that 'the customer is always right' even when the customer is not, a lesson which management uses both to warn the players and to mandate certain behaviors from them. Beware of the negative fan behavior and attitudes, but do not let yourself be affected by it" ("Guide" 9). This section, like the ones covering the topics listed above, seem to focus more on image than character.

Although the terms are related and sometimes interchangeable, they are not synonyms. One's image may or may not accurately reflect one's character. The introduction of character issues at the beginning of the guidebook leads to advice about image in the body of the document. Another interesting distinction arises. The professional standards defined throughout the guidebook also do not place responsibility on players to safeguard "the very nature of the game"; rather, the standards promote personal development and business goals: "We hand you this manual to help guide you in your personal appearance. We ask you to follow the rules of behavior for your own good as well as that of the future success of girl's baseball" (1).

For Dickson, according to his definition, the issue of character encompasses more than one's personal development and a league's business goals, stretching to a baseball immortal's or Hall of Famer's "effect on the very nature of the game." This notion narrows the definition of character to the crucial point, especially in regard to defining baseball immortality. In his definition of "baseball immortal," Dickson offers no clarification of the phrase "an effect on the very nature of the game." Since no definition is provided, perhaps some illustrations will help in building a definition by example.

I want to argue that there are two members of the Hall of Fame who definitely had "an effect on the very nature of the game," a negative impact I will argue, calling into question their status as baseball immortals, according to Dickson's definition of that label. The term character should be applied in the narrow sense when considering the impact on the game of these two inductees. The term, performance, as usual in these discussions, involves statistical records when appraising their achievements.

The first example is Cap Anson. Anson's plaque at the Baseball Hall of Fame reads:

> Greatest hitter and greatest National League player-manager of the 19th century. Started with Chicagos in National League's first year 1876. Chicago manager from 1879—1897, winning five pennants. Was .300 class hitter 20 years. Batting Champion 4 times [*Players* 21].

Based strictly on this statistical evidence defining his performance on the field, Cap Anson deserves the title "greatest," if not one of the greatest players during the latter part of the nineteenth century. Judging his performance on this basis alone, he definitely belongs in the Hall of Fame. But, according to Dickson's definition of a baseball immortal or Hall of Famer, should Cap Anson receive such recognition?

A character issue remains regarding Anson. In the narrow sense of that term, he promoted prejudice against African-American baseball players, "being almost solely responsible for imposing the color line," throughout organized baseball, according to Sol White in his *History of Colored Base Ball* (qtd. in Peterson 29). In that same work, White seeks an explanation:

> Just why Adrian C. Anson, manager and captain of the Chicago National League Club, was so strongly opposed to colored players to white teams cannot be explained. His repugnant feeling, shown at every opportunity, toward colored ball players, was a source of comment throughout every league in the country, and his opposition, with his great popularity and power in baseball circles, hastened the exclusion of the black man from white leagues [Peterson 30].

Even if holding Cap Anson as "almost solely responsible for imposing the color line" appears overstated, Anson's negative impact on the game involving teams with African-American players had an "effect on the very nature of the game" for the next fifty years until Jackie Robinson broke the color barrier. This negative effect, a result of Anson's attitudes and actions, should deserve consideration as much, if not more, than performance ratings.

Anson's prejudicial attitudes were not uncommon in the 1880s among ballplayers. Many others shared his attitudes and supported the gentlemen's agreement of white players to boycott any game in which an African-American tried to play. But those lesser known players did not become candidates for the baseball Hall of Fame, for baseball immortality. Should Anson's high profile actions expressing his attitudes to bar African-American players be taken into account in considering him as a Hall of Fame representative? Certainly his influence in establishing the gentlemen's agreement carries weight. According to Dickson's definition, and the prevailing attitudes of most people today, such consideration against Anson certainly would be justified.

Another example is Charles Comiskey. Comiskey's plaque at Cooperstown reads:

> Charles A. Comiskey "The Old Roman" started 50 years of baseball as St. Louis Brown's first-baseman in 1882 and was first man at this position to play away from bag for batters. As Browns' manager-captain-player won 4 straight American Association pennants starting 1885. World Champions first two years. Owner and president Chicago White Sox 1900–1931 [*Players* 49].

Not mentioned in these key details is Comiskey's role in promoting, through neglect, the so-called Black Sox scandal. Not only is there evidence that Joe Jackson tried to notify Comiskey of the corrupt activity on his ballclub but also that Comiskey deliberately failed to respond:

> If he really wanted the whole story, he could have had it from the horse's mouth. Had not Jackson indicated willingness to talk? What else was necessary to start the snowball rolling? Less than two weeks after the Series, Comiskey did receive a letter from Joseph Jefferson Jackson, written by his wife, and postmarked Savannah, Georgia. The letter simply stated he had information that the Series had not been played on the square and offered to reveal what he knew. Comiskey quietly filed the letter, and did not bother to reply [Asinof 130].

Even more worrisome than Comiskey's lack of response to Jackson's invitation was the owner's deliberate attempt to confuse and deflect the issue, participating in the covering up:

> On the following day, the Great Whitewash began. Charles Comiskey, owner of the Chicago American League Baseball Club, was quoted in the public press as follows: "There is always a scandal of some kind following a big sporting event like the World Series. These yarns are manufactured out of whole cloth and grow out of bitterness due to losing wagers. I believe my boys fought the battles of the recent World Series on the level, as they have always done. And I would be the first to want information to the contrary—if there be any. I would give $20,000 to anyone unearthing any information to that effect..." [Asinof 129].

If we accept that the Black Sox scandal clearly had "an effect on the very nature of the game," and if we accept the claims that Comiskey played a role in the scandal, does it not follow that his inaction and action had "an effect on the very nature of the game"? If so, his character deserves some scrutiny not only for these ill effects but also for the potential injustice to Joe Jackson, who remains banned from baseball and from consideration by the Hall of Fame while Charles Comiskey remains in good standing and immortalized at Cooperstown.

If we agree that these two examples raise a legitimate question about the logic of connecting character and performance in bestowing baseball immortality, does it mean that we need to review all Hall of Fame inductees in terms of the character/performance litmus test? I don't think so, because the character traits of most inductees, while not altogether admirable, did not have a destructive effect on the very nature of the game. For example, Babe Ruth displayed many questionable character traits, but they did not ultimately have a negative impact on the game. I offer the two examples above as obvious case studies, but I don't assume that all regular players or all Hall of Fame inductees deserve such scrutiny.

Scrutiny of character *connected* to performance has intensified in the political arena of American society and in the business sector, especially in view of scandals involving large corporations such as Enron. Scandals in these arenas have a serious effect on our political and financial lives. Why has character *disconnected* from performance remained an acceptable position in baseball, even in the choice of our baseball immortals or Hall of Famers? It is an intriguing issue in American culture that baseball writers and fans seem to underrate character and overrate performance in the sporting arena, while in appraising other professionals they might seek a more balanced view of the two. Perhaps baseball serves strictly as entertainment for its patrons, not seeming as serious as politics or business, and therefore not inviting the same concerns about character and performance among writers or fans that arise in these other areas. Perhaps "an effect on the very nature of the game" does not prove as worrisome as the results of a scandal on our political system or a bankruptcy on our financial portfolios. But this distinction makes no sense, especially if we agree with Walt Whitman that baseball "belongs as much to our institutions, fits into them as significantly as our constitution, laws: is just as important in the sum total of our historic life" (qtd. in Rader xv).

WORKS CITED

Asinof, Eliot. *Eight Men Out*. New York: Henry Holt and Company, 1963.
Browne, Lois. *Girls of Summer*. New York: Harper Collins, 1992.
Dickson, Paul, ed. *Dickson Baseball Dictionary*. New York: Facts on File, 1989.
Giamatti, A. Bartlett. *A Great and Glorious Game*. Ed. Kenneth S. Robson. Chapel Hill, NC: Algonquin Books, 1998.
"Guide for All American Girls." *National Baseball Hall of Fame Primary Sources*. (Dec. 13, 1999): 15 pp. 27 Feb. 2003 www.baseballhalloffame.org/edu.
James, Bill. *Whatever Happened to the Hall of Fame?* New York: Simon and Schuster, 1994.
"Larsen Is Sued for Non-Support." *Cincinnati Enquirer*. (Oct. 9, 1956): 39.
"Lynx to Retire Jamey Carroll's Number 3." *Ottawa Linx Press Box* (Mar. 26, 2003): 2 pp. 30 March 2003 www.ottawalynx.com/lynxpressbox03
Peterson, Robert. *Only the Ball Was White*. New York: Oxford UP, 1970.
Players of Cooperstown: Baseball's Hall of Fame. Lincolnwood, IL: Publications International, 1994.
Rader, Benjamin G. *Baseball: A History of America's Game*. Urbana: U of Illinois P, 1992.
Stein, Irving M. *The Ginger Kid: The Buck Weaver Story*. William C. Brown Communications, 1992.

14

Forces of Darkness and Light: The Cultural Significance of Transitions in Baseball History

DAVID SHINER

> I raised my head. The offing was barred by a black bank of clouds, and the tranquil waterway leading to the uttermost ends of the earth flowed sombre under an overcast sky—seemed to lead into the heart of an immense darkness.
>
> —Joseph Conrad, *Heart of Darkness*

Writers in the Western world have traditionally employed such terms as "darkness" and "blackness" to suggest the presence of evil. Such usages, natural though they might seem, are culturally bound; they are conspicuously absent from the literature of Africa, for example. This difference does not necessarily make our own cultural metaphors less fitting, but it does highlight their culturally specific implications. The distinction between "clean," "light," and "white" as terms of approval on one hand, and "dirty," "dark," and "black" as words of condemnation on the other, was especially widely used in the United States around 1920. The Red Scare following the Russian Revolution of 1917 raised the stakes on behalf of "whiteness," the figurative label given to all "true patriots" as well as to Russians opposing the Revolution, "White Russians." Temperance was ushered in when those opposing it found themselves unable to combat the rhetoric uniting the "cleaning up" of the "dirty" effects of alcohol with "liberation" from those effects. The racist overtones of each of these crusades were undeniable; for example, the Ku Klux Klan was prominent in both movements. It can hardly be coincidental that recorded lynchings of blacks were the most numerous in United States history during that period.

In baseball, the sudden transition from the finesse game of the "dead-ball era" to the power game introduced and dominated by Babe Ruth in the 1920s was similarly due in part to the speed with which the public came to believe that the outgoing era was too "dirty" and that only a thorough "cleaning up" could rescue it. In this case, too, the assumptions and implications of the crusade went far beyond the relatively small world of professional baseball. Again, racism was a component of the movement, although not a consciously intended one. The social consequences of the ideas associated with temperance and the Red Scare are well documented. The same is not true of the transition in baseball during the same period. This essay is intended as a step in that direction.

CLEANLINESS AND DIRTINESS

The year is 1920. A World War, the most monumental in history up to that time, has recently ended. Attendance at baseball games is about to reach record heights. A new commissioner, baseball's first, takes office. Babe Ruth, nearing his prime, turns twenty-five. A new communications medium, radio, begins to capture the imagination of the public; within a couple of years the World Series will be broadcast on it, and eventually millions of Americans will listen to baseball broadcasts regularly.

In 1920, Major League Baseball—that is, baseball in the highest level of the white professional leagues—moved with startling haste into a new era. While this process had begun long before 1920, it climaxed in that year due largely to two events: the death of Cleveland Indians shortstop Ray Chapman as the result of being hit in the head by a pitched ball and the discovery of an attempt by members of the Chicago White Sox to throw the previous season's World Series. These two incidents contrived to lead to a new age in baseball, one based on very different principles from those of the old era.

The "dirtiness" which led to the demise of the old era was of two kinds. One was that of the Black Sox and others who traded wins for money. The other was the condition of the baseballs themselves. Before 1920 pitchers had been allowed to "doctor" the baseball with saliva and other so-called "foreign substances," and baseballs would be removed from play only if they went into the grandstands and could not be retrieved. As a result, the balls in play were often dark, sometimes barely visible. When spitball pitcher Carl Mays threw the pitch that killed Chapman in August 1920, one form of dirtiness was exposed as toxic. When eight Chicago White Sox players were indicted for throwing the 1919 World Series a couple of months later, another was. Those events led to the sharpening of a distinction between cleanliness and dirtiness that informed subsequent events in baseball in a more sweeping way than ever before or since.

The affiliation of blackness and darkness with evil pervaded the public imagery surrounding the game's greatest scandal. As soon as the confessions of Eddie Cicotte, Happy Felsch, and Joe Jackson became public, the print media branded them and their co-conspirators "Black Sox" and their apparently guiltless teammates "Clean Sox." This imagery has pervaded accounts of the scandal ever since, as witness the following: "When the eight members of the Chicago White Sox attained lifelong ignominy by changing the hue of their hose to black, baseball entered upon its darkest hour" (Allen 201). The use of and reaction to such symbols and metaphors helped create a new paradigm, one that figured prominently in the overhaul of Major League Baseball in 1920.

The novel treatment of the baseball itself fit neatly into the new paradigm. "Dark" and "dirty" pitches such as the spitball had had a long history before 1920, but so far as is known the issue of whether they should be banned had never before come to a formal vote among members of Major League Baseball's ruling body, the National Commission. Similarly, the notion of throwing a dirty ball out of play, although somewhat controversial, was contrary to league policy until late 1920. Deadball era outfielder Fred Snodgrass described the rare introduction of a new baseball in Lawrence S. Ritter's *The Glory of Their Times*. The umpire, Snodgrass declared, would "throw the ball out to the pitcher, who would promptly sidestep it. It would go around the infield once or twice and come back to the pitcher as black as the ace of spades. All the infielders were chewing tobacco or licorice, and spitting into their gloves, and they'd give that ball a good going over before it ever got to the pitcher" (91). Such shenanigans, *de rigueur* prior to 1920, practically disappeared after Chapman's death. At that point the National Commission mandated that any ball that was "even slightly scuffed or soiled" was to be tossed out of play immediately (Seymour 427).

It is well worth remembering that not long before 1920 the over-the-fence home run had been as controversial in its own way as the dirty baseball. Several prominent turn-of-the-century baseball authorities such as Henry Chadwick felt that receiving credit for hitting a ball over a fence was contrary to the spirit of the game. In support of their arguments is the likelihood that fences were originally intended as boundaries rather than targets. For a brief period in the late nineteenth century, power hitting had come to the fore, but it was soon nullified by the development of "trick pitches" such as the spitball and tricky strategies like the sacrifice bunt and the hit-and-run play. Clever strategy, instead of brute power, continued to inform the thinking of baseball men throughout the deadball era. "You couldn't hit the ball over the fence in most parks in those days," Snodgrass told Ritter, "because the ball was too dead" (91). It was a rare individual in a rare stadium who could muscle a baseball over a fence more than once a month. Even after the more lively cork-centered baseball was introduced in 1910, some organizations responded by raising their outfield fences, thus keeping many long hits in the park.

Hitting for power, then, was possible but rare in the deadball era, and not held in particularly high esteem. This lack of appreciation was demonstrated in a variety of ways. In 1913, for example, Brooklyn first baseman Jake Daubert led the National League with a batting average of .350, followed by Philadelphia right fielder Gavvy Cravath at .341. The offensive statistics for the two players were as follows:

Player, Team	G	AB	R	H	2B	3B	HR	RBI	BB	SB	Avg
Daubert, Brooklyn	139	508	76	178	17	7	2	52	44	25	.350
Cravath, Philadelphia	147	525	78	179	34	14	19	128	55	10	.341

After the season, a committee of baseball writers awarded Daubert the MVP "for his good hitting and all-around work" (Richter 124). Such a decision can hardly seem credible to us today. Cravath's offensive statistics exceed Daubert's in every category except batting average and stolen bases, completely dominating them in the power categories. Daubert was probably a little better defensively, but neither man played a key position. Furthermore, Cravath's Phillies finished second in the league, while Daubert's Dodgers were sixth. But Daubert had a better batting average, and he was a better bunter and base stealer; Cravath was pretty good too, but he was "only" a slugger. At any rate, that was the way baseball people viewed the matter before 1920.

Rube Bressler, a longtime Major Leaguer whose career spanned both eras, astutely summarized the change that took place as a result of the events of 1920 when he told Ritter that baseball during the deadball era "was a matter of manipulation, see, not power.... All the great artists of the old days maneuvered. It was manipulation, then; today it's power. Manipulation and power, two entirely different things" (196) . The hit-and-run play, the bunt, the holding of the bat so as to "hit 'em where they ain't"—in all such cases, power was sacrificed in favor of what Bressler termed manipulation. From the hurling side, the same was true of pitches, such as the choice of the spitball as opposed to the fastball.

The manipulative strategies of the deadball era, though on the one hand artistic, always had a "dark" side to them, one bordering on "dirtiness." This connotation is evident in a term such as "stealing," which implies an ethical marginality from which power seems untainted. Similarly, players would regularly feign being hit by pitches and engage in similar stunts to try to fool umpires to their team's advantage. On the harsher side was the spiking of players, which was "dirty" if overdone but generally within the spirit of the game. The masters of this brand of play had been the Baltimore Orioles of the "Gay '90s," who had mastered what we now call "small ball." They employed every imaginable play, legal or not, and were both criticized as a "dirty" and celebrated to a remarkable degree. The less extreme manipulations undertaken by their successors in the early years of the 20th century were widely considered among the fundamentals of winning baseball but were readily prone to ethical disapproval. That disapproval was simmering just below the surface prior to the events of 1920.

The fixing of the World Series and the death of Ray Chapman helped create a setting in which disapproval turned into outright denunciation. At the same time, a young, unschooled ex-pitcher was delighting fans by hitting home runs in unprecedented numbers. Given those circumstances, as baseball analyst Bill James has written, "the owners did not do what they would quite certainly have done at any other time, which would have been to take some action to control this obscene burst of offensive productivity, and keep Ruth from making a mockery of the game. Instead they gave Ruth his rein, and allowed him to pull the game wherever he wanted it to go" (*Abstract, 1985* 124). Off the field, baseball's new commissioner, Kenesaw Mountain Landis was given that same latitude when desperate owners disbanded the National Commission and accepted his demand for supreme and practically unlimited power as baseball's first Commissioner.

Ruth on the field, and Landis off of it, helped the fans forget the darkness and dirtiness of America's game by transforming it from a contest of manipulation to one of power. Before 1920, Ty Cobb had been baseball's greatest star, reaching the pinnacle of his profession by bunting, stealing bases, spiking opponents, and generally using all the strategies that manipulative baseball had to offer. During that era nearly every baseball insider and enthusiast would have said with Cobb that the game was intended to be "an act of skill rather than simple power" (Cobb 145). That view, at least in its starkest form, eroded quickly after 1920.

Cobb, like Snodgrass and most other baseball men of the deadball era, believed that baseball was a subtle and intricate game whose mastery took intelligence. That view too changed with the new era. Ruth, according to teammate Leo Durocher, was "dumb in anything that took any intelligence," but felt that fact was irrelevant to his talent for baseball because he was a "natural" (43). Ruth's power overcame the strategies of manipulation in the most practical manner imaginable: it won ball games. It seemed self-evident that one-run strategies could not prevail over three-run homers. "Babe Ruth," James has written, "was a cyclone who swept up precious strategies of the generations before him and scattered them in ruins" (*Abstract 1983* 66). New York manager Miller Huggins' recognition of the value of Ruth's slugging prowess was vital to the Yankees' great success in the 1920s.

Baseball was far from the only sport in which power was becoming the dominant force. The emergence of Babe Ruth as the marquee star of the diamond was closely followed by that of Bobby Jones in golf, Bill Tilden in tennis, Red Grange in football, and Jack Dempsey in boxing— "power" men all. Like the good guys in the movies, they wore white and they hit hard. Along with powerful moguls such as Judge Landis, they would dominate the American sports scene in the 1920s. Perhaps this worship of power was not coincidental at a time when corporations were enjoying the power of a boom economy and the nation itself was emerging as a world power following World War I.

As 1920 drew to a close, however, it was not power but cleanliness that was next to godliness in the eyes of the public. The victory of the Indians over the White Sox in the 1920 American League pennant race was widely perceived and expressed as the triumph of cleanliness over dirtiness, of good over evil. The day after the Indians clinched the flag, the front page of the *Cleveland Plain Dealer* featured a three-column by eight-inch drawing of a Cleveland ballplayer looking toward a giant pennant off on the horizon. Overlooking the scene, up in the clouds, was Ray Chapman. Underneath him were inscribed the words, "It pays to play clean" (Sowell 263). To play clean, or at least appear to, and to win were the joint aspirations of sports-minded Americans. By virtue of their power, Landis and Ruth combined to lead Major League Baseball toward the seeming realization of those goals.

Some aspects of the cleaning up of baseball bordered on the comical. In a baseball magazine of the early 1920s, for example, the Spalding Company saw fit to place an ad that read in part, "All Spalding baseball uniforms are made by us in our own sanitary factories.... Our employees receive the benefits that an abundance of light and air in the workroom brings to them. When you put on your Spalding uniform, you have our assurance that it was made under clean and healthful conditions" (qtd. in

Foster 33). The idea that "it pays to play clean" had evidently pervaded the consciousness of the baseball public in quite unforeseen ways.

Not all the consequences of the new paradigm were as innocuous or benign. One such effort was an increased "whitening" of Major League Baseball, which was in part a consequence of Landis' rise to power. Prior to 1920, teams from the black and white major leagues often played each other after the end of the regular season. In the 1920s, however, Landis limited post-season exhibition games so that Major League Baseball would not have its supposed superiority threatened. Exhibitions between the races would henceforth be limited to games between black all-stars and white all-stars. In later years Negro League stalwarts would give their version of the reason for Landis' decision: "We beat the Athletics in 1925," recalled Jake Stephens in an interview with John Holway some fifty years after the fact. "We beat them three straight ball games.... We even beat them 18–3! That's when Judge Landis made a ruling that never would a big league club play a Negro League club intact again" (*Black Diamonds* 10). Just as darkness and dirtiness were to be extinguished in favor of cleanliness and light, so too was blackness to be suppressed in deference to whiteness during Landis' reign.

The Negro National League was another product of the year 1920. Unlike the white major leagues, the Negro Leagues retained the rules and strategies of the deadball era. Spitballs, emery balls, stealing, spiking, and all the rest were part of the Negro Leaguers' stock in trade. While white baseball aspired to a squeaky-clean image *a la* the Marquis of Queensbury rules, the Negro Leaguers, as Kansas City Monarchs star Newt Allen put it, "played by the 'coonsbury' rules. That's any way you can think to win, any kind of play you think you could get by on" (Holway, *Voices* 96).

"Getting by" was hardly a matter of choosing manipulation over power. On the contrary, sluggers like Josh Gibson, Buck Leonard, and Mule Suttles were among the biggest stars in the Negro Leagues. However, the presence of power men did not lead to the diminishing of manipulative strategies. Having nothing to prove with respect to the superiority of lightness over darkness, of power over manipulation, the Negro Leaguers utilized both styles of play. That synthesis would not take root in Major League Baseball for many years.

INTEGRATION

The year is 1945. Another World War, the most monumental in history, has recently ended. Attendance at baseball games is about to reach record heights. A new commissioner, baseball's second, takes office. Babe Ruth, nearing his death, turns fifty. A new communications medium, television, begins to capture the imagination of the public; within a couple of years the World Series will be broadcast on it, and eventually millions of Americans will watch baseball broadcasts regularly.

By 1945, the deadball era was a dim memory. So were the Black Sox, scuffed baseballs, and the manipulative strategies of the deadball era. The devotion that Major League Baseball in general and Judge Landis in particular had displayed toward cleanliness and whiteness no longer fit the dominant cultural paradigm as well as it had twenty-five years earlier. For many reasons, including the facts that blacks had fought with distinction in World War II and that such highly visible and generally popular dark-skinned athletes as Jesse Owens and Joe Louis had graced the sporting world, white baseball was becoming ready for integration—the integration not only of black and white but also of manipulation with power.

In 1945, baseball's most successful and celebrated young manager was Leo Durocher of the Brooklyn Dodgers. As a teammate of Babe Ruth in the 1920s, Durocher had been unable to hit for power, and his basic physical tools were nothing special. But he could run, he could bunt, and he could play the field. He was also a fiery competitor and a student of the game, which endeared him to Miller Huggins. Durocher said the Yankee manager, who during the deadball era had been much the same type of player, "loved me like a father, and I loved him like a son" (35). Huggins would often talk strategy with Durocher, becoming his first managerial model and mentor as well as his surrogate father. One day in the Yankee dugout, the older man told the younger, "There are a lot of guys around here with strong backs and weak minds. You have a strong mind and a weak back. Let them do all the hitting. You use your head. And as long as you live, there will be a place for you in baseball. You'll be there when they're all gone" (34). And so he was.

Durocher's self-confessed baseball philosophy was, "Win any way you can as long as you can get away with it" (3). It was the approach not only of Ty Cobb and the other deadball-era players but also of Newt Allen and his fellow Negro Leaguers. Durocher's phrasing, however, put a new slant on the matter. In the deadball era, playing hard had always been distinguished from playing dirty. If a player such as Cobb were accused of dirty play, as happened often, he would be honor-bound to dispute the charge. Durocher had no particular qualms with such charges: if others considered his brand of baseball "dirty," then so be it. When discussing the acquisition of catcher Mickey Owen, for example, Durocher reviewed an earlier incident in which Owen had "made his own contribution to the cause of clean baseball by taking a whack at me. In the interests of clean baseball, I whacked him back. In other words, my kind of player" (119).

Jackie Robinson was that sort of ballplayer too, "the kind of player," Durocher told sportswriter Ed Linn, "who—like me—had to be driving and scratching and yelling to be at his best" (182). That attitude appealed to Dodger General Manager Branch Rickey, who signed Robinson to a Dodger contract in October of 1945. As Dodger announcer Red Barber later wrote, Rickey had quickly sized up Robinson as "the most competitive man he'd known since Ty Cobb" (58). Supported by Durocher, Robinson would reintroduce the electrifying strategies that had been the trademark of Cobb and his mates from the deadball era, such as steals of home, which were new to the fans of the 1940s unless they were old-timers or followers of Negro League baseball.

In the deadball era, stolen bases had been about ten times as common as home runs. That ratio changed quickly and radically in 1920. By Jackie Robinson's rookie year, homers outnumbered steals by a margin of more than two to one. The reason was evident: speedsters were instructed to play it safe on the basepaths so that they would still be there when the power hitters stepped up to the plate. On the Boston Red Sox of the 1940s, for example, Dom DiMaggio and Johnny Pesky batted just ahead of Ted Williams. Both DiMaggio and Pesky were fast men and capable baserunners, but they were rarely permitted to attempt a steal. When Pesky asked his manager, Joe Cronin, for permission to steal more often, Cronin responded, "You've got the best hitter in baseball coming up behind you, and he hits the ball and you're going to score. You damn well won't run" (Halberstam 230). Not every team had a Ted Williams, but all had power men whose job was to hit the ball out of the park. Faster players were ordinarily expected to get on base and stay there until the next hit. "The game," Ty Cobb complained, "has degenerated into a high-scoring slugging match with thin, whippy bats as weapons and the home run as the universal objective. Players limp along on one cylinder" (145).

Jackie Robinson presaged the type of player who would operate on more than one cylinder, combining the skills of manipulation and power. Nowadays we speak respectfully of "30–30" men, players who have hit 30 home runs and stolen 30 bases in a single season. But this is a very recent phenomenon. Before Robinson's debut, no player in the history of the white major leagues had ever accumulated more than six "12–12" seasons— that is, seasons in which he hit at least 12 home runs and stole at least 12 bases—in an entire career. Robinson broke that record by accomplishing this feat in each of his first seven years in the league. He demonstrated that power and speed were not mutually exclusive, and his example set the tone for the Dodgers. His double-play partner, Pee Wee Reese, had never stolen more than 15 bases in a season before Robinson's arrival. In 1948, the year he turned thirty, Reese stole 25. He continued at that rate through age thirty-five while compiling double-digit home run totals almost every year during that span. Called up to the Dodgers a few months after Jackie, Duke Snider posted four 12–12 seasons in his first five full years in the big leagues, a feat no player had accomplished before Robinson. In short, Brooklyn was discovering what Negro Leaguers had always known, that power and speed were best regarded as complementary rather than contradictory. And the Dodgers prospered, finishing either first or second in the National League in every one of Robinson's ten seasons with them.

The signing of Jackie Robinson and the death of Judge Landis began the long, slow decline of the power game as the unrivaled master of Major League Baseball. The new commissioner, Happy Chandler, and his successors would never successfully claim the far-reaching powers exercised by Judge Landis. On the field, Robinson would soon be followed by a host of other former Negro Leaguers, many of them also power-speed men like Minnie Minoso and Sam Jethroe. Soon to follow were young men, black and white, who would combine the skill and manipulative strategies of the deadball era with the natural grace and power of the Ruthian age: Willie Mays, Henry Aaron, Mickey Mantle, Al Kaline, to name a few. Fittingly, Durocher would come to love the youthful Mays as a son, just as Miller Huggins had loved Durocher a quarter-century earlier.

Slowly, slowly, the old biases had been chipped away. No longer were the taboos against blackness and its symbolic compatriots as strong as they had been a generation earlier. Black and white players were now permitted to join forces on the baseball field. The strategies of power and manipulation would eventually follow suit. Now that the biases of the previous generation were being reconsidered, it was also becoming possible to think of these strategies as complementary rather than exclusionary. This trend has continued ever since, as attested by various phenomena: the breaking of stolen base records by the likes of Maury Wills, Lou Brock, and Rickey Henderson; the shattering of home run records by Henry Aaron, Roger Maris, Mark McGwire, and Barry Bonds; and the surfeit of players who have accumulated both home runs and stolen bases in record numbers, led by Bonds who became the first major leaguer to hit 500 homers and steal 500 bases in his career.

In 1945 Major League Baseball took its first steps toward racial integration since the nineteenth century. Those steps signaled the demise of the most drastic effects of the cleaning up of baseball in 1920. The results of those changes would not bear fruit for yet another generation, but the signing of Jackie Robinson sewed the seeds. Once again, just as twenty-five years earlier, one era was fading away and another was about to begin.

WORKS CITED

Allen, Lee. *100 Years of Baseball: The Intimate and Dramatic Story of Baseball from the Game's Beginnings Up to the Present Day*. New York: Bartholomew House, 1950.
Barber, Red. *1947, When All Hell Broke Loose in Baseball*. New York: Doubleday, 1982.
Cobb, Ty, with Al Stump. *My Life in Baseball: The True Record*. New York: Doubleday, 1961.
Durocher, Leo, with Ed Linn. *Nice Guys Finish Last*. New York: Simon and Schuster, 1975.
Foster, John B., ed. *Spalding Official Base Ball Guide for 1923*. New York: American Sports Publishing, 1923.
Halberstam, David. *Summer of '49*. New York: William Morrow, 1989.
Holway, John B. *Black Diamonds: Life in the Negro Leagues from the Men Who Lived It*. Westport, CT: Meckler, 1989.
_____. *Voices from the Great Black Baseball Leagues*. New York: Dodd Mead, 1975.
James, Bill. *The Bill James Baseball Abstract 1983*. New York: Ballantine, 1983.
_____. *The Bill James Historical Baseball Abstract 1985*. New York: Villard, 1985.
Richter, Francis C., ed. *Reach Official American League Base Ball Guide for 1914*. Philadelphia: A. J. Reach, 1914.
Ritter, Lawrence S. *The Glory of Their Times: The Story of the Early Days of Baseball Told by the Men Who Played It*. New York: Macmillan, 1966.
Seymour, Harold. *Baseball: The Golden Age*. New York: Oxford UP, 1971.
Sowell, Mike. *The Pitch That Killed*. New York: Macmillan, 1989.

15

Lessons to Be Learned from *Only the Ball Was White*: Similarities Between the Negro Leagues and African-Americans in Baseball Today

DAVID C. OGDEN

More than forty years have passed since the remaining four teams of the Negro American League played their last season. That season, 1960, heralded the end of that league, and by the late 1960s there were few traces of the once thriving business of black professional baseball. In the decades that followed, black involvement in Major League Baseball has had its share of ebbs and tides. Today, that involvement seems to be at one of its lowest ebbs. According to some scholars, basketball "has become the preeminent American sport," particularly for African-Americans (Boyd and Shropshire 10) while baseball has been relegated to the periphery of black culture. The number of African-American youth playing baseball at a competitive level seems to bear this out. That number is significantly low, compared to the overall percentage of black youth in the overall population (Ogden, "Youth Select" 323).

During the first half of the twentieth century, however, black culture fully embraced baseball. Denied a place in Major League Baseball, African-Americans created their own cultural framework for the game. During those early decades, "an entire subculture doted" on black teams in such cities as Chicago and Philadelphia, and in smaller and rural communities with concentrations of blacks (Ribowsky xv). Baseball served as a hub for social activity in black communities. Former Kansas City Monarchs' Manager Buck O'Neil recalls church services being rescheduled to accommodate "blackball" patrons when his team was playing at home: "They started church at ten o'clock, so they could get out an hour earlier and come to the ballgame," said O'Neil. "They were proud, very proud [of the Monarchs]. It was the era of dress-up. If you look at the old pictures, you see the men have on ties, hats, everybody wore hats then. The ladies had on fine dresses" (Ward and Burns 227).

Negro League players became celebrities in their respective communities. In 1942 Negro American League games drew an estimated two million spectators and 51,000 attended the annual East-West Game, the Negro Leagues' equivalent of the All-Star Game (Rader 145). Black baseball, noted Ribowsky, "was perhaps the first national black business, arising at a time when even local black business was a long shot at best to succeed" (xiii).

But individual teams and leagues struggled to survive. In *Only the Ball Was White*, Robert Peterson points out several reasons for the instability and tenuousness of the Negro League and its teams (80, 126). Chief among those were 1) the lack of finances to sustain the leagues, 2) the lack of leadership and support in managing league operations, and 3) the lack of instruction for players. As popular as baseball was among blacks before 1950, the black version of the professional game never achieved the footing to establish itself as a permanent fixture in American culture, certainly not like its white counterpart. Such instability has grown into a gulf between baseball and African-Americans.

Research indicates that baseball no longer evokes a sense of cultural ownership or community for African-Americans (Ogden, "African-Americans" 206). African-American youth are not playing baseball in numbers proportionate to their overall population. Surveys of 130 youth traveling, or "select," teams from twelve Midwestern states during the summers of 2000 and 2001 show that less than two percent of the almost 1,400 players on those teams were African American. In contrast, more than thirteen percent of the youths (under age eighteen) in the cities where the select teams are based are African-American.

Select baseball differs from other forms of youth baseball in that players compete for roster positions via tryouts or are recruited from all-star teams of recreational leagues. Recreational leagues, on the other hand, usually take any and all players, regardless of skill levels. I interviewed more than sixty select team coaches and officials from ten Midwestern states between 1999 and 2001. In their recorded discussions, segments of which are transcribed in this paper, the coaches and officials cited numerous reasons why few black players are found on select teams. Some of those reasons echo the problems of the Negro Leagues cited by Peterson.

Parallels Between the Negro Leagues and Black Youth Involvement Today

Black leagues and teams of pre–1950 America failed to flourish due to a lack of finances and figureheads. The near absence of African-American players on Midwest youth select teams can be attributed to similar reasons, according to the youth baseball coaches and officials interviewed. Peterson's explanations for the constant faltering of the Negro Leagues (i.e. lack of finances, leadership and instruction) should be considered within the context of the plight of African-Americans during the first several decades of the twentieth century and the social barriers they faced. But those reasons still parallel and share common themes with some of the explanations most frequently given by the coaches and officials today for the low numbers of Africans-Americans on their and their opponents' teams.

Lack of Finances: Peterson said the Negro Leagues and the majority of its teams were "consistently underfinanced" (80). Many teams, lacking a permanent home field and thus a stable local audience, were forced to barnstorm. Teams survived day-by-day, with their paychecks depending on the draw at the gate in the particular town where they were playing. According to Ribowsky, teams "could vaporize at a moment's notice," leaving the players to seek other employment or an opening on another team's roster (52).

While young black players in the Midwest aren't necessarily cut adrift, the majority play in recreational leagues where the competition and funding are limited, compared to select teams of the same age. Arnold Snell has umpired in youth select leagues for five years and has been involved in the RBI (Reviving Baseball in the Inner Cities) program, a partnership of Major League Baseball and the Boys and Girls' Clubs to fund and sponsor baseball leagues for inner city and underprivileged youth. Even with the RBI funding, said Snell, inner city teams don't have the money that the primarily suburban-based select teams have.

Other officials and coaches echoed Snell's comments regarding the number of financial sponsors each select team usually has. Often, parents of select team players must contribute at least three to four hundred dollars for each player's registration, uniforms, and/or equipment, not to mention lodging and travel expenses during team road trips. In one Kansas City league in the RBI program, the registration fee was $25 and in an Omaha inner city YMCA league, the fee was $23 for members and $48 for non-members.

"I see these [select team] players swinging $250 or $300 bats," said Tim Latham, a youth league umpire for nineteen years and former high school coach. "The money's not there in the inner city. Money's so much of it." Hubert Moss, a youth baseball coach for thirteen years, noted that teams in his inner city Omaha youth league wouldn't be able to play for days after it rained because their league didn't have the funds to pay for such things as drying compound (Ogden, "African-Americans" 202). "Grass is overgrown on our field, and every time it rains, water stands for a long time," said Moss. "Those guys out west [in the suburbs] have money"(Ogden, "Youth Select Baseball" 328). Reflecting the fate of many black teams and leagues, Moss's team folded before its 2001 season ended, primarily due to lack of interest among the youth and lack of community support (Brunt 1-C).

Lack of Leadership: Moss is a good example among community leaders and supporters for inner city youth baseball, but the leadership ranks in most black communities are thin. The same was true in the early years of black baseball. When one of its earliest pioneers, Octavius Catto, was killed in 1871, there was no one to fill the void. Catto's Philadelphia team, the Pythians, folded, as did the amateur league in which it played (Ribowsky xv).

In the early decades of the twentieth century, Andrew "Rube" Foster helped to form and then dominated the Negro National League. In doing so, he wrested control of black professional baseball in the Midwest from white booking agent Nat Strong. When Foster was committed to a mental hospital during the last years of his life, "his beloved Negro National League skidded precipitously toward oblivion" (Peterson 114). Other black baseball leaders, such as Gus Greenlee, maintained their power through the backing of gamblers and numbers racketeers, a situation that prompted Branch Rickey to label the Negro Leagues as a front for illicit business practices (Rampersad 123).

The lack of leadership for black youth baseball may be traced to the few black role models baseball has. Many coaches and officials noted the need for such role models, both locally and nationally. Part of the reason for the scarcity of African-American role models simply may be the dwindling number of African-Americans at higher levels of the game. Among NCAA Division I level baseball players in 1999, three percent were African-American (Lapchick and Matthews 19). In Major League Baseball African-Americans accounted for thirteen percent of the 2001 rosters, a thirty-year low (although some of those players, such as Barry Bonds, Derek Jeter, and Ken Griffey, Jr. have gained high profiles). Only the National Hockey League ranks lower in men's team professional sports (Lapchick and Matthews 19).

Black role models, especially those playing at the college or professional levels, are important to increasing interest in baseball among youngsters, said Ivan Chambers, a director for the Butler-Gast YMCA in Omaha: "I'd like to get a group of black baseball players to come and speak to our kids. We need to take them to Golden Spikes' [Omaha's Triple-A affiliate for the Kansas City Royals] games or UNO [University of Nebraska at Omaha] games so they can see black players hit home runs or pitch." Snell said the prominent black role models are found in other sports: "When you flip on the TV and see a commercial, nine times out of ten it's going to be basketball, and nine times out of ten it's going to be black athletes."

Lack of Instruction: Teaching the fledgling Negro League players the fundamentals of the game was a luxury. As Peterson notes, "The Negro ballplayer learned as he played, because there was no other way. The big Negro teams rarely had coaches, and the manager was usually a player himself with little time to spend drilling young rookies on the fine points of baseball" (126). During his first year with the Kansas City Monarchs, Jackie Robinson learned that spring training "consisted of actually playing baseball games rather than getting prepared for the coming season" (Rampersad 116). Shortstop Bill Yancy, who played on numerous Negro League teams (including the Philadelphia Giants, the New York Black Yankees, and the Brooklyn Eagles), said spring training never began more than two weeks before the regular season. That left little or no time for working with young players (Peterson 126).

According to baseball coaches today, inexperience and a lack of teaching remains an obstacle for young African-American ball players. Of the sixty coaches and officials interviewed for this research, eight had coached or currently coach African-American players. Six of the eight said their black players had little if any experience before joining their teams. Seth Rowland had two African-American players on his Rock Island, Illinois team of twelve to fourteen-year-olds. One of the two had never played organized ball before the 2001 season, and the other had played Little League but received little instruction. "He's learning the game," Rowland said of the second player. "Defensively, he has a tough time, so it's tough to work him into the line-up. But we like to get him in for experience. It's unbelievable the talent [black players] have. I just wish we could work with it some more."

Of the fifty-two players on Scott Hodges' three high school teams in 2001, three were African-American, and only one of them had played select ball as a youth. Hodges is head baseball coach at Omaha's Central High School and coach of an Omaha select team for thirteen to fourteen-year-olds. Of the three African-American players on his high-school team, one had played youth select ball. Of the other two, "one kid didn't play any spring ball or select ball, and one kid is just a part-time player. He doesn't play in the summer, so his skills are lacking."

Mike Carnazzo, general manager of the Omaha Cats (a youth select team) and the Omaha Baseball Federation, relates a similar tale. In his twenty years of coaching youth baseball, he estimates that he has had "several dozen black players" on his teams. In most cases, those players had little or no experience before playing on his team. He recalls one of those youths who "couldn't catch a baseball" when he began playing on one of Carnazzo's teams. He became what Carnazzo described as "a superior player" and another select team lured him away.

But such success stories for young African-American players seem to be rare, according to the coaches. Most black youths play in recreational and RBI leagues. Patrick Pinkins umpires for select team tournaments and coaches an RBI team in Kansas City. He said the skill levels the select players bring to the diamond are a stark contrast to those of his RBI players:

> If we were to bring one of our [RBI] teams out here to play in one of these [select] tournaments, I feel that that would be a big mistake because we aren't as developed as the kids out here playing in tournaments. We have a lot of kids [in RBI] who are just now playing baseball at the age of twelve. These kids out here playing in the [select] tournaments have been playing since they were four or five years old.

The reason for black players' lack of experience most frequently given by the coaches was a lack of early instruction. Several coaches echoed Pinkins sentiments. Said Steve Mach, coach of a team for twelve to fourteen-year-olds, the St. Louis Cougars:

> A lot of inner city kids don't have ... the type of training that the kids in the suburbs have. I would say it's due to the lack of people wanting to teach the inner city kids how to play baseball.

We don't have as many coaches willing to show them how to play baseball." Although I see some wonderful coaches in the minority areas who are devoted to it, I don't think you see the overall numbers who are committed. I think you see one good coach for an entire team, and that's sad. In baseball, there are so many things to work on. We're blessed [the Cougars] with having four good people who are willing to give up their time and do all this.

Future Implications

Black baseball and the Negro Leagues were the result of blacks being denied the opportunity to play at the highest professional level. MLB's RBI program resulted from young blacks' lack of opportunity to play at the highest levels of competition (i.e. select baseball) for their age groups, or even in recreational leagues, for that matter. Former Detroit infielder John Young began the RBI program in 1989 after observing how few black youths in south-central Los Angeles played baseball and how few opportunities there were to do so. But comparing RBI teams and select teams invokes once again the relationship between pre–1950's Negro teams and Major League teams. Negro League star infielders Judy Johnson and Buck Leonard said the teams for which they played "were not of major league quality" and may have been "equal to that of Triple-A leagues, the highest minor leagues in organized baseball" (Peterson 81).

RBI coach Patrick Pinkins described a similar situation in that RBI players, many of whom are minorities, have not had the opportunity to develop the skill levels of their counterparts on the mostly white select teams. He is not the first to note such a disparity. Anthony Dickson, RBI director for the Boys and Girls' Clubs of Greater Kansas City, agreed that the teams from his RBI league couldn't compete with suburban select teams (Ogden, "Youth Select" 333). Part of the reason could relate to the number of playing opportunities the youngsters have. While RBI teams may play as many as twenty games in a season, select teams play from fifty to 150 games per season (Ogden, "Youth Select" 332). In short, said Robert Kitsh, coach of the St. Louis Barons select team, "Inner city kids don't get the exposure week in and week out that kids in suburbia do."

There remains the question of whether black youngsters aren't playing because of lack of opportunities or lack of interest, especially in light of the coaches' views. Some feel that disinterest, rather than lack of opportunities, is to blame for the dwindling number of blacks in baseball.

While the expense of playing select ball was cited by coaches and officials as one of the most frequent deterrents to African-American participation, some of those interviewed, such as Ivan Chambers, do not agree. He said fees for select youth basketball leagues can be as costly as those for select baseball, but African-American parents will "pay those fees. I've seen parents pay $200 or $300 for basketball. Those parents will buy those one-hundred-and-some-dollar basketball shoes. I think that a lot of the parents push the kids toward basketball rather than baseball." Former Minnesota Twins pitching ace and 20-game-winner James "Mudcat" Grant also doesn't think money is the issue:

> I think it's a lack of interest. African-American families are buying what their children like. We don't have enough children who like or want to play the game of baseball. I don't think they're motivated to play baseball anymore. Certainly they don't see us. They don't see ex–Major League ball players, or very seldom they do.... Kids emulate what they see, who they see, and so on. If we're not there, the people they see on TV the most and whom their parents watch the most is where the interest is going to be. We have a big viewing audience of basketball and football in African-American communities, but not baseball.

When did African-Americans' interest in baseball begin to decline? Some argue that it was when Major League Baseball began integrating in 1947 (Early 41). Ironically, blacks' fulfilled dream of integrating the Major Leagues spelled doom for the Negro Leagues, which finally folded in 1960, and baseball may have ceased to be a reason and nucleus for community in African-American culture. With 78% of NBA players and 67% of NFL players being African-American (Lapchick and Matthew 18), the focus on sports has seemingly shifted in African-American culture. Tracking that focus in the next years and decades is a ripe field for research, as is the rise and seeming fall of baseball in black culture and the historical relationship between African-Americans and what once was their national pastime.

WORKS CITED

Boyd, Todd, and Kenneth Shropshire. "Basketball Jones: A New World Order?" *Basketball Jones: America Above the Rim.* Ed. Todd Boyd and Kenneth Shropshire. New York: New York UP, 2000: 1–11.
Brunt, Cliff." Baseball Striking Out Among Black Youths." *Omaha World Herald* 29 July 2001, metro ed.:1-C, 9-C.
Early, Gerald. "Why Baseball *was* the Black National Pastime." *Basketball Jones:*

America Above the Rim. Ed. Todd Boyd and Kenneth Shropshire. New York: New York UP, 2000: 27–50.

Lapchick, Richard E., and Kevin Matthews. *2001 Racial and Gender Report Card.* Boston: Center for the Study of Sport in Society, Northeastern University, 2001.

Ogden, David C. "African-Americans and Pick-up Ball: The Loss of Diversity and Recreational Diversion in Midwestern Youth Baseball." *Nine: A Journal of Baseball History and Culture* 9.2 (2001): 200–207.

_____. "Youth Select Baseball in the Midwest." *The Cooperstown Symposium on Baseball and American Culture, 2001.* Ed. William Simons. Jefferson, NC: McFarland, 2002: 322–335.

Peterson, Robert. *Only the Ball Was White.* Englewood Cliffs, NJ: Prentice-Hall, 1970.

Rader, Benjamin G. *Baseball: A History of America's Game.* Urbana: U of Illinois P, 1994.

Rampersad, Arnold. *Jackie Robinson: A Biography.* New York: Knopf, 1997.

Ribowsky, Mark. *A Complete History of the Negro Leagues: 1884 to 1955.* New York: Birch Lane Press, 1995.

Ward, Geoffrey C., and Ken Burns. Baseball: An Illustrated History. New York: Knopf, 1994.

Coaches and Officials Cited: Omaha: Mike Carnazzo, Ivan Chambers, Hubert Moss; Kansas City, KS: Anthony Dickson, Tim Latham, Patrick Pinkins, Arnold Snell; Rock Island, IL: Seth Rowland; St. Louis: Robert Kitsh, Steve Mach; James "Mudcat" Grant, Minnesota Twins.

16

From "Game Winning Home Run" to "Walk-Off": Baseball Jargon and the Discourse of Modern American Life

WILLIAM A. LEHN

THE LINE UP: BATTER UP

The language of baseball has become entrenched in the discourse of modern American culture. Whether we call them baseball terms, jargon, lingo, clichés, vernacular, or slang, the bottom line is that words normally associated with the game have crossed over into the everyday vocabulary of American society, and they are going international as well. Since Abner Doubleday was credited with inventing the game played "between the lines" in 1839, the use of certain terms became synonymous with the language of baseball. Everyone is familiar with the most obvious terms such as "getting to first base" used in romance or "ballpark figure" used in business transactions. This study will explore the introduction and development of specific phrases and their relative ease of acceptance into mainstream sports lingo. For the purposes of this paper, I will limit my analysis to two terms, "walk-off home run" and "Tommy John Surgery." Additionally, I will investigate term borrowing and show how certain idioms of baseball foster a universality of language and understanding between different cultures who do not share the same language. Lastly, I will also explore the correlation and the reasons behind baseball jargon being sometimes supplanted by football terms in the American vernacular, a possible changing of the guard in the American sports landscape and its implications in a post-9/11 society.

Before any discussion of baseball terms can be made, a little discourse theory needs to be set down to provide a perspective on the terms. First of all, what is jargon and why is jargon used? William Lutz talks about the origin of jargon in his book *Doublespeak*. Doublespeak is "language that pretends to communicate but really doesn't" (1), but jargon is another form of doublespeak where specialized language is used by different discourse communities (groups of like-minded speakers) and serves an "important and useful function" (3). Jargon's function is "a kind of verbal shorthand that allows members of the group to communicate with each other clearly, efficiently, and quickly" (Lutz 3). To be a member of this group is to understand what is being said implicitly. Robert P. Watson, in his essay "Wittgenstein on Language: Toward a Theory (and the study) of Language in Organizations," offers insight into this contextual usage of jargon. Wittgenstein contends that a single word may have many meanings "but one must also know the context and meaning by which it is used" (364). Additionally, Watson offers that "Language is not simply a way to articulate the practices of an organization, but language shapes the thoughts of bureaucrats [and sports fans] and frames the nature of organizational and public issues" (366). This notion can be applied to the vernacular used in baseball, its meaning and its understanding. The purpose of jargon or vernacular is to convey meanings inside a discourse community and keep the context of the conversation apart from other groups, but sometimes, as in the case of baseball terms, jargon expands beyond the community, bringing terms "up to the plate" for speakers who are not members of the group where the terms originated.

GOING DEEP: "GAME WINNER" TO "WALK-OFF"

The initial focus of my paper addresses the use of the term "walk-off home run," now used ad nauseum in broadcasting of baseball games and being force fed to fans of baseball and in the mainstream of public discourse. According to the *New Dickson Baseball Dictionary*, Jeff Pearlman, in an article in *Sports Illustrated*, credited Dennis Eckersley with coining the term after he gave up the now legendary game ending homer to hobbled Los Angeles Dodger Kirk Gibson in the 1988 World Series opener.

While doing my own research during spring training, I met Roger Craig in Tiger Town a.k.a. Lakeland, Florida; he has been in baseball for over fifty years. He told me that until recently he never heard of that term in all his life. I then caught up with Paul Olden, WFLA announcer and the voice of the Tampa Bay Devil Rays in St. Pete, and he doesn't use the term in his broadcasts. He used to use it, but when it was put into "the baseball lexicon a couple of seasons ago ad nauseum," he went back to "game winning home run." After that, I had the opportunity in Winter Haven to interview Tom Hamilton, the radio voice for the Cleveland Indians since 1988. During our conversation, he told me that over the last five or six years the expression has become "much more popular" but did not know where it originated. "With the proliferation of ESPN, it spreads the word quicker than anything."

I also met Russ Schneider in the Cleveland Indians' pressroom; Russ is the author of ten books on the Tribe and was a sportswriter and columnist for *The Plain Dealer* in Cleveland for thirty-two years. In the course of our conversation, the term "walk-off home run" came up, and I asked him the origin. According to Schneider, Indians' slugger Al Rosen coined the term in 1953. He explained to me that "Al said that a walk-off home run is the greatest thrill you can have, while you are running around the bases, the other team is dejectedly walking off and everybody is waiting for you at home plate." This claim would put the origin of this term thirty-five years earlier than *The New Dickson Baseball Dictionary* did in attributing it to Eckersley in the 1988 Series. It would also precede the home run Bill Mazeroski hit off the New York Yankees' Ralph Terry in the bottom of the ninth to win game seven of the 1960 World Series; the first time a home run had ever ended a World Series and the last until Joe Carter did it again in 1993 off Mitch Williams to enable the Blue Jays to defeat the Philadelphia Phillies in six games.

From the subjects of my interviews, it is apparent that the media, especially ESPN broadcasters ignited the explosion of this term in the last couple of years. On the popular Internet search engine "Google Search," I came up with 1,880 hits of the term in quotes (to search for the exact phrase) and 56,000 without quotes. The term is relevant in discussions in every level of baseball from the majors down through the minors, collegiate, Pony, Babe Ruth, and even Little League. "Walk-off home run" is even being used in girl's softball game accounts as well; that's fair, Title IX is working effectively.

This term is now becoming common in discourse in America. Two different websites are selling pictures depicting Jim Thome and Derek Jeter after a walk-off homerun. Shaun Kinley's rendition of Thome, a limited edition lithograph drawn by the artist, retails for $725 autographed, and a photo of Jeter's walk-off homer off Byung-Hyun Kim in the 2001 World Series goes for $430 autographed, complete with a certificate of authenticity at sportsgifts.com. So not only is the public eating this phrase up, America is at its best because profit is involved. William Lutz discusses what happens when a word becomes a thing to provide an understanding of how certain terms in baseball transcend their original context and take on a new meaning that can sell merchandise. In *The New Doublespeak*, Lutz explains that terms can become a signal reaction. "A signal reaction is a reaction that occurs whether or not the conditions warrant ... when we identify the symbol with the thing for which it stands, when the word becomes the thing" (49–50). Terms like "walk-off home run" do just this and thus are appropriated for merchandising as is the case with the Jeter and Thome images. Indeed, in the case of Thome, given that the image is a drawing, we only know the home run he is depicted hitting is a "walk-off" because the artist and merchandiser designate it as such. It is unlikely that Thome looks any different hitting any other home run. Likewise, the Jeter photo must be identified by the language or the viewer would otherwise not know from the image itself the particular home run the Yankee shortstop is hitting.

Two other instances ratify "walk-off home run" as becoming very engrained in the psyche of America even beyond baseball; one has to do with terrorism and the other business. The terrorism reference was published in *The Hartford Courant* on September 8, 2002. In the article "When the Normal Cyclings of the Day Stopped. Forever," Colin McEnroe used the term to illustrate its suddenness and uneasy finality while describing the attack on the World Trade Center on September 11, 2001. He states that "The collapse of the World Trade Center was a walk-off home run, a screaming shot from home plate to hell. Nothing to be done. Just go home. The normal cyclings of the day ground to a sickening stop in midrotation." Here the term relates to how the attacks just made people stop whatever they were doing and walk away feeling not "quite right" inside. To relate the term to business, the Chicago White Sox recently decided to sell the naming rights to Comiskey Park to help finance its renovation, though it was built only in 1991. The park will now be known as U.S. Cellular Field. While this is the topic for another paper about how advertisers are constantly invading our lives, the story was published in *Crain's Chicago Business* on February 8, 2003. In an article entitled "No Grand Slam at the Ball Park," Jeremy Mullman and Steven R. Strahler contend that this deal "is more of a stand-up double than the walk-off home run it's been billed." While this article references an aspect of baseball, the use of the term here applies to the deal itself rather than any on the field event.

Both these references to "walk-off home run" illustrate John Austin's Speech Act Theory. The term becomes an illocutionary force when uttered. The force used in the Chicago story implies that the deal isn't all that it's cracked up to be, and with the terrorist attack the truth is in the metaphoric reference to the horribly stunning spectacle of the act. Both uses of the term "walk-off home run" strike a nerve and hit a home run when considered in light of Austin's requirements of felicity conditions. As Margaret Wetherell, Stephanie Taylor, and Simeon Yates note in their *Discourse Theory*, "they [felicity conditions] lock utterances directly into the psychological and social concerns" (44). The term walk-off home run used in these contexts moves the finality it denotes on the ballfield into political and economic areas deeply important in the social and political scheme of the world beyond sport.

Though this term has passed beyond baseball, like other such terms, it could become passé. Ken Silverstein, a radio personality for WKNR in Cleveland, Ohio puts it best: "we lived without it for so long, from the thirties up until the nineties ... the problem is that [an expression like this] becomes gobbled up by every broadcaster and writer in the country and gets overused. It's like I want to ban the word because everyone thinks they're so cute in using it" (interview). Felicity conditions or not, once a term drops out of the discourse of the community in which it originated, rarely does it maintain signifying power in others, but the uses of "walk-off home run" outside of baseball suggest that the term may be entering the larger discourse community of the general public.

CALL TO THE BULLPEN: TOMMY JOHN SURGERY

The term "Tommy John Surgery" refers to the surgery performed by Dr. Frank Jobe in 1974 on pitcher Tommy John, then of the Los Angeles Dodgers. His name became synonymous with the procedure, medically termed "elbow ligament replacement surgery," because he was the first player to have the surgery, and he successfully returned to win 164 more games. Since John's landmark operation, the surgery has been performed on hundreds of pitchers and is highly successful. According to Stan McNeal in an article on *SportingNews.com*, John had a one in a hundred chance of recovering, but today "because of refinements in the surgery and improvements in the rehabilitation process.... Doctors now place chances of complete recovery at 90 percent" (1).

Because of this unparalleled success, the term "Tommy John Surgery" became a synecdoche. While the definition varies between theorists, Richard Lanham, quoted in *Semiotics: The Basics*, by Daniel Chandler, explains it as "the substitution of part for whole, genus for species or vice versa" (65). Common examples of synecdoche are phrases such as "lend me your ears," "get your butt over here," or "I was stopped by the law." Further investigation reveals that the term is used by Major League Baseball as one reason why a player is on the disabled list. While every other player with an injury (groin, back, dislocated shoulder) has a medical term that denotes his injury, players who are on the DL for elbow ligament surgery are referred to as "Tommy John."

Watson offers that "Jargon is specialized language used by members of a profession or those in a select group or organization ... it is possible that it [the term being used] is utterly unknown by nonmembers" (369). As with other baseball terms, the term "Tommy John Surgery" has begun to be used outside of baseball as well as becoming a synecdoche within it. During my interviews during spring training, I posed the question to several people. Paul Olden said, "I think the term Tommy John Surgery should be in the dictionary because it is in such universal use in baseball." Tom Hamilton also talks about reconstructive elbow surgery as Tommy John Surgery in his broadcasts. He says the term is now "pretty self explanatory ... kind of like an appendectomy." Kris Benson, the Pittsburgh Pirates pitcher who had the procedure done in 2001, agrees. He says, "Unfortunately it's a common injury nowadays, and they're [the general public] pretty up on what it is." John Felke, a reporter for "ESPN On The Go" added, "It's indicative the way that sports has permeated our culture. Also very helpful, you can tell a relative baseball novice that he [a player] had Tommy John Surgery. They know it's something serious. It [the term] is part of the vernacular because it fits." Tommy John made his own reference to a synecdoche when he told people about his procedure in 1974. He says, "When they operated, I told them to put in a Koufax fastball. They did, but it was Mrs. Koufax's" (qtd. by Felke).

To further demonstrate the increased usage of this term, I once again performed a Google Search and came up with 4,390 references with the term in quotes, 52,300 with the term not in quotes. Aside from Lou Gehrig having amyotropic lateral sclerosis being named after him, no other player, current or former has a medical term synonymous with his name. Had Wayne Garland, whose career was cut short with shoulder problems, pitched as long or well as Tommy John did post-surgery, rotator cuff surgery might be known as Wayne Garland Surgery. I could bring up Steve Blass Disease, but it is not really a disease. The term is just a euphemism for a player who has lost the ability to throw strikes, and though it has found a place within baseball, especially among scouts, it has never entered the lexicon of the general public.

INTERNATIONAL OPERATIONS: HOME PLATE IS ALWAYS HOME PLATE, BUT HOME RUNS ARE NOT ALWAYS HOME RUNS

There are certain axioms in baseball which are not translatable but cross both cultural and language barriers. What are some of these terms and what do they say about the universality of the language of baseball? I recently had the luxury of interviewing a broadcaster who does the color commentary for the Ponce Lions in the Puerto Rican Winter League. In addition to his duties for Ponce, Pedro Lugo was also the Spanish color man for the twenty-two Montreal Expos' games played in Puerto Rico in 2003. He opened my eyes to some of the unique aspects of the language of baseball. During our conversation, he informed me that certain terms used in the Spanish broadcast remain in their English form. Aurelio Espinosa's work on the influence of English on New Mexican Spanish explains why: "As a rule, the English words adopted have no Spanish equivalent. In most cases the adoption of the English word has not been a case of fashion, luxury in speech, neglect of Spanish, or mere desire of imitating the language of the invaders, but an actual convenience and necessity" (qtd. in Smead 4). These certain words and phrases lose their luster and magic in the description of the game if they are translated, so they are borrowed from English and used in Spanish. Some examples are back-to-back homer, diving catch, squeeze play, foul ball, basket catch, steroids, in the gap, RBI, hit and run, closer, hot dog, clubhouse, bullpen, and home plate. Even Tommy John surgery is translated as *por cirujía de Tommy John* not *por cirujía del reemplazo de ligamento*.

Wittgenstein believes that "Words stand for things and are used in place of the actual phenomenon. Words also represent expressions and sensations. Words 'name' objects and have meaning" (362). If the denotation of a word is located in what it represents, then this borrowing of terms between different cultures and languages is nothing new, but the application of this rule to baseball discourse exposes the universality of the game's language.

However, when my conversation with Pedro Lugo came around to talking about home runs, something unique transpired as he mentioned terms that are not only unique to Spanish but also to specific locales. The calling of a homer is regionally specific in Puerto Rico. For the Ponce Lions, Lugo says "*se fue pa la calle*" or "it went to the street." For the Bayamon Cowboys, an announcer says "*cuadrangular*" (four corners) or the English "home run," and for the Carolina Giants the expression "*por encima de la verja*" or "went over the top" is used to signify a home run has been hit. Much of this has to do with the fact that although Puerto Rico is a small island, the radio broadcasts do not transmit over the mountainous terrain into other cities of this U.S. territory. Certain terms are used in geographically specific areas because the terrain prevents the slang from traveling via the airwaves thereby limiting the portability of the lingo. Peter Bjarkman, a noted authority on Latin American baseball, informed me that, like announcers in the U.S., those in Latin America like to put their own stamp on their broadcast so this may contribute to the variations. One can think of some similar terms in the U.S., such as Harry Carey's calls at Wrigley that described home runs as "on to Waveland Avenue," but here in the States because broadcasts are not often local, announcers tend to use similar terms such as "that's outta here" or "going, going, gone."

LAST LICKS: CHANGING OF THE GUARD, PERHAPS

The instances of baseball vernacular being spoken in everyday situations continue to increase. On a recent ESPN broadcast, the announcer Bill Raftery said that "They are going for the homerun" while explaining Texas Tech's attempt to beat St. John's in the semi-finals of the 2003 NIT Tourney. The inbounds pass with 2.9 seconds remaining in the game was never received, and the Johnnies beat the Red Raiders 64–63 to go to the finals. This is just another reminder that baseball invades and pervades the American consciousness on a daily basis, even entering into other sports discourse. Here the term is used instead of its football corallary— "the Hail Mary"—to denote a long desperation pass.

There is, however, a wave of change on the landscape of American discourse. Football terms are starting to supplant baseball expressions more and more in everyday language. When I asked Ken Silverstein about football replacing baseball in sports vernacular, he said it probably results from the popularity the NFL has achieved: "As a hunch, the NFL has been number one since the 80s." Some possible reasons are that teams are closer to equal in football. Each year most any team has a shot at winning the Super Bowl, while "with the revenue set up in baseball, only eight to ten teams have a realistic shot at winning the World Series." Sure there are anomalies in any given year, witness Anaheim in 2002, but when opening day starts the Yankees are usually the favorite to win the World Series; that's economics and that's possibly why baseball has fallen behind football in the public's heart.

One such instance of football's language replacing baseball's can be seen during the news coverage of the Iraq War. On April 2, 2003, a MSNBC broadcaster proclaimed that coalition forces were entering the "red zone" around Baghdad enroute to their final conflict with the Republican Guard. While it may seem that in this instance it was a no-brainer to use this football term depicting a team being in a high percentage scoring situation as a metaphor for a military position, it demonstrates football's popularity among the American public. On the other hand, football has many times used the language of war. Announcers speak of "a battle of division powers," "blitzes," and "long bombs," and the gridiron has often been likened to "a battlefield."

Post 9/11, the mood has significantly changed, and because football is often associated with war, its terms will more often surface in a culture concerned with war. Baseball terms tend to be less aggressively charged. It is hard to imagine a newscaster saying "U.S. troops are rounding third toward Baghdad." Tom Hamilton, the voice of the Cleveland Indians put it all in perspective during an interview on March 13, 2003, less than a week before the commencement of the U.S. led coalition effort to "liberate" the Iraqi people from the regime of Saddam Hussein. When asked about war references during play-by-play and color analysis of games, Hamilton argued that we have to be careful because "there is no correlation between war and a baseball game. There is no place for calling a game a war." It becomes very trivial who went three for four or pitched a shut out when people's lives are being lost over foreign policy.

GAME RECAP: POST GAME REPORT

Baseball is undoubtedly a slice of American life. The rudiments of the game and its language run deep into the psyche of American social discourse. This is evidenced by the persistence of terms such as Tommy John surgery and the plethora of English terms carried over as the game becomes increasingly international. The New York Yankees issued 150 media requests to the Japanese media in Spring Training this year with the appearance of Hideki Matsui. Say what you will from a purist perspective about the Yankees and George Steinbrenner ruining the game, he has the future of the game at the forefront of his plans. Yes, there are problems with revenue sharing, mass player movement, and possible collusion with mid-level players. Those problems will work themselves out; the MLBPA is far too powerful to let them go unresolved. From my perspective, baseball, at present, doesn't mind being second fiddle to football in the American sports eye because it is looking to expand beyond the U.S. for the future, and NFL Europe notwithstanding, baseball has a large headstart. This international thrust is evidenced by the Expos playing some games in Puerto Rico, past series being held in Mexico and Japan, and MLB's quiet attempts to organize a baseball version of the World Cup. There will be an international flavor to this game in the coming decades, but one thing will remain constant, English. The word borrowing will only continue, and English terms being spoken in international broadcasts will be more commonplace while cross pollination from other languages will bring new terms into English, both in baseball and public discourse as well.

WORKS CITED

Benson, Kris. Personal interview. 13 March 2003.
Bjarkman, Peter. Personal interview. 11 Apr. 2003.
Chandler, Daniel. *Semiotics: The Basics*. London: Routledge, 2002.
Craig, Roger. Personal interview. 10 March 2003.
Dickson, Paul. *The New Dickson Baseball Dictionary*. New York: Harcourt Brace: 1999.
Felke, John. Personal interview. 12 March 2003.
Hamilton, Tom. Personal interview. 14 March 2003.
Isaacs, Stan. "Tracking Down the Elusive "Walk-off Home Run." *The Columnists Home Page.* last updated 2001. 6 March 2003. <http://thecolumnists.com/isaacs/isaacs38.html>.
Lugo, Pedro. Personal interview. 10 March 2003.
Lutz, William. *Doublespeak*. New York: Harper & Row, 1989.
Lutz, William. *The New Doublespeak*.New York: Harper Collins 1996.
McEnroe, Colin. "When the Normal Cyclings of the Day Stopped. Forever." The Hartford Courant. September 8, 2002. 6 March 2003. http://www.ctnow.com/news/local/northeast/columnists/hccolin0908.artsep08col,0,4559013.column?coll=hc-columnists-northeast>.
McNeal, Stan. "Tommy John Surgery Giving Players Another Chance." *SportingNews.com*. 1 May 2002. http://www.sportingnews.com/voices/stanmcneal/20020501.html.

Mullman, Jeremy and Steven R. Strahler. "No Grand Slam at the Ball Park." *Crain's Chicago Business*. February 8, 2003. 6 March 2003. <http://www.chicagobusiness.com/cgi-bin/news.pl?id=7883>.

Olden, Paul. Personal interview. 12 March 2003.

Raftery, Bill. "St. John's vs. Texas Tech." ESPN 1 Apr. 2003.

Schneider, Russ. Personal interview. 14 March 2003.

Silverstein, Ken. Personal interview. 14 March 2003.

Smead, Robert. "English Loanwords in Chicano Spanish: Characterization and Rationale." *Bilingual Review* 23.2 (1998): 113–124.

Watson, Robert P. "Wittgenstein on Language: Toward a Theory (and the study) of Language in Organizations." *Journal of Management History* 3.4 (1997): 360–374.

Wetherell, Margaret, Stephanie Taylor, and Simeon J. Yates. *Discourse Theory and Practice*. Sage: London, 2001.

17

Nineteenth-Century and Black Baseball in Indianapolis

W.C. MADDEN

When did baseball first come to Indianapolis? While Union soldiers in Indianapolis may have played some ball games during the Civil War, no accounts of those games were ever recorded by the press. The first published accounts of organized baseball games in the capitol of Indiana came after the conflict in 1866. The Base Ball and Cricket Club of Indianapolis gathered for a picnic on August 11, according to an article in *Indianapolis Daily Journal*. A tin cup went to the poorest player on the team. Town ball was being played around the state as well, and two teams met at Camp Morton in Indianapolis in a "match" game for the state championship. A team from LaPorte beat the Westerns, an Indianapolis team, 49–21, in a marathon that spanned four hours and fifteen minutes. Underhand pitching was the rule back in those days, which accounted for some of the high scores and long games.

The following year, more and more baseball games were played in Indianapolis. The Star City Club of Lafayette and the Washington Nationals, one of the most famous amateur baseball clubs at the time, came to Indianapolis to take on two local clubs. The two teams battled in the second game of a July double-header at Camp Burnside. Some 5,000 cranks first watched the Actives of Indianapolis beat Lafayette, 54–31 in a six-inning affair. Then the Washington team beat the Western Club of Indianapolis, 106–21, in nine innings in the nightcap. Later that month, the first Negro baseball was played in Indianapolis. The Eagles, a team of African-American workers from the Bates House hotel, played the Mohawks, a team composed of barbers. Baseball had come to Indianapolis to stay.

Professional baseball first came to Indianapolis in 1869, when the undefeated Cincinnati Red Stockings, the first professionally paid team, came to town. They wore beards, short pants, and long red stockings. The undefeated professionals whipped the team of Indianapolis scrubs at a converted cornfield at the northeast corner of Delaware and South streets. The Red Stockings would win fifty-seven games and tie one in their trip around the country that year. The two teams met for a rematch the following year in Cincinnati, and Indianapolis gave the Reds the thumping of their life, but the final score of that game is unknown. The Indianapolis team was led by a battery made up of brothers: pitcher Aquilla and catcher Ben Jones.

The first professional team in Indy, formed in 1876, was called the Westerns. They played their games at a park located at Delaware and South streets. W.B. Pettit organized the team. The following year the nickname was changed to the Blues, the color of their uniforms, and the team won the pennant in the International Association by beating every Canadian team they played. Their only loss was to a team from Hartford, Connecticut. The team was built around a battery of pitcher Eddie Nolan and catcher Frank "Silver" Flint, both of St. Louis. The pitcher became known as "The Only Nolan," because he was the only pitcher on the team. By this time, pitchers were throwing overhand and The Only Nolan had a great curveball. Flint had the task of catching those curves with his bare hands as no mitts were used back then.

Nolan's curveball came under the scrutiny of Butler University Professor David Starr Jordan, who thought it was contrary to nature. Jordan thought an optical illusion was involved. Butler's faculty even supported Dr. Jordan's position. So the Indianapolis team challenged Dr. Jordan to a demonstration. The test was made at a fire station. Two poles were placed a few feet apart and across them was stretched a piece of sheer paper. About ten feet back were placed two other poles also plastered with paper. Nolan pitched a ball powdered with chalk through the two sheets of paper. The professor traced the route of the pitch and saw it was not a straight line. Dr. Jordan wouldn't have believed it if he hadn't seen it with his own eyes. On a side note, the university didn't begin a baseball program until 1901.

The following season, the Blues moved to the League Alliance, considered by some to be the first minor league. The Blues joined the National League in 1878 and played home games at South Street Park. Indianapolis opened the season on May 1 in Chicago and lost 5–4 before 2,500. The

Blues blew a 4–2 ninth-inning lead, and Nolan was tagged with the loss. The game reflected how the season would go for the Indianapolis nine. Besides Nolan and Flint, the other players on that team included Joe Quest at second, Orator Shaffer in rightfield, Russ McKelvy in center, Ned Williamson at third, Art Croft at first, Fred Warner at short, subs Candy Nelson and Jim Hallinan, and pitchers Jim McCormick and Tom Healey. The team ended next to last with a 24–36 record, and Nolan finished the season 13–22. John Clapp managed the team, which lost $5,000. Clapp had nothing left to pay players, so the team broke up.

Pro baseball didn't return to Indianapolis until 1883. The independent team compiled a stellar record of 95–47 against teams from the National League, American Association, and Northwest League. The following year, Dan O'Leary reorganized the Indianapolis Hoosiers and joined the American Association, considered a major league back then. The team played at Seventh Street Park and was managed by Jim Gifford and then Bill Watkins. The poor squad began the season losing its first three games to St. Louis and finished next to last with a 29–78 record. Pitcher Larry McKeon led the league in losses (41). In all, thirty-four players took part during the season. League officials decided to oust the Indianapolis franchise from the league after the season.

The Hoosiers began the 1885 season in the Western League with Bill Watkins at the helm. The team played its first game on April 18 and lost to Milwaukee at Washington Park. The Hoosiers bounced back from the poor start and won the first half of the season with a 13-2-1 record. The second half opened with the league taking on the court over Sunday baseball. Blue laws in Indianapolis forced the club to play out of town at Bruce Park located at College Avenue and Twentieth Street. When attendance dropped, several teams folded, but not in Indianapolis. A league meeting was held at the Indianapolis Grand Hotel to replace the departed teams, but financial considerations ended any speculation with replacements. The Western League disbanded. The final standings left the Hoosiers with a 27-4-1 record. J. W. Keenan hit three home runs to lead the league, while McKeon topped the league in wins with eleven. O'Leary sold his superstars to Cincinnati for $10,000, an extraordinary price back then. He sold the rest of the team to Detroit, including farm boy "Big Sam" Thompson, who would later make his way to the National Baseball Hall of Fame in 1974.

In 1887, John T. Brush purchased the St. Louis franchise of the National League and moved it to Indianapolis. He changed the name of the team from Maroons to Hoosiers. Brush was a real Scrooge and proposed an A-to-E grading system for players with salaries ranging from

$2,500 to $1,500. The team played at Athletic Park on the corner of Capitol Avenue and 16th Street, accessible by mule streetcar. Sunday games were played beyond city limits at Tinker Street Park and Bruce Park to dodge the city law that prohibited games on the Sabbath. The Hoosiers opened the season with a loss to the Detroit Wolverines on April 12. The team continued to perform dismally on the field with way too many errors. The poor team went through three managers that season—Watch Burnham, Fred Thomas and Horace Fogel—and ended up in last with a 37–89 record. On October 20, the Hoosiers held an exhibition game against the Cuban Giants, a team of black players. About a thousand fans braved the cutting winds to witness the game. The two teams met again the next day. The Hoosiers were leading 2–0 when the Cubans walked off the field in protest of the umpire, Tug Arundel, who was a catcher for Indianapolis. Egyptian Healy was the ace of the pitching staff and finished the season with a league leading twenty-nine losses against a dozen wins.

The team improved a little in 1888 with Harry Spence as manager, finishing next to last with a 50–85 mark. Henry Boyle won 15 games for the Hoosiers and lost 22. Indianapolis changed managers again in 1889 with Frank Bancroft, but he couldn't do much better and was replaced mid-season by Jack Glasscock, who finally pulled off a winning mark (34–32). Remarkably, the team had a pitcher with a winning record: Amos "The Hoosier Thunderbolt" Rusie went 12–10. He would later enjoy a great career with Brush's New York Giants and eventually be named to the Hall of Fame. But that year the Hoosiers ended up next to last.

The National Brotherhood of Baseball Players forced a reorganization of the National League in 1890, so Brush sold his players to the New York Nationals for $69,000, ending the franchise. Indianapolis would not host another major league team until the Federal League was formed.

After a couple years without a pro team, Indianapolis sponsored a team called the Rainmakers in 1892, in the reconstituted Western League. Their name was typical of the weather as rain washed out fourteen games, and the team began with eight losses before they posted a victory. Finishing last with a 15–39 record, this team as well as the league disbanded after the season. Two years later, the Western League was again back in operation thanks to Ban Johnson, a sports editor for the *Cincinnati Commercial-Gazette*. Brush again became the owner of the Hoosiers. He also owned the Cincinnati Reds of the National League, so in an early version of the farm system he began sending players to Indianapolis for more seasoning. The Hoosiers started off slowly but got hot when Brush sent some Major League players to Indianapolis, a move that irked league

President Johnson. In the long run, the move didn't help the Hoosiers much as they finished the season in sixth place with a 60–64 record.

The next season opened on May 1, and Indianapolis received lots of reinforcements from Cincinnati, particularly Bill Phillips and George Hogriever. Phillips finished the season with a 12–4 record, while Hogriever hit .402. Infielder Motz and outfielder Jack McCarthy led the league in hitting with .420 averages. Those performances helped the Hoosiers win the league championship with a 78–43 record. The league tried to prevent the "farming" of players, but Brush continued the habit, since it wasn't against any league rules.

The 1896 season saw the Hoosiers finish second to the Minneapolis Millers. After the regular season, the two teams met in a playoff series, and Minneapolis beat Indianapolis four games to two. The 1897 season began with a bang as the Hoosiers, who began calling themselves Indians for the first time, shut out the Grand Rapids Gold Bugs, 10–0. That game began a winning streak that lasted three more games. Indianapolis continued to dominate the league the remainder of the season and easily won the pennant with a 98–37 mark. A trio of Indianapolis pitchers dominated the league: Jot Goar, who was purchased from the Pittsburgh in the National League, led in ERA (1.30) on his way to a 28–8 record, Frank Foreman was 27–9, and Bill Phillips was 30–10. The Hoosiers faced Columbus in the postseason five-game series and won three games to two. Each player received a $75 bonus, which was quite a sum back in those days.

The 1898 season got off to an uncertain start when Watkins left to manage Pittsburgh and took a couple of key players with him. However, that didn't seem to matter much when Bob Allen took the Indianapolis helm, and the team started off the season with a 16–2 mark. The Hoosiers stayed at the top until August when they began to melt under the hot sun and finished second behind Kansas City. Phillips continued his winning ways with a 29–8 mark on the season. Some 90,000 fans saw the Hoosiers play that season in their Ohio Street park.

The Hoosiers were back up at the top of the hill the next season as well, but in a different way. After a sluggish start, Indianapolis began to get some momentum and won twelve straight in July. When the first-place Minneapolis Millers came to town late in the season, the Hoosiers won three of four to games to take charge. Although the team won a game less than the Millers, they had three less losses and won the pennant.

Johnson decided to rename the Western League the American League and turn it into a major league. The Indianapolis franchise joined the American League for 1900, but it was still considered a minor league at that point. Watkins was fired from Pittsburgh, so he bought the remaining Indianapolis stock and became its owner and manager. He decided to establish a new park on Washington Street near Rural. The team acquired some new players as well and got off to a fast start in first place until a series of injuries began to take their toll. The Hoosiers finished the season in third.

After the season, American League owners decided to reorganize and move more franchises into cities occupied by the National League to directly challenge it. Watkins decided to try and form the American Association to compete with the American League, but his attempts failed. Instead, he had to settle with joining the Western Association. He was able to keep some of those players under contract and reserve, but the rest of the players and the franchise were moved to Philadelphia to become the Athletics. Still, the Indianapolis team got off to a good start, but attendance was poor and Watkins soon had to let players go because he could no longer afford to pay them. He finally decided to sell the team to Matthews, Indiana. The poor team went from a 46–26 record to 56–78 and sixth place.

BLACK BASEBALL IN INDIANAPOLIS

Interest in baseball by the black population reached the professional level in July 1902 with the founding of the Colored Baseball League. It was short-lived, folding two months later. However, the Indianapolis Unions and the Indianapolis ABCs continued to play. The ABCs were so named from their affiliation with the American Brewing Company. In 1905, the ABCs played a double-header exhibition at Northwestern Baseball Park during the Great Emancipation Celebration, which celebrated the end of slavery. The following year, the ABCs played against the Nebraska Full Blooded Indians and won 9–8. The black team also played other local semi-professional teams named the Indianapolis Crescents and Indianapolis Reserves. Promotions, which are especially prevalent today in minor league baseball in Indianapolis, were held by the ABCs as well in 1911. A female pitcher tossed a few innings for Louisville in a game against the ABCs in Indianapolis. A boxing match preceded another contest.

The following year, the owner of the ABCs, Randolph Butler, sold the team to Thomas A. Bowser, a white Indianapolis bail bondsman. The black team manager, George Abrams, quit the team in protest and formed his own team, the X-ABCs, which he later renamed the Abrams Giants.

Abrams returned to the ABCs the following year, though. Another ownership change came to the ABCs in 1914 when Charles Isam Taylor bought half interest in the team. C.I., as he liked to be called, brought with him some talented players, including Dizzy Dismukes, George Brown, Morten "Morty" Clark, George Shively, and Bingo DeMoss. Taylor's brothers, James and Ben, also played for the team. He also signed a great local player, Oscar Charleston, a future Hall of Famer. All that talent led the ABCs to a disputed "Colored Championship Series" over the Chicago American Giants in 1916. During the war years, the team played some military opponents—the local Speedway Aviators and Camp Grant from Rockford, Illinois. Some team members were also called to the war themselves.

After the war, the ABCs joined the Negro National League when it was formed in 1920. Their first game was on May 2 and some 6,000 fans watched the ABCs beat the Chicago Giants. The team played well and finished second that season. The Indianapolis franchise dropped to fifth place the next season. Then Taylor passed away and left the team to his wife. The team rebounded to its best-ever season record in 1922 (46–33) to finish second again. In 1923, the ABCs caught fire at the beginning of the season and charged into first with an 11–1 record, but the success didn't last, and the Kansas City Monarchs won the league championship. Charleston, Frank Warfield, and Elvis Holland became known as the "Indianapolis Bunch." A mass exodus of players occurred in 1924, and the team fell out of the league. The ABCs returned for three more seasons before dropping out again due to lack of funds. It returned to the league again once more in 1931.

The Depression hit the Negro National League hard in the 1930s and it died out, but other Negro leagues continued, so the ABCs joined the Negro Southern League and finished with a 14–19 record in 1932. The following year, the Chicago American Giants moved to Indianapolis after they had problems finding a home field in the Windy City. The team continued to wear Chicago uniforms and played for a season in Indy before moving back to Chicago. That cavity was soon filled with a team called the Monarchs. Other semi-pro teams sprung up in the mid–1930s, including the Zulu Cannibal Giants, a barnstorming team whose players wore shirts and headdresses like the African tribe. The last time the ABCs suited up came in 1940 as a semi-pro team. Beer had become legal again in 1934, and some brewery teams started playing semi-pro ball and providing opponents for the ABCs. The Sterling Beers were led by former Chicago White Sox pitcher Reb Russell and managed by Clyde Hoffa. Later came the Gold Medal Brewery team. By 1939, several factories had teams, such as the Kingan Packers.

Several teams had very short lives in Indianapolis. The Indianapolis Athletics were born in 1937 as part of the Negro American League. The team played so poorly on the field that they didn't last a season. The Atlanta Black Crackers moved into Indianapolis and played as the ABCs for a short time in 1939. Then the Indianapolis Crawfords joined the league in 1940 when Oscar Charleston decided to move his Toledo team to his hometown. That move was brief, too. The Ethiopian Clowns adopted Indianapolis as their home city in 1944 when they joined the Negro American League. The team dropped its on-field antics and became serious about playing baseball. They adopted the name of Indianapolis-Cincinnati Clowns and recruited talented players, such as Willie "The Devil" Wells, who played in 1947. Wells would later find a spot in the Baseball Hall of Fame.

The Clowns won NAL pennants in 1950 and 1951. Then they won the league championship series over the Birmingham Black Barons in 1952. Hank Aaron played for the Clowns for two months early in the season, yet he never got to play a game in Indy as most Clowns' games were on the road. He soon signed with the Boston Braves and, as is well known, went on to be enshrined in the Hall of Fame after setting Major League Baseball's career home run record. In 1953, the Clowns signed the first woman to play in professional black baseball—Toni Stone. Although signed as a gate attraction, she played second base and hit a respectable .243. The following year, the Clowns signed up Mamie "Peanut" Johnson as a pitcher on the squad.

Oscar Charleston joined the Clowns in 1954 and managed it to the NAL title with a 43–22 mark. After the season, Charleston suffered a stroke and died in Philadelphia. Charleston was honored in 1998 when Indianapolis dedicated a park in his name. When the Society for American Baseball Research (SABR) began a chapter in Indianapolis in 2001, members decided to call themselves the Oscar Charleston Chapter.

With the disbanding of the Negro Leagues by 1960, the Indianapolis Clowns became the Harlem Globetrotters of baseball and went back to clowning around. Traveling the country, the Clowns played only about four games a year in Indianapolis at Bush Stadium. The team became integrated and played on and off until 1989. The Clowns were the last great barnstorming team, and their demise marked the end of an era.

VINTAGE BASEBALL IN INDIANAPOLIS

Nowadays, the old-time game is evoked by vintage baseball teams playing by nineteenth-century rules in and around Indianapolis: the Freetown Village Ball Team, Indianapolis Blues, and the White River Base Ball Team of Conner Prairie in nearby Fishers. Freetown Village, a living history museum, and the Indianapolis Blues play by the rules of 1870, while the White River team has adopted the rules of 1886. The big difference between the two eras is that pitching was still underhanded in the 1870s. By the 1880s, pitching was done overhand or sidearm. There were other more subtle differences, and teams decide before a game what rules to follow.

The White River club is a member of the Vintage Base Ball Association, a national association that formed in 1996. As an Association member, the White River nine is required to play six full games against other VBBA teams. The team played a dozen games in 2002 and was scheduled to play the Cincinnati Red Stockings, Ohio Buckeyes, Saxton's Band, Hobart, and other teams at a tournament in Detroit, Michigan in 2003. Several members of the club belong to SABR, so they study and research how the game was played way back when Indianapolis was among the several America cities where baseball emerged from its infancy to become a local and national pastime.

WORKS CONSULTED

DeBono, Paul. *The Indianapolis ABCs*. Jefferson, NC: McFarland, 1997.
Madden, W.C. *Baseball in Indianapolis*. Great Britain: Arcadia Publishing, 2003.

18

Interviewing a Local Legend: Preacher Roe and Ozark Culture

DAVE MALONE

Several hours from St. Louis, in southern Missouri, you will find that you are still in Cardinal baseball country. If you take Highway 63, some of it still two-lane blacktop, south out of Rolla, Missouri, you'll eventually land in the tiny burg of West Plains. Before long, you are likely to find yourself on one of the town's two main thoroughfares: Porter Waggoner Boulevard, named for the country singer, or Preacher Roe Boulevard, honoring baseball great Elwin Charles "Preacher" Roe.

Preacher Roe pitched for one of the greatest teams in baseball, the Brooklyn Dodgers of the late 1940s and early 1950s. Roe's teammates included Roy Campanella, Jackie Robinson, Duke Snider, Gil Hodges, and Pee Wee Reese. With that team in the field, Roe shut out the New York Yankees in the 1949 World Series, sending the bowed heads of Phil Rizzuto and Joe DiMaggio to the locker room. In 1951, Roe would go 22–3 and be honored by *The Sporting News* as the pitcher of the year. Preacher Roe spent seventeen years in pro ball and a successful eleven-year stint in the Majors with a record of 127–84.

One might expect that a player with such a successful career would coach professionally, whether as a manager or a pitching coach. In Roe's case, one might also think he would use that Southern drawl to call a few games in the booth for the Cardinals and consider a career as a professional broadcaster, as former Cardinal Dizzy Dean had done. Surely, Roe could have made a living in Brooklyn, New York, off of his glory days. But in 1954, after his career ended with the Brooklyn Dodgers, Roe did not stick around the Big Apple. Instead, he decided to return home to the Ozarks and its rolling hills. Preacher Roe and his wife Mozee would land in West Plains, Missouri, only about fifty miles as the crow flies, northeast of his hometown of Viola, Arkansas. Mozee Roe's family owned several supermarkets, so Roe and his wife decided to try their hand at the grocery business and ended up on the corner of Highway 63 and Broadway in West Plains for almost twenty years.

Preacher Roe was very aware of what Viola, Arkansas, and the Ozarks gave to him, and he would touch the community upon his return to the area. This would be appropriate, for the community that nurtured him while growing up proved to be the place that he would very richly give back to.

Preacher Roe's baseball career began with dirt roads, cow pastures, and lawn-chair grandstands. As a boy, Roe, with his brothers and friends, would walk eight miles from Viola, Arkansas, up to Moody, Missouri to play baseball on Saturdays. The area was not a hot bed for entertainment, so baseball was one way that a community got together. One summer, when Preacher was about ten years old, quite a few heated games were played between the Roes and a team of candidates for local sheriff. At that time, there were nine Democrats seeking the office. According to Roe, his family's team consisted of his father, the six Roe boys, his sister's husband, and their son—filling out the nine-member roster. They fielded teams on Saturdays, and according to Roe, "They'd play for blood." Roe was an outfielder while one of his older brothers pitched, and his father caught the game. They would play throughout the summer, wherever they could in various towns. They'd use small fields, often without a fence, constructing white markers for doubles and home runs as needed. Sometimes, the people of the town would erect small grandstands; otherwise cars and chairs would have to do for seating.

After a few summers of walking trips to Moody, Missouri, to play ball, Preacher Roe would turn into a decent player. When Roe was fifteen, he graduated to the men's team. This meant playing on Sundays, and Roe admits, "I got a pretty good jump on it." The young Roe's love for the game was not only shared by the communities surrounding his hometown of Viola, but fortunately for the boy, also by his father, Dr. Charles Roe. Although his father was a doctor, he had played two years of pro ball, a year at Memphis and then another at Pine Bluff in the Cotton States League (Kahn 294). His father's appreciation for the game would make for a family of ballplayers and *aficionados*, and the family tutelage would be invaluable to Roe.

In his youth, Preacher was probably not the most prominent candidate of the six boys for a pitching career. In March of 2003, I interviewed

Preacher Roe, and we talked about his younger brother, who was heavier and taller than he was. Despite this, their dad apparently had Preacher in mind for a pitcher, which I queried him about. Roe responded, "Well, in the first place, I was left-handed ... my brother younger than me was a little heavier, he was taller and he could throw hard but he was hot-tempered as hell. He never could have done any good, because he didn't know how to control it." His brother would go to college (so would Preacher but without completing a degree) and eventually go on to earn a doctorate in mathematics.

Preacher's patience would be for the game, not college. Commenting on his brother, Roe said, "He got the brains, and I guess I had a better curveball." Though Roe was rather self-effacing during our interview, he did offhandedly say of his older brothers, they "didn't have the ambition or idea that they could be a Major Leaguer." Nurturing from father and family, the couple of years playing ball at Harding College, and the summer and semi-pro games that Roe would play became the foundation that would eventually get him to the show. This sort of nurturing and support was probably all that was needed for someone who would show such consummate skill. Despite this encouragement, Roe actually said that he never thought to himself that he could definitely play Major League Baseball (Kahn 295).

Several factors would become important in the nurturing of Roe's talent, and one has to wonder, without these influences, if Roe would have remained just another good ole boy in the Ozarks. Perhaps, after college, he would have come home, taken a job, and pitched for the West Plains' city team. Maybe he would have thrown harder than anyone they'd seen. But without those years of coaching from his father and playing those Roe vs. Sheriff games, Roe might not have had a decent curve, or maybe his fast ball would have been slower and wilder than it would become when he was in college.

The support of Roe's parents and the love of the game in the Ozarks certainly precipitated and facilitated his achievement. Roe, who attended college at Harding in Searcy, Arkansas, said of the combination, "My college baseball was just the aftermath of my dad's help. My dad was an ex-professional player and a good teacher. I had good coaching in college, too" ("Preacher Roe" 295). Roe set a state record in a thirteen-inning game in 1937, where he threw 26 strikeouts. But he may not have been done; the game was called for darkness (Butler). At Harding, Roe averaged 18 strikeouts a game but did suffer from a lack of control, often walking as many as he struck out (Kahn 298).

Between his sophomore and junior years, he hooked up with a semi-pro league. An Arkansas Tech baseball coach had seen Roe pitch at Harding, and had him come out to Russellville, Arkansas, for a tournament. Roe actually got paid for pitching that summer, twenty dollars a week and room and board, which according to Roe, in the 1930s, was good money. In the semi-pro league, the forty-four game season was split into four series of eleven. The winner of one eleven-game series would play the winner of the next. In the middle of that season, Roe and the team's other pitcher, a right-hander, pitched all complete games and won all of them as well as the three-game playoff following. Their team's relievers never saw the mound. This performance would get some attention from the scouts for both pitchers.

In a 1984 interview with *The West Plains Gazette*, Roe claimed that his first real break came because of a Kansas City barber's bet and a semi-pro tournament. The barber, formerly of Viola, would brag about the boys he knew back home in Viola, including the talents of one certain pitcher. One team manager who was playing in the tournament said you bring the boy up, and "if he wins a game, I'll pay his way, and if he don't, you pay his way" (Hampton 10). Preacher went up to Kansas City, Kansas, but was unaware of the bet. Once at the park, the manager told his catcher to take Roe and the regular pitcher, Carter, and have them throw. It was decided that Roe would pitch, and pitch he did. According to Roe, in the tourney, he pitched 56 innings, gave up 4 hits, and struck out 54 batters. Roe won three games, and his team won the tournament. The scouts there paid close attention to Roe the following year at Harding.

Roe would eventually sign with the Cardinals in 1938 but would remain in the minors until finally getting a break with the Pittsburgh Pirates in 1944. After four years with the Pirates, Roe was traded to the Dodgers in 1948 with Billy Cox and Gene Mauch in exchange for Dixie Walker and two lesser-known players. When the Dodgers came to St. Louis, the support by the Ozark community for Preacher Roe was obvious. It was love. It was typical fashion for Roe to leave 150 or more tickets for fans for a game he played in St. Louis. These dedicated fans would make the four-hour trip from the Ozarks to Sportsman's Park. For a Preacher Roe night on September 19, 1952, hundreds of Ozarkers traveled up to see their local hero on the mound. That evening, Roe was given a brand-new, baby-blue Cadillac. Roe's college coach from Harding, M.E. "Pinky" Berryhill brought up the car, paid for by friends and fans from the Ozarks. Appreciative of the gift, Roe gave his 1949 Worlds Series uniform to Harding College (Hampton 15). That night, Roe pitched a shutout against the Cardinals. His last shutout would happen not only in front of dedicated Ozark fans but also his family, who were on hand that night.

Things weren't always so financially lucrative for Roe. Four hundred dollars a month was his starting pay in professional baseball. He says that in 1939, "That was pretty good money" (Hampton 11). Though it seemed decent pay for playing ball, it was not enough for him and his wife, Mozee, to live on. In the off-season, Roe would teach and coach basketball in Hardy, a small town in northern Arkansas, not far from either Viola or West Plains. The school would start his ninth-grade math class late, given that Roe could not arrive in September. He coached four basketball teams of boys and girls. Commenting on that experience, Roe said, "I had some of the greatest kids you could congregate yourself around." This kind of love for children may have affected his later decision to be a coach to a multitude of youngsters.

Roe's attention to children would begin in Brooklyn. In those days, the players parked their cars on the street just like the fans. Roe said walking out of Ebbets Field, the kids would cover him up. He'd tell them to line up by his car, and he'd sign autographs for an hour or more, while his wife read a magazine and sat inside the car with him. Coming back home to the Ozarks, Roe would be a mentor for young boys and girls, which is obvious in his comment: "To be a ballplayer was to be a hero ... I realized the responsibility and I always tried to meet that head-on.... I always treated everybody right, especially the kids" ("Preacher Roe" 297).

When Roe was teaching and coaching at Hardy, Arkansas, the state had very little money. For educators, this meant the trimmed eight-month school-year budget was slashed to five months. For the eight-month school year, the Hardy school ran on five month's money. To help, people in the community donated, and Roe was among them. During his last two years at Hardy, he gave his salary back to the school.

His benevolence would not stop here. While Roe was a Brooklyn Dodger, he would come back home to the Ozarks in the off season. At nearby Salem, Arkansas, the people in the town wanted to put up some lights for their baseball field, but they lacked the funds. Roe commented, "The bank wouldn't let them have the money, unless I would agree to pitch a game every year until it was paid for." While Roe is certainly philanthropic and at times self-effacing, he has some acumen and he's toughly humble. Fearful that he might end up with the remaining bill, Roe said, "I couldn't keep myself that open. As long as I'm able." He also made the stipulation that neither he nor any other players would be paid for their efforts. "We're going to pay for them lights," he said.

To raise the money, teams would be gathered up from the local communities. Roe would not be in charge; a man from a local team would be the one officially who got the teams together and chose the lineups. However, Roe would take four of five men down from West Plains. In the games played for the ballpark lights at Salem, Roe said they could make $4000 in one day. Curious to know who would dare bat against the Brooklyn Dodger pitcher, I asked him who would comprise these teams. After recounting a slew of names, he said, "Just local boys." He said they'd gather up local players from local towns, and "they played to get to play." He said, "If there was a crossroads store, they might have a boy down there who played somewhere, and he was the hero. We'd have him come in."

One such boy was Bill Virdon, whom Roe first saw at one of these Salem games. While Roe was pitching one afternoon, a ball had been hit hard off him deep into centerfield, where Virdon was playing. According to Roe, "I saw this person cruise after that ball." Roe asked a friend, John Cordell, "Who in the world is that?" He was told, "He's going to be our next major-leaguer from West Plains." Roe's response, "I knew when I saw that boy going after that ball, that he wasn't no farmer." How true this would be. Not long after, in 1955, Virdon would become the National League Rookie of the Year, as a St. Louis Cardinal. At these games in Salem, Arkansas, no one was paid, except for one year when a minor league team of professionals garnered wages. That day, the bank netted 170 dollars. Eventually, the lights were paid for, and the park was appropriately named Preacher Roe Park.

One evening, not long after Roe's retirement in 1954 and during his second year at the Preacher Roe Supermarket, a man and his son showed up at the Roes' front door. They visited for a while, and then another father and another boy were at the door. Eventually, Roe looked up to see thirteen fathers and seventeen boys. They voiced their desire for a baseball team (having checked with Roe's wife Mozee first). Mozee apparently was supportive, willing to give up Preacher at the store some so that he could travel to games. There was no Little League at that time in West Plains, and Roe ended up coaching various teams from the ages of 11–22 years old for the next ten years. At eighteen, the boys played American Legion. The closest team was one hundred miles away. Even then, Roe coached and met for practice when he could, though he couldn't always with family obligations. He said of his wife, "She had a lot of nerve for a country gal," in response to the fact that when he was a Brooklyn Dodger, she couldn't travel with the team and had to drive herself and their young children to road games. So one might imagine, running a store and helping boys play baseball may have seemed a comparatively small task.

Roe's influence on the community is obvious in many ways from his coaching basketball at the Hardy schools and returning his salary, to raising funds for the lights at Salem, to coaching baseball in West Plains when there was no Little League. Roe's family, Harding College, the betting barber, and the baseball loving communities surrounding Viola, Arkansas, and Moody, Missouri, all contributed to the making of Preacher Roe, but Roe's giving in return contributed to forming a legend of past, present, and future in this area of the Ozarks. At the age of eighty-eight, Roe is still involved in the community and sports. He now plays golf, having picked up the game about twelve years ago. I heard from a friend, who works at Southwest Missouri State–West Plains with me (Roe is very supportive of the college), that she saw him recently at a local event. And there he was, she said, a man of many years but large stature and a strong sense of self. She said, "I saw him sign baseball after baseball. And graciously."

WORKS CITED

Butler, Rick. "The Day Preacher Roe Fanned 26 in One Game." *Searcy Daily Citizen*. 22 Dec. 2000. 7 Feb. 2003 <http://www.rootsweb.com/~arwhite/wchs/TheDayPreacherRoe.htm>.
Kahn, Roger. *The Boys of Summer*. New York: Harper & Row, 1972.
Hampton, Terry. "Our Own Boy of Summer." *West Plains Gazette*. 26.2 (1984): 6+.
Roe, Preacher. Personal Interview. 20 March 2003.
Roe, Preacher. "Preacher Roe." *For Love of the Game*. Ed. Cynthia Wilber. New York: Morrow, 1992. 293–302.

19

Which Ball Is in Play? Lasting Images of Stan Musial at Wrigley Field

ROBERT E. MEYER

Most baseball fans in the Chicago area favor one of our city's two baseball teams with an ardor that borders on tribalism. I still recall arguments among the boys in my grade school over whether the Cubs or White Sox were the better team. The insistence of the Cub fans in favor of their heroes was testament to the intractability of youth, since, in those days, the 60s, as in these, the Cubs rarely finished above .500. The White Sox, by contrast, enjoyed, or perhaps endured, a series of first-division finishes, almost always behind the hated Yankees, a point that could be used by either side in a Cubs/Sox argument. I regarded these debates with the amused detachment of one who is above the fray. Mine was the voice of reason. Since my father regularly took me to games on both the north and the south side of town, I could state without fear of contradiction (one of my favorite phrases in my grade-school days) that there was much to be said in favor of both teams.

It was only recently that I came to understand the reason for my ambivalent baseball upbringing, my dual loyalties to the conflicting causes of the Cubs and the White Sox. My father had (secretly?) been a fan of the St. Louis Cardinals! I don't know why it took me so long to figure this out. When we went to White Sox games, the opponents varied—sometimes the Yankees, sometimes the Orioles, whoever happened to be in town on the weekend. But when we went to see the Cubs, (and we sometimes went to mid-week games in the summer, when I was not in school) the opponent was always the Cardinals. The explanation for this was simple, although my father never mentioned it, apparently preferring to hide his allegiance behind a mask of objectivity. Born and raised in Iowa, in the days when there was only one relatively permanent Major League Baseball team west of the Mississippi, he had been a lifelong St. Louis Cardinals fan. And so it happened that I was present for two memorable but decidedly minor events in baseball history, both of which involved the Cubs and Cardinals, and their great star, Stan Musial.

The first of these incidents coincided with my initiation to Major League Baseball, my first game as a fan in the stands at Wrigley Field, which would be memorable in itself, although I remember little of it for a variety of reasons. For one thing, in the summer of 1959 I was only five years old and therefore lacked the experience, the knowledge of the game, and the aesthetic sense necessary to appreciate fully the intricate patterns of movement and mind that become apparent to the true connoisseur of baseball. I also lacked the necessary height to see beyond the shoulders and backsides of the people in front of me, most of whom stood throughout the most interesting and puzzling part of this particular game.

By now, if you haven't already lost patience, you're probably wondering what happened on that fateful day that would make it so memorable. All right, here it is—drum roll—I was present for the famous "two-balls-in-play" incident. What follows is essentially my father's version of this event, seen vaguely through the fog of my own memory of him telling me what I saw, or tried to see, over 40 years ago.

With a count of three balls and something on Stan Musial, the Cubs' pitcher threw an inside pitch that flew past everyone, rolling to a stop near the brick wall that serves as a backstop at Wrigley Field. "Ball four," said the umpire, and Musial headed for first base. The Cubs' catcher, thinking the ball was actually a foul tip, argued with the umpire instead of retrieving the ball. This encouraged Musial to break for second. At this point, the umpire, apparently having forgotten about the first ball and, perhaps, feeling that this was the best way to end the confusion (boy, was he wrong!), handed a new ball (the infamous "second ball") to the Cubs' catcher, who, at that point, suddenly became aware of Musial's progress toward second. He must have hurried his throw, because it went wildly into the outfield, further encouraging Musial to advance to third. At this point, the dubious prospect of circling the bases without actually hitting the ball must have entered his mind. However, unbeknownst to Musial, the Cubs' third baseman, Alvin Dark (my father always mentioned his name, emphasizing his "heads-up play" as a model for a budding ballplayer like me), had hustled to the backstop and retrieved the original ball. Musial, distracted by the wild throw from the catcher, never saw Dark peg the first ball (are you following this?) to the Cubs shortstop, Ernie Banks, who was still positioned between second and third.

"As Musial ran past," my father would say, as he recited the story, "Banks slapped him on the rump with his glove hand." The irony of this moment clearly amused my old man. There was Musial, not the fastest runner on the field, hustling to third, only to be brought down by the cruel and unexpected reality of a second ball in play. The umpire called Musial out. What, one might wonder, was Musial's response to this obvious injustice, which was made all the more egregious by the fact that it was caused by an umpire's procedural error? "He didn't say a word," my father told me, in reverent awe, although how he could have known I don't know now and didn't question then. "He just made a left turn and went to the dugout."

If that is what Musial did, he must have passed the Cardinals' manager on his way out to argue the ruling. The lengthy ensuing rhubarb (again, my father's term) was captured, at least partly, by my father's 8mm home-movie camera, which he had fortuitously brought to the park that day, but which, less fortuitously, he had kept nestled in his lap during Musial's unique at-bat. Ironically, the footage my father did manage to capture, with little crowds of Cubs and Cardinals milling around the infield, the colors muted in the overcast light, may have served to dim my own recollections of the scene, eventually even replacing them. Many was the time I watched this footage in our darkened living room, with the smell of heated celluloid, and the flickering projections of the players, coaches and umpires trying to figure out what in the world had happened. Over the years, these artificial images must have supplanted any real ones that I may have had, and now, with the home movies long ago lost in a flooded basement, I have only the strange residue of memories once removed.

Oddly enough, it's the idea of Musial in the dugout, resigned to the fact that ours can be an unjust world, that sticks in my mind. I contrast it to the sight of George Brett storming out of the dugout after having a home run against the Yankees ruled invalid in the famous pine-tar incident. Like many notable moments in baseball history, especially in the age of videotape, it has been replayed over an over until it becomes a hackneyed but defining moment. I wonder if Brett's volcanic reaction to this perceived injustice contributed to the eventual ruling in that case in which his home run was later restored, and the game replayed from that point. Perhaps Musial should have argued more, or at least some. But then he wouldn't have been Musial. In any case, it didn't matter. The Cardinals won the game, and their protest was dropped. I also wonder what would have happened if my father had raised his movie camera a minute or two earlier. As far as I am aware, no film or videotape of the "two-balls-in-play" incident exists. If my father had been more "on the ball," my name might be as famous, at least in some circles, as that of Abraham Zapruder.

This brings me to a second memorable game at Wrigley Field, again involving Stan Musial and the Cardinals, and one for which I can call on my own distant though undiluted memories. The occasion was notable for a number of reasons, not the least of which is that it was the only time I can recall playing hooky from school with my father. In the fall of 1963 I was just beginning fourth grade, and school still held some excitement for me. I had not yet experienced the disillusionment that would come when I learned that my teacher—the fabled Miss Freese—was not the paragon of kindness that I had been led to expect by my older sister but a petty martinet who thought that good penmanship counted more than eloquent expression. (There, I have my revenge at last!). Nor had I undergone the trauma that was the nation's lot when President Kennedy was assassinated in November of that year, nor the more personal loss that would follow soon after. None of that had happened yet, and September was still a magical time of year, a time of limitless possibilities. I actually looked forward to going to school each day! Nevertheless, when, on a September evening, my father announced unexpectedly that the next day I would be permitted to miss school to go to a baseball game, I was ecstatic.

"It's Stan Musial's last game at Wrigley Field," my father said, his matter-of-fact tone belying the significance he attached to this event. He held Musial, arguably the greatest player in Cardinals' history, in the highest esteem. Musial who, to my father's way of thinking, embodied everything that was good in sports, and by extension, in humanity—dignity, ability and a sense of fair play—had announced his retirement and was now in the midst of what amounted to a farewell tour of National League ballparks. His stop at Wrigley Field would be one of the highlights of that tour, and we had two box-seat tickets.

I have always had a sense, upon emerging from the dank concrete ramps and walkways that form the underbelly of Wrigley Field into the dazzling greenery of the playing field itself that I have entered another world, one where beauty and grace of movement are honored, a place where we pause and pay homage. The exquisite foliage—the wide expanse of grass, the ivy on the walls—creates a stunning visual effect, almost too rich for the squinting eyes of the pilgrims who have come to worship at this verdant altar, after passing through the grays and browns of the urban landscape. As I look back on that day, I think it was a fitting place to pay tribute to "Stan the Man."

Our seats were behind the first-base dugout—the Cardinals' dugout—just a few rows back, and, due to my father's busy schedule, we arrived just as the game was about to start. Soon, Stan Musial himself emerged from the dugout and stood in the on-deck circle waiting for his turn at bat. He looked unmoved but not bored, old but not tired, (he was forty-two, my age as I write this, although he would soon be a grandfather, while my oldest is in the third grade). He was trying to treat this game as just another in what had, up until then, been an endless succession of games. In fact, when Musial retired, he held the National League records for most hits in a career (3600, later broken by Pete Rose) and consecutive games played in the national league (a respectable 917, but well below Lou Gehrig's then-record of 2,130). No one knew it at the time, of course, but Billy Williams, the Cubs' rookie who was standing in left field while Musial waited to bat, was destined to break the latter record in 1971. For that matter, no one knew that another of the outfielders on that Cub team—Lou Brock—also had a date with baseball history, as a World Series hero and all-time base-stealer, not for the Cubs, of course, but for the Cardinals!

When Musial came to bat, he received an enthusiastic ovation, a testament to his standing in the minds of Cub fans—barely outnumbering the Cardinal fans that day, among whom my father secretly counted himself—who recognized in him a greatness that transcended his ability to play the game. The excitement was palpable as Musial—a lifetime .340 hitter who had wrought havoc on Cub pitchers for over two decades—stepped up to the plate. All around me grown men, including my own father, were craning their necks, their attention riveted on this moment, trying to freeze it in their memories. They were hoping for something dramatic to happen. Perhaps it occurred to my father that in years to come he would tell the story of this day to the son I might some day have, his grandson. But life does not follow a script (baseball certainly doesn't) and instead of driving the ball off the ivy in right field, Musial hit a magnificent popup that seemed to my young eyes to go into temporary orbit before it returned to earth where it was easily gathered in by a Cubs' infielder. As the ball was being returned to the pitcher, Musial circled around Ernie Banks—a first baseman now—and quietly trotted to the dugout.

When the Cardinals took the field for the Cubs's turn to bat in the first inning, Musial and centerfielder Curt Flood warmed up by playing catch on the lush outfield grass. As the Cubs' leadoff batter stepped up to the plate, Musial tossed the warm-up ball a few rows up into the left-field bleachers as a memento of the occasion, a gesture that was enthusiastically appreciated by the fans out there. I watched as they scrambled for the ball, seeming to bobble it from one to another like some sacred object floating above their grasp. Eventually, the ball made its way down to the first row without anyone catching it and popped back onto the field, coming to rest a few feet away from where Musial stood. By this time, one or two pitches had been thrown to the Cub batter, and Musial had to stand ready to field his position. Between pitches, however, he walked over, picked the ball up, and threw it into the stands again—with the same result! A mass of groping arms stretched out to receive the gift, but in its uncoordinated efforts, succeeded only in rejecting it. The ball returned to the field a second time. (Looking back, I shudder to think what some of today's players would be inclined to do in such a situation, especially in the absence of the public relations training they apparently receive).

By this time I was growing anxious. A sensitive boy, I found the situation embarrassing and undignified. As the Wizard of Oz said, this was spoiling his exit. I looked to my father, whose knitted brow reflected a restrained sense of concern. For a third time, Musial offered the souvenir to the teeming throng. Again, it was returned to him. I squirmed in my seat.

If only I had been clever enough to remark that, once again, Musial was having to deal with two balls in play. Though that particular witticism escaped me, and the connection between these two disparate moments linking the great Stan Musial and the small Robert Meyer, only recently occurred to me, I do recall another sensation—one of awe. For it was at that moment, despite the embarrassment, despite the strange feeling of guilt by association—what must he think of us bumbling Chicagoans?—that I had the first rumblings of insight into the greater significance of baseball in my life. Musial tossing the ball into the stands was like the minister at the wedding who, after the groom has dropped the ring, calmly goes on with the ceremony, sanctifying the moment beyond the unruly mob's ability to sully it. The thing will be done, before God and these witnesses. We are forgiven. The community gathers for this event, validating and defining itself at the crucial moment.

Finally, on the umpteenth attempt, someone managed to grab the ball and hold it. You could not buy such a treasure, although nowadays people think they can. The passing of money would defile it, removing the spiritual value with which it was imbued by Stan the Man's touch. A general but subdued sigh of satisfaction was heard from all around the park. I was not alone; others had noticed this bizarre comedy and were relieved to see it end satisfactorily. I remember little else about the game, other than a Cub loss, partly as result of Curt Flood's home run late in the game. As for Musial, he was pulled after the third inning, confirming the occasion as the token appearance of an elder statesman.

The next year—1964—was my first in little league. I played for a team sponsored by the local bowling alley, sporting red caps and hose, vaguely reminiscent of the Redbirds. When the coach handed out the uniforms, I was given number six, Stan Musial's number. This seemingly chance occurrence must have given my father no small measure of delight. Seeing me take my position—like Stan the Man, I was a left-fielder most of that year—with a red number six on my back, he must have indulged in the hopeful delusion that I was a Musial-in-the-making. Never mind that I batted right-handed and that my swing was so slow that a strikeout after a foul ball down the first-base line was considered a good at-bat.

For some reason—perhaps having to do with my father's work schedule, perhaps due to an illness about which the rest of my family remained unaware—he and I did not attend any major league games in 1964. In fact, Stan Musial's last game at Wrigley Field as a player was also my father's last game there as a spectator. He kept the news of his failing health from my mother, my sisters, and me as long as he could, in keeping with his generally stoic attitude toward life. From the couch in our living room, he watched the 1964 World Series—won in seven games by his beloved Cardinals—with former Cub Lou Brock playing left field and running wild on the bases. He offered clues neither to his devotion to the Cardinals nor the severity of his disease. It is only now that I understand my father well enough to take comfort knowing that, when my father died of cancer in 1965, at the age of thirty-five, the Cardinals were the reigning champions of Major League Baseball.

I remember reading an interview with Stan Musial in which the reporter asked if he was disappointed about missing out on the Cardinals' great season. The reporter wondered if Musial had retired one year too early. With typical humility, Musial said that if he had still been on the team there wouldn't have been any championship for the Cardinals because Lou Brock wouldn't have been there. And so I'm left to ponder the meaning of this strange coincidence: the first time and the last time I saw Stan Musial in action, he had to deal with two balls in play. On both occasions, he refused, by virtue of a degree of dignity that was rare even then but seems almost unknown today, to be diminished by circumstances.

Although I've never seen it in person, I understand that a bronze statue of Stan Musial stands outside Busch Stadium in St. Louis. To the millions of baseball fans who come to watch the Cardinals each year—some of whom may have witnessed his prowess in person—this colossus must imbue Musial with almost god-like eminence. For myself, I remember Musial as a good sport, a man who could rise above the little indignities that sports—and life—always seem to send our way. And in case anyone wonders, I'm still a Cubs fan *and* a Sox fan with just a little Cardinal red in my blood. I can live with that.

Contributors

Andrew Anderson teaches at Ithaca College in upstate New York, where he is developing a new professional/technical writing concentration for writing majors. His work centers on integrating American studies and cultural studies courses with this program. He once got Eddie Murray's autograph while in the lobby of a hotel at a writing teachers' convention and Carlton Fisk's while at a rock concert.

Matthew C. Brennan is Professor of English at Indiana State University, where he teaches courses in Romanticism and poetry writing. He has published two critical studies—*Wordsworth, Turner, and Romantic Landscape* and *The Gothic Psyche*—and three small-press volumes of poetry. His essay and poems have appeared in various literary journals as well as in the baseball journals *Nine* and *Elysian Fields Quarterly*.

Peter Carino is Professor of English at Indiana State University, where he teaches a variety of courses, including one on baseball literature. He has been coordinator or co-coordinator of the Indiana State Conference on Baseball in Literature and Culture since its inception in 1995. In addition to two writing textbooks, he has published essays on composition pedagogy, writing centers, American literature, and baseball literature.

Andrew Hazucha is Associate Professor of English at Carson-Newman College, where he teaches eighteenth- and nineteenth-century British literature. When not lecturing on Wordsworth and ecocriticism, he coaches and plays shortstop for the faculty men's intramural softball team, which recently won the IM season championship game against a team comprised of students twenty years his junior.

Contributors

Scott Jensen is Associate Professor of Speech Communication Studies at Webster University. He recently taught his first baseball course, the Rhetoric of America's Pastime. Ever the optimist, he continues to dream of a Chicago Cub world championship in his lifetime and hopes that baseball will always grace the Jensen household as he and his wife, Gina, raise their own t-ballers and Little Leaguers.

Ronald Kates is Assistant Professor of English at Middle Tennessee State University. In addition to teaching freshman writing, Renaissance drama, and a variety of interdisciplinary writing classes, he regularly teaches a sports in literature course. He is a long-suffering Cubs fan.

William A. Lehn is a Master's degree candidate at Youngstown State University, where he teaches writing while he explores his love of sport under the guise of seeking higher education. He hopes to pursue a doctorate in American Studies with an emphasis on baseball literature and linguistics. As he watches his beloved Mets sink further into the abyss, he tries to recall the chant of his favorite lefty reliever, "You Gotta Believe!"

W.C. Madden is the author of ten books, most of which treat baseball topics. Much of his work covers aspects of the game in Indiana, including a book on Indianapolis Bush Stadium. He has also written extensively about women's professional baseball, and his interest in automotive history led him to write *Haynes-Apperson and America's First Practical Automobile*. He is also the owner of Madden Publishing.

Dave Malone directs the writing center and teaches composition and film courses at Southwest Missouri State University–West Plains. He has published three books of poetry and is currently writing screenplays, one about baseball. Though a Kansas City Royals fan, he is in the early stages of researching a book on the Brooklyn Dodger pitcher Preacher Rowe, the subject of his essay in this collection.

Robert E. Meyer is Associate Professor of English at Barat College of DePaul University. His varied teaching includes courses in composition, film, drama, and the history of the English language. An ever hopeful champion of the underdog, he coaches his son's Little League team, and he eagerly awaits the next appearance of either the Cubs or White Sox in the World Series, with admittedly dim prospects for success.

David C. Ogden is Assistant Professor of Communications at the University of Nebraska–Omaha. He has taught at UNO since 2001 and prior to this appointment was Assistant Professor at Wayne State College in Nebraska. His research focuses on cultural trends in baseball, specifically the history of the relationship between African Americans and baseball.

Jeffrey Powers-Beck teaches various courses in the English Department at East Tennessee State University, where he is an Associate Professor. His research interests include baseball literature and the role of Native Americans in baseball.

Frank D. Rashid is Professor of English and Chair of the English and Modern Languages Department at Detroit's Marygrove College. He is also a founding member of the Tiger Stadium Fan Club, which fought unsuccessfully to prevent stadium subsidies and to preserve Tiger Stadium as the home of the Detroit Tigers.

Ron Rembert teaches in the Religion/Philosophy Department and sometimes offers a course in Baseball and American Culture through the History Department at Wilmington College. Growing up in Texas, he rooted for the St. Louis Cardinals until his favorite boyhood team, the Houston Colt .45s brought Major League Baseball to his hometown.

Joseph Schuster chairs the Department of Communications and Journalism at Webster University in St. Louis. He has published articles about baseball in *Sport* magazine, the Cardinals' *Game Day* magazine, and elsewhere, and his fiction has appeared in several journals, including the *Kenyon Review*. One Sunday at a Cardinals' game, his son said, "I wish this game would go 100 innings; then we'd never have to leave." To Joe Schuster, that sounds pretty close to heaven.

David Shiner teaches philosophy and has been a member of the faculty and administration at Shimer College in Illinois since 1976. A prolific writer on baseball topics, he has been invited to present his work at several baseball conferences and was the keynote speaker at the United Kingdom's annual SABR meeting in 2000. His book *Baseball's Greatest Players: The Saga Continues* was published in 2001.

Trey Strecker teaches English and sports studies at Ball State University, where he is an Assistant Professor, and serves on the advisory board for the interdepartmental major in sports studies. He plays 1886-vintage baseball with the White River Base Ball Club at Conner Prairie Museum in Indianapolis.

Joan M. Thomas is a freelance writer who lives and works in St. Louis. Her writings on the Cardinals and baseball in general have appeared in local St. Louis magazines and various SABR publications. A regular presenter at the ISU Conference, she also compiles and designs cookbooks. She is a staunch supporter of the St. Louis Cardinals.

Despite the objections of purists, **Warren Tormey** roots for his hometown Arizona Diamondbacks and regards their thrilling victory over the Yankees in the 2001 World Series as the culmination of his experience as a baseball fan. He teaches American literature, sports literature, and various writing courses at Middle Tennessee State University. He still sees occasional duty in rightfield for the school's undergraduate club team and looks forward to life with Kim, Bunny, Myron, Julius, and Thea.

Gerald C. Wood is Professor and Chair of the English Department at Carson-Newman College, where he has taught a variety of courses over the years. His research interests include the representation of baseball in mass media.

Toby Ziglar, an Atlanta Braves fan through the lean as well as the fat years, is an Assistant Professor in the Department of Religion at Carson-Newman College. He is a fanatical participant in a fantasy baseball league and the league's self-appointed Chaplain.

Index

Aaron, Hank 155, 184
Abrams, George 182
Abrams Giants 182
Acheson, Dean 50
Aethlon: The Journal of Sport Literature 115
AFL-CIO 64
Alexander, Grover Cleveland 21
Alger, Horatio 29
Algren, Nelson: *Chicago City on the Make* 3, 49–60, 74
All-American Girls Professional Baseball League 141–142
Allen, Bob 18
Allen, Lee 148, 156
Allen, Newt 153
All-Star Game 158
All-Story Magazine 86
American Association 179
American Communist Party 51
Angell, Roger 16
Anson, Cap 142–43
Archer, Dennis 103
Arundel, Tug 180
Asinof, Eliot: *Eight Men Out* 3, 61–62, 65, 71, 72, 74, 144, 145; *Man on Spikes* 61
Atlanta Black Crackers 184
Atlanta Braves 106, 111, 113, 126, 128–130
Attell, Abe 68–69
Austin, John 170
Austrian, Alfred 71

Babe Ruth League 168

Baker, Dusty 126
Baker, Ron 6
Ballparks: architecture 113; Astrodome 17; Bank One Ballpark 118; Busch Stadium 119; Bush Stadium (Indianapolis) 184; Comerica Park 95, 103, 118; Comiskey Park (old) 56–57, 61, 62, 119, 169; cookie cutters 17, 119; Dodger Stadium 17, 127; Fenway Park 35; financing and construction of 4; Fulton County Stadium 126; Jacobs Field 96; Kingdome 17; Metropolitan Stadium 45; Miller Park 118; Oriole Park at Camden Yards 96; preservation of 4; retro design 113; Sportsman's Park 189; Tiger Stadium 4, 93–104; Turner Field 126, 128; U.S. Cellular Field (New Comiskey Park) 56–57, 169; Wrigley Field 5, 52, 56–57, 119, 124–127, 131–134, 173, 194–199; Yankee Stadium 16
Baltimore Orioles 150, 193
Bancroft, Frank 180
Banks, Ernie 12, 134, 195, 197
Barber, Red 154
Barnett, Larry 1
Baseball (cf. Major League Baseball): as cultural institution 4; ethnicity and 19–27, 76–77, 98; fantasy baseball 107; fatherhood and 28–38; language of 166–175; literary subject matter of 3; as marker of time 111; Native Americans in 19–27; nine-

205

teenth-century 177–185; pace of 117; playing technique 146–156; religion and 4, 106–115; in small towns 85; status as national pastime 173–175; youth-select teams 157–164;
Baseball and Cricket Club of Indianapolis 177
The Baseball Encyclopedia 12
Basinger, Kim 38, 48
Basketball 15, 164
Bayamon Cowboys 173
Becker, Howard 77, 81, 82
Bellah, Robert 110, 115
Bellamy, Robert 130, 135
Benson, Kris 171, 175
Berryhill, M.E. "Pinky" 189
Bertolino, Terry 21, 27
Betzhold, Mike 101, 102, 104
Billman, John 2, 19–27; "Indians" 2, 19–27; "Sugar City" 24; *When We Were Wolves* 2, 19, 24, 27
Bingham, Hiram 50
Birmingham Black Barons 184
Bjarkman, Peter 173, 175
Black Sox scandal 3, 5, 49, 51–55, 60–74, 77, 138, 143–144, 147–48
Blass, Steve 172
Block, Marylaine 45, 47
Bloomer Girls 23
Bly, Robert 40, 47
Bonds, Barry 17, 117, 155, 161
Boston Braves 184
Boston Red Sox 6, 46, 109, 154
Bostwick, Kyle 140
Boswell, Thomas 16
Bowser, Thomas 182
Boyd, Todd 164
Boyle, Henry 180
Boys' and Girls' Clubs 159, 163
Brady, James 124–125
Brennan, Matt 2
Bressler, Rube 149
Brett, George 195
Brickhouse, Jack 134
Brignano, R.C. 84, 88
Brimley, Wilfred 38, 48
Brock, Lou 155, 197, 199
Brooklyn Dodgers 5, 149, 153–155, 186, 189–191
Brooklyn Eagles 161

Brown, George 183
Brown, Nat 61
Browne, Lois 141, 145
Browns Stadium (Cleveland) 96
Brunt, Cliff 164, 164
Brush, John 179, 180
Bull Durham 16, 120
Burnham, Watch 180
Burns, Bill 66, 69, 70
Burns, Ken 17, 115, 158
Burroughs, Sean 57
Bush, George W 55, 102
Bush, Rudolph 57, 59
Butler, Rick 188, 192

Cagan, Joanna 96, 105
Caldwell, John 132, 134
Campanella, Roy 186
Campbell, Joseph: *The Hero with a Thousand Faces* 29, 31, 38
Cannon, Raymond J. 74
Carey, Chip 4, 130–135
Carey, Harry 4, 124–135, 173
Carey, Skip 4, 126–134
Carillo, Mary 174, 176
Carlisle Indian School 22, 23
Carlton, Steve 10
Carnozzo, Mike 162, 165
Carolina Giants 173
Carroll, Jamey 140
Carter, Gary 16
Carter, Joe 16, 131, 133, 168
Casey, Ethan 101, 102, 104
"Casey at the Bat" 118
Cash, Norman 94
Castro, Fidel 17
Catto, Octavius 160
Cey, Ron 129
Chadwick, Harry 148
Chambers, Ivan 161, 164, 165
Chandler, Dan 171, 175
Chandler, Happy 155
Chandler, Joan 125, 134
Chapman, Ray 147, 150, 151
Charleston, Oscar 183
Chase, Hal 77
Cherokee All-Stars 20, 22
Chicago American Giants 183
Chicago Cubs 21, 30, 193–200; fans 3, 49, 56–58, 124–135, 193, 198, 200
Chicago Tribune 12, 13, 50, 126, 131, 135

Index

Chicago White Sox 52, 49–59, 60–74, 169, 183, 200; fans 3, 51, 53, 56–58, 137–138, 147–148, 193
Chidester, David 110, 114, 115
Cicotte, Eddie 52, 54, 64, 66–68, 70–72, 74, 148
Cincinnati Red Stockings 178
Cincinnati Redlegs (Reds) 23, 52, 180
Civil War, U.S. 177
Clapp, John 79
Clark, Morten "Morty" 183
Clemente, Roberto 9
Cleveland Indians 147, 151, 168, 174
Cleveland Plain Dealer 151, 168
Close, Glenn 38, 48
Cobb, Ty 15, 51, 85, 150, 153, 154, 155, 156
Cochrane, Mick 39–47
Collins, Robert: "Catch" 42, 47
Comiskey, Charles 13, 54–55, 56, 60, 61, 65, 66, 67–73, 143–144
Conrad, Joseph 146
Coover, Robert 85
Coren, Robert 57
Corso, Gregory 112; "Dream of a Baseball Star" 12, 21
Costner, Kevin 120
Cotton States League 187
Cottrell, Robert 52, 54, 59
Coveleski, Stanley 87–88
Cox, Billy 189
Cox, Bobby 126, 129
Craig, Roger 168, 175
Cravath, Gavvy 149
Crawford, Wahoo Sam 23
Croft, Art 179
Cronin, Joe 154
Cuban Giants 180
Curse of the Bambino 109

Dacey, Philip: "Mystery Baseball" 120
Dark, Alvin 194
Daubert, Jake 149
Davis, Robert 86
Davis, Robert H. 83, 87
Dean, Dizzy 130, 186
DeBono, Paul 183
DeMause, Neil 96, 105
DeMoss, Bingo 183
Dempsey, Jack 151
Detroit Lions 96

Detroit Tigers 93–105
Detroit Wolverines 180
Diaz, Laz 57
Dickson, Anthony 163, 165
Dickson, Paul 137, 140, 142, 145
Didrikson, Babe 22
Dillinger, John 51
DiMaggio, Dom 154
DiMaggio, Joe 16, 186
Dismukes, Dizzy 183
Doubleday, Abner 166
Drew, Bettina 50, 51, 59
Durkheim, Emile 111, 115
Durocher, Leo 151, 153–155
Duvall, Robert 38
Dyersville, IA 15

Early, Gerald 77, 82, 164
Eastman, Monk 69
Eckersley, Dennis 167, 168
Egyptian Clowns 184
Elia, Lee 124
Ellis, Dock 1
Elysian Fields Quarterly 95, 100, 105
Engler, John 97, 105
Erskine, Carl 1
Espinosa, Aurelio 172
ESPN 168, 171, 173
Evans, Christopher 107, 112, 113, 115

Faber, Irwin "Red" 137–138
Fear Strikes Out (film) 2, 42, 47
Federal League 65, 180
Felber, Bill 118, 122
Felke, John 171, 175
Felsch, Happy 52, 70, 148
Field of Dreams 2, 28, 29, 34–38, 39, 40, 42, 47
Figg, L.G. 23
Fisk, Carlton 112
Flint, Frank "Silver" 178, 179
Flood, Curt 197, 199
Fogel, Horace 180
For the Love of the Game 116, 120, 123
Ford, Henry II 101
Forman, Frank 181
Forsch, Bob 16
Fort, Rodney 96, 100, 102, 105
Foster, Andrew "Rube" 160
Foster, John 152, 156
Foxx, Jimmy 42

Franks, Herman 16
Freidman, James 125, 135
Fullerton, Hugh 65, 70, 77, 80

Gamboa, Tom 57
Gandil, Chick 52, 61, 64, 66–70
Garagiola, Joe 128
Gardiner, Judith 133, 134
Garland, Wayne 171–172
Geertz, Richard 111, 112, 115
Gehrig, Lou 171, 197
Giamatti, Bart 136–137, 140, 145
Gibson, Josh 152
Gibson, Kirk 167
Gifford, Barry 131, 35
Gifford, Jim 179
Gillette, Gary 118, 122
Glasscock, Jack 180
Gleason, Kid 71
Goar, Jot 181
Goldstein, Tom 95, 100, 105
Gomez, Lefty 163
Grand Rapids Gold Bugs 181
Grange, Red 151
Grant, Jim "Mudcat" 164
Gratz, Roberta Brandes 97, 105
Green, Guy Wilder 20, 22–27
Greenberg, Eric Rolfe: *The Celebrant* 3, 16, 76–82
Greenlee, Gus 160
Greenstein, Teddy 57, 59
Gregorich, Barbara 20, 23
Griffey, Ken, Jr. 161
Groh, Heine 62
Gund Arena 96
Guyette, Curt 95, 105

Halberstam, David 154, 156
Hall, Donald 39, 42, 43, 47; *Fathers Playing Catch with Sons* 39
Hall of Fame 5, 16, 136–38, 140–145, 179, 180, 184; Veterans Committee 138–140
Hallinan, Jim 179
Hamilton, Tom 168, 171, 174, 175
Hampton, Terry 189
Hancock, John Lee 38
Hano, Arnold 89
Harlem Globetrotters 184
Harris, Arne 127, 132
Harris, Mark 84; *The Southpaw* 84

Hartford Courant 169, 175
Hassey, Ron 126
Haugh, David 57, 59
Hawkins, Joel 21, 27
Healey, Tom "Egyptian" 179, 180
Henderson, Ricky 155
Herzog, William II 107, 112, 113, 115
Hinkley, John 124
Hirschberg, Al 48
Hirsley, Michael 57, 59
Hodges, Gil 186
Hodges, Scott 162
Hoffa, Clyde 183
Hogriever, George 181
Holiday 54
Holland, Elvis 183
Hollander, Russell 40, 46, 47
Holway, John 152, 156
Hornby, Richard 81, 82
Horvath, Brooke 47
House Committee on Un-American Activities 49
House of David 19, 21
Hrabosky, Al 1
Huggins, Miller 153
Huitt, Ralph 53, 58
Humphrey, Hubert 125
Hussein, Saddam 174

Ilitch, Mike 95
Indianapolis ABCs 5, 182, 183
Indianapolis Blues 178
Indianapolis Clowns 5, 183, 184
Indianapolis Daily Journal 177
Indianapolis Hoosiers 179, 180, 181
Indianapolis Rainmakers 180
Indianapolis Westerns 177, 178
Iraqi War 114, 174
Isaacs, Stan 175
IWW 64, 65; "Wobblies" 73

Jackson, Shoeless Joe 15, 17, 34–37, 51, 54, 62, 66, 73, 144, 148
James, Bill 137–38, 145, 150, 156
Japanese Baseball: Central League 114; Pacific League 114
Jeter, Derek 161, 168, 169
Jethroe, Sam 155
Jobe, Dr. Frank 170
John, Tommy 170, 171
Johnson, Ban 180, 181

Johnson, Ernie 128
Johnson, George 26
Johnson, Judy 163
Johnson, Mamie "Peanut" 184
Johnson, Walter 85
Johnstone, Ronald 108, 115
Jones, Acquila 178
Jones, Ben 178
Jones, Bobby 151
Jones, James Earl 18, 30
Jordan, David Starr 178
Jung, Carl 122

Kahn, Roger 188, 192
Kaline, Al 155
Kansas City Monarchs 108, 152, 158, 161, 183
Kansas City Royals 57, 161
Kapos, Shia 57, 59
Katt, Jim 46
Keenan, J.W. 179
Kennedy, John F. 196
Kepley, David 57
Kerr, Dickie 64, 70
Ketchell, Stanley 86
Killebrew, Harmon 46
Kim, Byung-Hyun 169
Kinley, Shaun 168, 169
Kinsella, W.P. 9–18; advice for writers 10; *Dixon Cornbelt League and Other Baseball Stories* 18; "The Eddie Scissons Syndrome" 13; "Eggs" 9, 10–11; and *Field of Dreams* 13–14; *Go the Distance* 18; "K-Mart" 9, 11–12; on Hollywood 14; on writing 10, 12; "Searching for January" 9; *Shoeless Joe* 2, 9, 10, 13–14, 18, 40, 48; "Shoeless Joe Comes to Iowa" 12
Kitsch, Robert 163, 165
Klapp, Gordon 64
Kleinman, Morris 53
Klempley, Rita 61, 74
Kostner, Kevin 18, 38
Koufax, Sandy 171
Kubek 128

Lancaster, Burt 14, 18, 38, 47
Landis, Kenesaw Mountain 52, 55, 73, 74, 150, 151, 152, 153, 155
Lanham, Richard 171
Lapchick, Richard 161, 165

Lardner, Ring 3, 65, 70, 83, 84; "A Busher's Letters Home" 89
Larimer, George Horace 83
Larson, Don 139
Leach, Sandy 23
Leonard, Buck 152, 163
Levinson, Barry 29, 38, 41, 48
Lindell Athletic Club (Detroit) 94
Linn, Ed 154
Liotta, Ray 38, 47
Little League 106, 110, 168
Lloyd, Vince 126
Los Angeles Dodgers 57, 111, 112, 127, 129; fans 127
Los Angeles Examiner 86
Los Angeles Morning Herald 86
Louis, Joe 154
Lugo, Pedro 172, 173
Lutz, William 167, 169, 175

Mach, Steve 162,
Mack, Connie 85
Madigan, Amy 38, 47
Maharg, Billy 66, 69, 79
Major League Baseball: civic pride and 110; deadball era 85, 117, 147, 148–150, 154, 155; economics of 93–105; efforts to internationalize 175; fans 110–111, 113–114, 118, 120; marketing of 118; memorabilia 113–114; nicknames 117; percentage of African Americans in 161; Players Association 175; racial discrimination in 143, 152, 157; radio and 147; RBI (Reviving Baseball in Inner Cities Program) 159, 162, 163; strike of 1994 115, 121; television and 119, 124–135, 153; World War I era 89, 146–52
Malamud, Bernard: *The Natural* 40, 48
Malden, Karl 41, 47
Mantle, Mickey 155
Marc, David 132, 135
Maris, Roger 155
Marquard, Rube 80
Martin, Kenyon 117
Matsui, Hideki 175
Matthews, Kevin 161, 165
Matthewson, Christy 3, 16, 76–82, 85, 87
Mauch, Gene 189

May, Allen 53, 59
Mayer, Robert 40–41, 48
Mays, Carl 147
Mays, Willie 16, 155
Mazeroski, Bill 168
McCarrell, Stuart 49, 59
McCarthy, Jack 181
McCarthy, Joseph 3, 50, 55; Army-McCarthy Hearings 50
McCarthyism 49, 53, 55
McCarver, Tim 130
McCormick, Jim 179
McCovey, Willie 16
McEnroe, Colin 169, 175
McGee, Willie 16
McGrady, Tracy 117
McGraw, John 76, 77, 85
McGuire, Mark 17, 117, 155
McKelvy, Russ 179
McKeon, Larry 179
McNeal, Stan 170, 175
Merkle's Boner 77
Minneapolis Millers 181
Minnesota Twins 45, 46, 164
Mintz, Norman 97, 105
Mitchem, Gary 6
Montreal Expos 16, 175
Mooney, Paul 21
Morris, Jim: as character in *The Rookie* 32–34
Moss, Hubert 160, 165
Most, Marty 28, 38
MS-NBC television 174
Mulligan, Robert 47
Mulman, Jeremy 169, 176
Munsey's (magazine) 86
Munson, Thurman 16
Murakami, Masonuri 16
Musial, Stan 5, 193–200
Myers, Randy 57

Nathan, Daniel 52, 58
National Basketball Association (NBA) 117, 164
National Brotherhood of Baseball Players 180
National Football League (NFL) 96, 164, 173–174, 175, 176
National Hockey League (NHL) 161
The Natural (film) 2, 28–32, 39, 41, 48, 120

Nebraska Indians 182; *see also* Green, Guy Wilder
Negro Leagues: 5, 108–109, 152–155, 158–164; East-West Game 158; in Indianapolis 182–184
Nelson, Candy 179
New York Black Yankees 161
New York Giants 35, 76, 77, 79, 87, 180
New York Mets 109, 124
New York Yankees 16, 112, 120, 121, 139, 168, 174–175, 193
Nidetz, Steve 129, 135
NIT Tournament 173
Nolan, Eddie "The Only" 178, 179
Noll, Roger 95, 105
Northwest League 179

O'Brien, Jack 86
O'Connor, Terrible Tommy 51
Ogden, David 98, 107
Olden, Paul 168, 171, 176
O'Leary, Dan 179
Oliva, Tony 46
Oliver, Al 1
Olson, John 20, 22–24
Omaha Baseball Federation 162
Omaha Golden Spikes 161
O'Neil, Buck 108, 158
Orondonker, Richard 88
Ottawa Lynx 140
Owen, Mickey 153
Owens, Jesse 153

Paige, Satchel 21
Palm, Kristin 96, 105
Palmer, Jim 130
Pappas, Milt 1, 43
Passi, Louis 56–57
Peddie, Ian 50, 59
Perkins, Anthony 47
Perkins, Cy 217
Perlman, Jeff 16
Pernell, Benjamin 21
Pesky, Johnny 154
Peterson, Pete 81, 82
Peterson, Robert 143, 145, 158, 161, 165, 166
Petrash, Jack 28, 37, 38
Philadelphia Athletics 152, 182
Philadelphia Giants 161
Philadelphia Phillies 117, 149, 168

Index 211

Philadelphia Pythians 160
Phillips, Bill 181
Piersall, Jimmy 47; *Fear Strikes Out* 2, 40, 41, 42, 44, 48
Pinkins, Patrick 162, 163, 165
Pittsburgh Pirates 132, 171, 181, 189
Players' League 65
Ponce Lions 172, 173
Pony League 168
Preston, Kelly 121
Puerto Rican Winter League 172

Quaid, Dennis 38
Quest, Joe 179
Quirk, James 96, 100, 102, 105

Radar, Benjamin 127, 130, 135, 145, 158, 165
Raftery, Bill 173
Rampersad, Arnold 160, 161
Rapport, Ron 57, 59
Rawls, John 93
Reagan, Ronald 124
Redford, Robert 38, 48
Reese, Pee Wee 155, 186
Reese, Rich 46
Reiff, Lester 86
Rephlo, Mary 57
Rhubarb (film) 16
Ribowsky, Mark 158, 159, 160, 165
Rice, Grantland 3, 89
Richter, Francis 156
Rickey, Branch 154, 160
Risberg, Swede 52, 53–54, 67, 71
Ritter, Lawrence 89, 148, 148, 156
Rizzuto, Phil 128, 130, 186
Roberts, Keith 109, 111, 112, 115
Robinson, Jackie 5, 153–56, 161, 186
Robinson, Philip Alden 14, 18, 34, 38, 47
Rodriquez, Alex 117
Rodriquez, Emmanuel 117
Roe, Dr. Charles 187–188
Roe, Edwin "Preacher Roe" 5, 186–192
Roe, Mozee 187, 190, 191
Rollins, Jimmy 117
Romond, Edwin 43; "Something I Could Tell You About Love" 39, 42, 48
The Rookie 2, 29, 32–34, 38
Rose, Ava 125, 135

Rose, Pete 15, 16, 136–37, 140, 197
Rosen, Al 168
Rosenbloom, Steve 131, 135
Rothschild, Richard 131, 135
Rothstein, Arnold 54, 61, 66, 68–69
Roush, Ed 62
Rowland, Seth 161, 165
Rudd, Robert 28, 38
Runyon, Damon 86
Rusie, Amos 87
Ruth, Babe 15, 71, 147, 150, 151, 153

Safer, Morley 15
St. Louis Browns 66
St. Louis Cardinals 6, 16, 102, 119, 121, 186, 189, 191, 193–200
St. Paul Saints 46
Salinger, J.D. 13, 16
San Diego Padres 111
San Francisco Giants 16, 111
Santiago, Jose 46
Saturday Evening Post 3, 83, 87
Sayles, John 3; *Eight Men Out* 3, 60–74; *Matewan* 3, 60–64, 75; *Union Dues* 60
Scarry, Elaine 93, 99, 100, 102, 103, 104, 105
Schalk, Ray 64
Schneider, Russ 168, 176
Schwarzbaum, Lisa 120, 123
Scully, Vin 130
Seidel, Michael 125, 128, 130, 132, 135
Selig, Bud 15
Seymour, Harold 20, 27, 148, 156
Shaffer, Orator 179
Shively, George 183
Silverstein, Ken 170, 173, 176
Simmons, Lon 118
Simons, William 165
Smead, Robert 172, 176
Smith, Curt 133, 135
Smith, Gavin 63, 75
Snell, Arnold 159, 165
Snider, Duke 155, 186
Snodgrass, Fred 148, 149, 150
Sobchack, Vivian 133, 135
Society for American Baseball Research 184, 185
Solomon, Eric 79, 82, 87, 89
Sosa, Sammy 17, 57, 117, 132
South, Charles 57

Sowell, Mike 151, 156
Spalding Company 151
Speaker, Tris 15
Speech Act Theory 170
Spence, Harry 180
Sport (novel) 3, 39–47
Sporting News 170, 186
Sports Illustrated 12
Star City Club 177
Stein, David 119–20, 122, 123
Stein, Irving 138, 145
Steinbrenner, George 175
Stevens, Jake 152
Stone, Steve 127, 131, 133, 134, 135
Stone, Toni 184
Strahler, Steven 169, 176
Stump, Al 156
Sugrue, Thomas J. 105
Sullivan, Neil J. 95, 105
Sullivan, Sport 61, 66–67, 69, 72
Super Bowl 174
Suttles, Mule 12
Sutton, Don 129, 134, 135

Taft, Philip 65, 75
"Take Me Out to the Ballgame" 127
Tampa Bay Devil Rays 33
Taylor, Charles Isam 183
Taylor, Stephanie 170, 176
Terkel, Studs 57, 59, 65
Terry, Ralph 168
Tesrau, Jeff 80
Thomas, Fred 180
Thome, Jim 168–69
Thompson, Big Sam 179
Thoreau, Henry David 93, 122
Tiger Stadium Fan Club 97, 98, 104
Title IX 168
Tobey, Senator Charles W. 53
Tobey, Dan 23
Tommy John Surgery 5, 166, 170–172, 174
Toronto Blue Jays 168
Total Baseball 118, 122, 123
Turner, Ted 126

University of Nebraska 23, 25
USA Today 11

Valdespino, Sandy 46
Van Loan, Charles 3, 83–89; *The Big League* 83; "The Drug Store Derby" 86; "The Golden Ball of the Argonauts" 86; "The Good Old Wagon" 88; "How I Broke into the Magazines" 86; *The Lucky Seventh* 83; "Making Good in the Big League" 87; "Matthewson, Incog." 87; "The Phantom League" 85; *Score by Innings* 83; *The Ten-Thousand Dollar Arm* 83
Veeck, Bill 127
Vintage Baseball 121–122, 184–85; teams 121–122, 184–185; Vintage Baseball Association (VBBA) 121, 122, 123, 184
Virdon, Bill 191
Vogler, Christopher: *The Writer's Journey* 29, 30, 31, 38

Wagner, Hans (Honus) 85
Walker, James R. 130, 134
Wanderer, Carl 51
Ward, Duane: "Isn't it pretty to think so?" 42, 48
Ward, Geoffrey 109, 115, 158, 165
Warfield, Frank 183
Warner, Fred 179
Washington Nationals 177
Washington Post 61, 74
Washington Senators 191
Watkins, Bill 179, 182
Watson, Robert 167, 171, 176
Weaver, Buck 52, 65, 74
Wells, Willie "The Devil" 184
West World 119
Western Association 181, 182
Western Club of Indianapolis 177
Western League 23, 179, 180, 181
Wetherell, Margaret 170, 176
WGN Chicago 124–135
White, Bill 128
White, Sol 143
Whitman, Walt 145
Wiles, Tom 47
Williams, Billy 197
Williams, Lefty 52, 70–71
Williams, Mitch 168
Williams, Ted 17, 154
Williamson, Ned 179
Wills, Maury 155

Winfrey, Oprah 132
Wittgenstein, Ludwig 167, 172, 176
Wood, Kerry 56
World Series 147, 153; *1905* 79; *1912* 80; *1918* 113; *1919* see Black Sox scandal; *1941* 112; *1945* 129; *1947* 112; *1949* 112, 189; *1952* 112; *1953* 112, 139; *1956* 139; *1960* 168; *1964* 199; *1993* 168; *1975* 112; *2001* 169; *2002* 174
World War I 61, 83
World War II 153
Wright, Richard 49

Wrigley, Philip K. 141
WTBS Atlanta 124–135

Yancy, Bill 161
Yates, Simeon 170, 176
Yinger, Milton 109, 115
YMCA 160, 161
Young, Coleman 101

Zapruder, Abraham 196
Zimbalist, Andrew 95, 105
Zimmerman, Dennis 96, 100, 105
Zulu Cannibal Giants 183

www.ingramcontent.com/pod-product-compliance
Lightning Source LLC
Chambersburg PA
CBHW032055300426
44116CB00007B/745